Gospel Light's

BIG REALLY BOOK

OF **KiDS' SERMONS** and **OBJECT TALKS**

Gospel Light

How to Make Clean Copies from This Book

You may make copies of portions of this book with a clean conscience if

- you (or someone in your organization) are the original purchaser;

- you are using the copies you make for a noncommercial purpose (such as teaching or promoting your ministry) within your church or organization;

- you follow the instructions provided in this book.

However, it is ILLEGAL for you to make copies if

- you are using the material to promote, advertise or sell a product or service other than for ministry fund-raising;

- you are using the material in or on a product for sale; or

- you or your organization are not the original purchaser of this book.

By following these guidelines you help us keep our products affordable.

Thank you,

Gospel Light

Gospel Light

Editorial Staff

Founder, Dr. Henrietta Mears

Publisher Emeritus, William T. Greig • **Publisher, Children's Curriculum and Resources,** Bill Greig III

Senior Consulting Publisher, Dr. Elmer L. Towns • **Product Line Manager,** Cary Maxon

Senior Managing Editor, Sheryl Haystead

Senior Consulting Editor, Wesley Haystead, M.S.Ed.

Senior Editor, Theological and Biblical Issues, Bayard Taylor, M.Div.

Editor, Karen McGraw • **Editorial Team,** Amanda Abbas, Debbie Barber, Mary Davis

Contributing Editors, Jay Bea Summerfield, Linda Mattia

Art Directors, Lenndy McCullough, Christina Renée Sharp, Samantha A. Hsu

Originally Published as *The Big Book of Kid Sermons and Object Talks* (Ventura, CA: Gospel Light, 1999), *Celebrate and Worship* (Ventura, CA: Gospel Light, 2000) and *Fruitful Lives Kids' Sermons and Object Talks* (Ventura, CA: Gospel Light, 2001).

Contents

The Really Big Book of Kid Sermons and Object Talks

Praise and Worship

Prayer

Salvation

Service to Others

Thankfulness

The CD-ROM included with this book will make your life easier! You can use the search engine included on the CD-ROM to locate the object talk file you want. What could be easier?

Kid Sermon and Object Talk Tips

Object talks can draw children in and help them apply the Bible truths to their lives. These object talks can be used as family devotions, children's sermons or supplements to any Sunday School curriculum. They can also augment any children's ministry program, day school or homeschool curriculum.

Getting the Most Out of an Object Talk

Preparation is the key to using *The Really Big Book of Kid Sermons and Object Talks!* Read a talk at least several days ahead to give ample time to gather the needed materials. You may find it helpful to practice some talks before presenting them.

Whenever possible, invite children to participate. Each time you present an object talk ask a different child to read the Bible verse aloud.

Occasionally describe situations in which knowing God's Word has helped you. Tell children how the Bible verse presented in the object talk has been important to you.

After giving the object talk, ask one or more of the Discussion Questions found in bold print at the end of each talk.

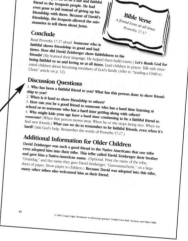

Suggestions for Using the Object Talks

• **Adult Worship Service** If the children in your church are in some or all of the adult service, consider using the object talk as the basis for a weekly children's sermon.

• **Newsletter** Encourage parents to use the object talk with their children. To support your church's parents in their significant job of teaching Bible truths to their children, insert the object talk into a family newsletter or e-newsletter you send every month.

• **Website** Instead of or in addition to a newsletter, post on your church's website an object talk every week or month for families to access and use for family devotions.

• **Parenting Classes** Distribute copies of selected object talks as part of classes on parenting and invite parents to use the object talks at home. Each object talk discusses a topic important to families, such as caring for others ("School Uniforms"), obeying God ("Stronger Than Sin") and forgiving others ("'Awe'some Forgiveness").

• **Holidays** Combine Christmas- and Easter-related object talks into a separate pamphlet and distribute to families to help them keep children focused on the biblical truths of these holidays.

• **Program Resources** Provide copies of object talks to leaders and teachers to use in supplementing their curriculums.

• **School Resources** Provide copies of object talks to teachers in weekday school or to parents who homeschool their children.

Leading a Good Discussion

A good discussion requires leaders to listen as much as—or more than—they speak. However, encouraging others to speak up can be difficult. The following questions are commonly asked about making a discussion truly productive, and not an unfocused, rambling monologue.

How do I keep the discussion on track?

Use the discussion questions provided with each Object Talk to focus on children's personal experiences. When Bible truths relate to daily life, interest in the discussion will grow.

How do I get the discussion back on track if a digression occurs?

If significant interest is shown in the new topic and it has real value and if you feel able to guide this new topic for discussion, then you may decide to stay with the new issue. Otherwise, use questions to bring attention back to the original topic. Move on to a new question, restate your question or rephrase it if the group did not understand what you asked.

If an outside interruption catches the group's attention, acknowledge it as matter-of-factly as possible, and then restate the question being discussed. You may also want to summarize some of the key points already made in the discussion.

What do I do when no one says anything or when kids are giving "pat" answers?

If you've asked a thought-provoking question, assume that kids need at least a few moments to think. Be silent for a bit (no more than 20-30 seconds), and repeat or rephrase the question. If you still get no response, give your own answer to the question and move on.

If silence is a recurring problem, evaluate the questions you ask. Are they too vague? Threatening? Do they require knowledge the kids do not have? Are the answers too obvious?

If the questions are fine, evaluate your response to what the group says. Are you unwilling to accept answers if they differ from what you consider to be the correct responses? Do you tend to always improve the students' answers? Work to create a climate of openness and trust.

Finally, add some variety to your approach in asking questions:

• Have students write their answers on paper. This allows them time to organize their thoughts. Then invite them to read what they wrote.

• Divide the class into smaller groups. You may ask all groups the same questions, or assign different questions to each group. Invite volunteers to share the answers for their groups.

The same suggestions apply when students are giving only "pat" answers. The root problem is often the same in either case: the discussion participants do not feel secure sharing what they really think.

Leading a Child to Christ

One of the greatest privileges of serving in children's programs is to help children become members of God's family. Some children, especially those from Christian homes, may be ready to believe in Jesus Christ as their Savior earlier than others. Ask God to prepare the children to receive the good news about Jesus and prepare you to communicate effectively with them.

Talk individually with children. Something as important as a child's personal relationship with Jesus Christ can be handled more effectively one-on-one than in a group. A child needs to respond individually to the call of God's love. This response needs to be a genuine response to God—not because the child wants to please peers, parents or you, the leader.

Follow these basic steps in talking with children about becoming members of God's family. The evangelism booklet *God Loves You* is an effective guide to follow. Show the child what God says in His Word. Ask the questions suggested to encourage thinking and comprehending.

a. **God wants you to become His child** (see John 1:12). **Do you know why God wants you in His family?** (See 1 John 4:8.)

b. **You and all the people in the world have done wrong things** (see Romans 3:23). **The Bible word for doing wrong is "sin." What do you think should happen to us when we sin?** (See Romans 6:23.)

c. **God loves you so much He sent His Son to die on the cross for your sins. Because Jesus never sinned, He is the only One who can take the punishment for your sins** (see 1 Corinthians 15:3; 1 John 4:14). **The Bible tells us that God raised Jesus from the dead and that He is alive forever.**

d. **Are you sorry for your sins? Do you believe Jesus died to be your Savior? If you do believe and you are sorry for your sins, God forgives all your sins** (see 1 John 1:9).

When you talk to God, tell Him that you believe He gave His Son, Jesus Christ, to take your punishment. Also tell God you are sorry for your sins. Tell Him that He is a great and wonderful God. It is easy to talk to God. He is ready to listen. What you are going to tell Him is something He has been waiting to hear.

e. **The Bible says that when you believe in Jesus, God's Son, you receive God's gift of eternal life. This gift makes you a child of God. This means God is with you now and forever** (see John 3:16).

Give your pastor the names of those who make decisions to become members of God's family. Encourage the child to tell his or her family about the decision. Children who make decisions need follow-up to help them grow in Christ.

NOTE: The Bible uses many terms and images to express the concept of salvation. Children often do not understand or may develop misconceptions about these terms, especially terms that are highly symbolic. (Remember the trouble Nicodemus, a respected teacher, had in trying to understand the meaning of being "born again"?) Many people talk with children about "asking Jesus into your heart." The literal-minded child is likely to develop strange ideas from the imagery of those words. The idea of being a child of God (see John 1:12) is perhaps the simplest portrayal the New Testament provides.

Group Music

Encourage one another to love and obey God and to do His work.

Teacher Materials

Bible with bookmarks at Psalm 147 and 1 Thessalonians 5:11, paper, photocopier, several CDs/cassettes of different vocal or instrumental groups (duets, trios, choirs, orchestras) and player.

Bible Verse

Encourage one another and build each other up, just as in fact you are doing.
1 Thessalonians 5:11

Prepare the Activity

Make five photocopies of Psalm 147:1-5.

Introduce the Object Talk

We can encourage each other to love and obey God and do His work. Let's look at some ways in which people work together to create something wonderful.

Present the Object Talk

1. Briefly play several examples of different types of musical groups. **What is the same about these different types of musical groups? What's different? What do the players or singers need to do in order to make their music sound good?** (Work together to follow the music. Play at the same tempo, or speed. Practice with each

other.) **Making music is only one way people work together. What are some other ways?** (Soccer players passing the ball to score a goal. Carpenters building a house.)

2. When there's a big job to be done, it's important to encourage each other to do the job. In Bible times, many people had to work together to rebuild the wall that had fallen down around Jerusalem. People who study the Bible think that Psalm 147 was written for a choir to sing when the wall was built.

The Really Big Book of Kid Sermons and Object Talks

3. Distribute copies of Psalm 147:1-5 to five volunteers. Volunteers read verses in the following manner: One child begins by reading verse one. Another child joins him or her on the second verse. Continue adding voices one at a time until all five volunteers read verse five together. Repeat with new volunteers as time allows.

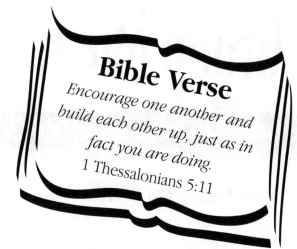

Bible Verse

Encourage one another and build each other up, just as in fact you are doing.
1 Thessalonians 5:11

Conclude

God gives us other people to help us and encourage us to do His work. Read 1 Thessalonians 5:11 aloud. **When we encourage others, we help them love and obey God.** Pray, thanking God that He gives us people to encourage us, and asking His help to encourage others to love and obey Him and to do His work.

Discussion Questions

1. **Why is it important to encourage other people?** (It is a way to follow God's command to love one another.)

2. **What does it mean to love and obey God and do His work?** (Do the things the Bible commands us to do such as love each other; give clothes, money and food to needy people; say kind words to one another instead of arguing; pray for others; etc.)

3. **What are some things you could do or say to encourage others to do God's work?**

Additional Information for Older Children

Psalm 147 was probably performed by two choirs made up of people called Levites. Levites (people from the tribe of Levi) helped the priests in the Tabernacle and, later, in the Temple. The first choir walked in one direction along the wall while the other choir walked along the wall in the opposite direction! Read about these choirs in Nehemiah 12:27-31,38.

Lighting the Way

God gives us courage in all situations.

Teacher Materials

Bible with bookmarks at Joshua 1:9 and
Psalm 59:16-17, object(s) used in dark areas
(night-light, flashlight, candle, lantern, etc.);
optional—paper, pencils.

Introduce the Object Talk

In all situations, we can count on God to
give us the courage we need. Let's look at
some things that people might use at
times when they are scared.

Bible Verse

Be strong and courageous. . . .
do not be discouraged, for the
Lord your God will be with you
wherever you go. Joshua 1:9

Present the Object Talk

1. Display object(s) you brought. **What is this? When do people use it? How does
it help them?** Volunteers respond. **Sometimes people use these kinds of lights
when it's dark. They might need to see where they are going, or maybe they
just want to see the light because it makes them feel safe. What are some
things younger kids might use to help them feel safe when it's dark?**

**2. When David, the man in Bible times who eventually
became King of Israel, wanted to feel
safe, he depended on God to give
him courage. David wrote several
psalms about times he needed
courage. Psalm 59 is a psalm David
wrote when Saul wanted to kill
him.** Read, or ask an older child to read,
Psalm 59:16-17 aloud. **Writing and
singing this psalm must have helped David remember and celebrate God's
help and care for him, because David wrote other psalms at other scary times**

in his life. (Optional: Children discuss times when they might need God's courage. Lead children to write a group psalm about one of the times mentioned. Read completed psalm aloud with children.)

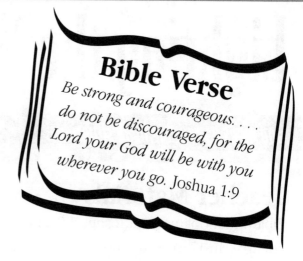

Bible Verse

Be strong and courageous. . . . do not be discouraged, for the Lord your God will be with you wherever you go. Joshua 1:9

Conclude

Just as David trusted in God to give him courage, we can also count on God to give us courage in all the situations we face. Read Joshua 1:9 aloud. **Just knowing God is with us wherever we go gives us all the courage we need!** Pray, thanking God for His gift of courage and that He is with us wherever we go.

Discussion Questions

1. What does it mean to have courage? (To do what is right even when it is hard or we feel afraid.)

2. When are some times kids your age need courage? (Taking a test at school. Performing in a music recital or acting in a play. Being around older kids who are mean.)

3. What can we do to get courage in hard situations? (Pray to God. Remember God's promise to be with us everywhere we go.)

4. Why can we always depend on receiving courage from God when we ask for it? (God always keeps His promises.)

Additional Information for Older Children

In many Bibles, the word *miktam* is written under the title of Psalm 59. No one knows exactly what this word means. Some people think it was a word that described the kind of words David was writing or the melody to which the words were sung. *Miktam* is written under the titles of all the psalms David wrote when he was in great danger. (Optional: Children look at Psalms 56—60.) **Since *miktam* is only written under the psalms David wrote when he was in danger, what do you think the word might have meant?**

Mirror Talk

No matter how bad it looks, God is with us.

Teacher Materials

Bible with bookmark at Psalm 118:6-7, one or more hand mirrors, paper on which you have printed the sentence "The Lord is with me" backwards (see sketch).

Materials for Children

Paper, pencils.

Bible Verse

The Lord is with me; I will not be afraid. What can man do to me? The Lord is with me; he is my helper. Psalm 118:6-7

Introduce the Object Talk

Because He promises to be with us, God can help us even when we're worried or afraid. Look at these words and see if you can figure out what they say and how God helps us in difficult times.

Present the Object Talk

1. In class, show words you printed to one or more volunteers and ask them to try to read the words. **How hard is it to read these words? Why don't they make sense when you first look at them?**

2. Hold words up to a mirror and invite several volunteers to read the words. Volunteers write sentence backwards and use mirrors to read words.

ｏｍｄｔｉｗｓｉｂｒｏＬｅｈＴ

Conclude

Sometimes we might feel like all the wrong things are happening to us. We might feel like we can't understand why sad things happen to us or to others. But if we remember that God is with us, we can ask Him to help us know what to do. Read Psalm 118:6-7 aloud. Thank God for promising to be with us even in difficult times.

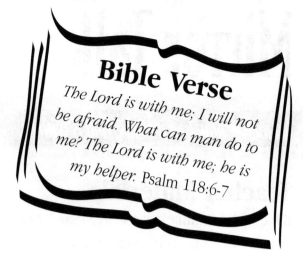

Bible Verse

The Lord is with me; I will not be afraid. What can man do to me? The Lord is with me; he is my helper. Psalm 118:6-7

Discussion Questions

1. **When is a time kids your age might feel afraid or worried?**

2. **What are some of the ways God helps us?** (Gives us parents and friends. Promises to hear and answer our prayers.)

3. **What other promises does God give us?** (To forgive us when we do wrong. To give us courage.)

Mission Impossible?

God encourages us when we're afraid.

Teacher Materials

Bible with Joshua 1:9 marked with a book-mark, 8½x11-inch (21.5x27.5-cm) paper, scissors.

Prepare the Object Talk

Practice cutting paper, following directions below.

Bible Verse

Be strong and courageous. Do not be terrified; do not be discouraged, for the Lord your God will be with you wherever you go. Joshua 1:9

Introduce the Object Talk

God gives us courage, even when we have something really hard to do. Look with me at this impossible task!

Present the Object Talk

1. Show paper and ask, **How might I fit my whole body through this paper?**

2. After children conclude that the task is impossible, fold the paper lengthwise. Cut the paper as shown in Sketch a, making an uneven number of cuts approximately ½ inch (1.25 cm) apart. Cut on the fold between the first and last sections as shown in Sketch b. Then carefully open up the folds and step through the circle you have made.

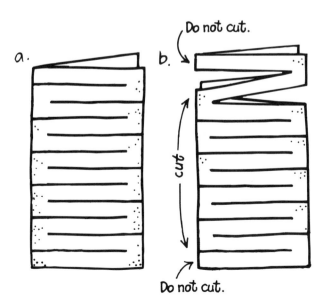

a.

b.

Do not cut.

cut

Do not cut.

Conclude

When something seems too hard to do or we're discouraged, God can help us by giving us courage and helping us know what to do. What does God promise to do? Read Joshua 1:9 aloud. Thank God for encouraging us when we're afraid.

Bible Verse

Be strong and courageous. Do not be terrified; do not be discouraged, for the Lord your God will be with you wherever you go. Joshua 1:9

Discussion Questions

1. **What might make a kid your age feel discouraged, or feel like giving up?**

2. **When is a time a kid your age might feel afraid and need to ask God for courage?**

3. **What are some ways in which God encourages us?** (Gives us friends and parents. Gives us promises of help in the Bible.)

Paper Challenge

Encouraging others can help them trust in God, too.

Teacher Materials

Bible with 1 Thessalonians 5:14 marked with a bookmark, one or more of these materials: toilet paper, crepe-paper strip, yarn, curling ribbon, narrow fabric strip.

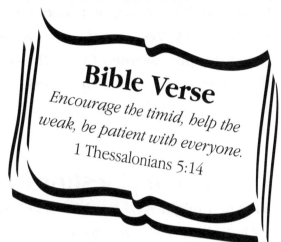

Bible Verse

Encourage the timid, help the weak, be patient with everyone.
1 Thessalonians 5:14

Introduce the Object Talk

God tells us in His Word that He wants us to help people who are weak. Watch to see what is weak in this experiment and what makes the weak item become strong.

Present the Object Talk

1. Invite a volunteer to come forward. Ask the volunteer to hold wrists together in front of him- or herself as you wrap one strand of toilet paper around the wrists. Challenge the volunteer to break free.

2. Repeat several times, each time adding one or two strands of paper before the volunteer tries to break free. Comment, **One or two strands of paper are weak and we can break them easily. The more strands of paper we add, the stronger the paper becomes.** Repeat with other volunteers and/or materials.

Conclude

When we try to trust in God by ourselves, it's like we are as weak as one strand of paper. We might find it hard to do what God says. But when others help us and encourage us, it's easier to trust God. We are stronger together—just as the papers were stronger when they were put together. Count the ways this verse says we can help others. Read 1 Thessalonians 5:14 aloud. Pray, asking God to show children ways of helping others to trust Him.

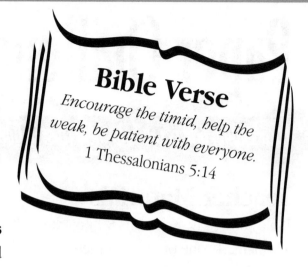

Bible Verse

Encourage the timid, help the weak, be patient with everyone. 1 Thessalonians 5:14

Discussion Questions

1. **When might it be hard for a kid to do what God wants? How could a friend help him or her to obey?** (Pray for him or her. Say helpful words to him or her.)

2. **What's something you know God wants you to do?** (Be honest. Stand up for someone who needs help.) **How could you also help a friend obey God in that way?**

3. **Who has helped you learn about God and trust in Him?**

A Faithful Watchman

God showed His faithfulness in keeping His promise to send the Savior.

Teacher's Materials

Bible with bookmark at Psalm 117:1-2, one or more items security guards use (flashlight, keys, billy club, walkie talkie, handcuffs, etc.).

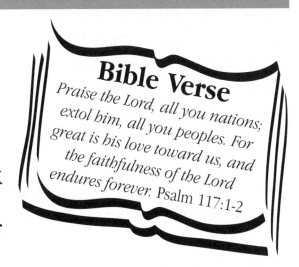

Bible Verse

Praise the Lord, all you nations; extol him, all you peoples. For great is his love toward us, and the faithfulness of the Lord endures forever. Psalm 117:1-2

Introduce the Object Talk

God showed His faithfulness when He kept His promise to send Jesus to be our Savior. Let's find out about someone who trusted God's faithfulness and was faithful to God.

Present the Object Talk

1. Show items you brought. **Watchmen, or security guards, use things like these to help them protect buildings and people and make sure that they are safe. Just like watchmen watch for problems and tell people what they**  **need to know to be safe, preachers pray for people and tell them what they need to know to become members of God's family and be saved from sin's punishment.**

2. In the early 1920s, a man in China changed his name from Ni Shu-tsu to Watchman Nee. He chose this name because his mother had prayed for him to be born while she listened to the night watchman make his rounds. When Ni Shu-tsu heard that his mother promised God that her son would love and obey Him, Ni Shu-tsu decided that the name Watchman would remind him and others of his plan to serve God.

For the rest of his life, Watchman did his best to be faithful in obeying

God. One day Watchman got a letter asking him to preach in the city of Chien-O. He wanted to go, but the boat trip to Chien-O cost 80 dollars and Watchman only had 10 dollars. Watchman asked for God's help and then went to the river. There was a small boat going to Chien-O for only seven dollars! Watchman Nee's faithful dependence on God meant others could hear about God.

Bible Verse

Praise the Lord, all you nations; extol him, all you peoples. For great is his love toward us, and the faithfulness of the Lord endures forever. Psalm 117:1-2

Conclude

Read Psalm 117:1-2 aloud. **What do these verses tell us about God? How did Watchman Nee show he was faithful to God?** (He obeyed God, even when he didn't know how God would provide for him.) Lead children in prayer, thanking God for His faithfulness.

Discussion Questions

1. **How has God shown faithfulness to us?** (He kept His promise to send Jesus. He makes us part of His family when we trust in Him. He keeps His promises to love and be with us.) Talk with interested children about becoming members of God's family (refer to "Leading a Child to Christ" article on p. 8).

2. **When might people today have a hard time trusting God's faithfulness? What could you say or do to encourage someone in a situation like this?**

3. **How does knowing about God's faithfulness help us?** (We can depend on Him.)

Additional Information for Older Children

During the same year he became a Christian, Watchman Nee began writing books and articles for newspapers. Many Christians still read and learn from Watchman Nee's books. In 1952, Watchman Nee was arrested and put in prison because of his belief in God. He died in prison on March 30, 1972.

Escape from Germany

Acting in ways that demonstrate belief in God shows faithfulness.

Teacher's Materials

Bible with bookmark at Proverbs 20:11, star cut from yellow construction paper or fabric.

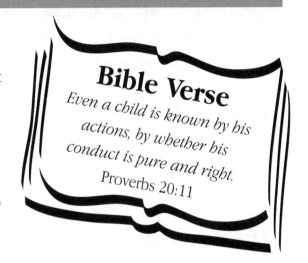

Bible Verse

Even a child is known by his actions, by whether his conduct is pure and right.
Proverbs 20:11

Introduce the Object Talk

When we're faithful to God, it means that our actions and words show obedience to God. Let's find out how one person showed His faithfulness to God in a very difficult and scary time.

Present the Object Talk

1. Show yellow star. **When people called Nazis were in control of Germany during World War II, Jewish people were forced to wear stars like this on their clothes. The Nazis wanted everyone to hate Jewish people. Not all of the German people agreed with the Nazis. A German man named Dietrich** (DEE-trihk) **Bonhoeffer** (BAHN-hahf-uhr) **dared to help people who wore yellow stars.**

2. Dietrich Bonhoeffer was a pastor in Germany during World War II. Many other German pastors would not help Jewish people, because they were afraid of Hitler and the Nazi army, but Dietrich said that this was not right!

Dietrich did more than just say that it was wrong to hate Jewish people; he did what he could to help them. One time Dietrich helped a group of Jewish people escape from Germany. He had papers that gave him permission to travel in and out of Germany. On one trip, he took some Jews with him. German guards stopped the car, but because of his permission papers, the guards let him leave Germany—along with the Jewish people in his car. Later, the Nazis found out what he was doing and arrested him. While he was in prison, Dietrich wrote several books about faithfully serving God. Dietrich was eventually killed because of his actions that showed his belief in God. People today still read the books he wrote and remember how important it is to be faithful to do what is right.

Bible Verse

Even a child is known by his actions, by whether his conduct is pure and right.
Proverbs 20:11

Conclude

Read Proverbs 20:11 aloud. **What are some actions that showed Pastor Bonhoeffer's belief in God? How did this pastor's actions make a difference?** Lead children in prayer, asking God to help them be faithful in showing belief in God.

Discussion Questions

1. How do kids your age show that they believe in God? (Don't go along with the crowd in doing wrong. Go to church. Read their Bibles. Pray and ask God for help when they have problems. Treat others kindly.)

2. How do you think your faithfulness to God might help another person?

3. When are some times you have seen other people show their belief in God? Briefly share your own answer before you ask for responses from children.

4. How can you show faithfulness to God when you are with your friends? When you are with your family?

Additional Information for Older Children

While in prison, Dietrich wrote many letters. His letters to the woman he was planning to marry were collected into a book called *Love Letters from Cell 92*. On the day Dietrich was killed, the prison doctor saw him praying in his cell. The doctor later said that in all his years as a doctor, he had never seen anyone more faithful about doing God's will.

Faith of a Mother

The habits we form by being faithful to God help us do what is right, even when trouble comes.

Teacher's Materials

Bible with bookmark at Proverbs 3:3, clock with hour and minute hands.

Introduce the Object Talk

The habits we form by being faithful to God help us do what is right at all times. Let's look at some different things we can do with our time.

Bible Verse

Let love and faithfulness never leave you; bind them around your neck, write them on the tablet of your heart. Proverbs 3:3

Present the Object Talk

1. Show clock. **How long does it take for the short hand to move from one number to another?** Children respond. **What are some things you can do in an hour?** (Watch [two] cartoon shows. Drive to [a location approximately 60 miles away]. Attend soccer practice.)

2. One person who lived a long time ago had a habit of doing something for two hours every day. Susanna Wesley, a woman who lived in England in the 1700s, prayed for two hours every day. Even though Susanna had many children to take care of and was very busy with all kinds of work, every day she stopped whatever she was doing to pray and think about God's Word for one hour in the morning and one hour in the evening. Susanna began this habit of showing love and obedience to God when her children were young, and she faithfully continued the habit throughout her life. She had two sons who not only became famous preachers and songwriters but also were people God used to tell the good news of Jesus all over England!

Conclude

Read Proverbs 3:3 aloud. **What are some habits Proverbs 3:3 talks about?** (Showing love and being faithful to God.) **How did Susanna Wesley obey this verse?** (She prayed and thought about God's Word every day.) **What are some other habits that show love and faithfulness to God?** Lead children in prayer, thanking God for His love and asking for His help in showing love and faithfulness to Him.

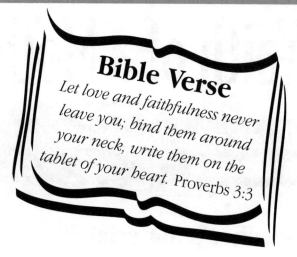

Bible Verse

Let love and faithfulness never leave you; bind them around your neck, write them on the tablet of your heart. Proverbs 3:3

Discussion Questions

1. **When you "bind [something] around your neck" or "write [it] on the tablet of your heart" (know it by heart), it means you are trying to keep that thing close to you so that you will never lose it. What is Proverbs 3:3 telling us not to lose?** (Love and faithfulness to God.)

2. **What does it mean to be faithful to God?** (To love Him with all your heart, soul, mind and strength. To obey God's commands no matter what.)

3. **What kinds of habits could you form that would show your faithfulness to God?** (Reading the Bible to learn more about God. Praying to God every day. Obeying God's commands.)

4. **How can these habits help you when things are hard?** (Knowing God's Word will help a person know the right thing to do, even in difficult situations. Praying to God will be comforting in times of fear or sadness.)

Additional Information for Older Children

One of Susanna Wesley's sons, Charles Wesley, wrote many songs called hymns that are still sung in churches today. (Optional: Use bookmarks or Post-it Notes to mark several of Charles Wesley's hymns in some church hymnals: "Love Divine, All Loves Excelling," "Hark! the Herald Angels Sing," "Jesus, Lover of My Soul," "O for a Thousand Tongues to Sing," "Christ the Lord Is Risen Today," etc. Children find and read some of the songs. **Can you find words or phrases that remind you of showing love? Of being faithful?**)

Faithful Friendship

Faithfulness to others means being a friend in good and bad times.

Teacher's Materials

Bible with bookmark at Proverbs 17:17, sleeping bag or pillow.

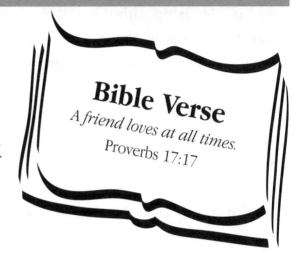

Bible Verse
A friend loves at all times.
Proverbs 17:17

Introduce the Object Talk

Showing faithfulness means being a good friend no matter what—in good and bad times. Let's find out how one man showed he was a faithful friend.

Present the Object Talk

1. Show sleeping bag or pillow. **When do you use this?** (Camping. Sleeping overnight at a friend's house.) **One way to show friendship is to stay overnight at a friend's house. One man showed friendship by doing more than staying overnight with his friends. This man chose to live with the people that he wanted to be friends with.**

2. David Zeisberger lived in the 1800s. During that time many Native Americans were being cheated out of the land they lived on. White people and Native Americans weren't usually friends.**

But David was a missionary who wanted to tell the good news about Jesus to a Native American tribe called the Iroquois (IHR-eh-kwoi). So David went to live with the Iroquois and learned to speak their language. He didn't try to make the people change the ways they dressed or ate. And instead of cheating the Iroquois out of their land, David helped them build towns of their own. David was a faithful friend.

Later when the members of David's church wanted to become missionaries to the Iroquois, the tribe didn't want these missionaries to come. White people had cheated them too many times! But one of the Iroquois called David a friend and a brother. Others who knew David agreed that David had proven to be a fair and faithful friend to the Iroquois people. He had even gone to jail instead of giving up his friendship with them. Because of David's friendship, the Iroquois allowed the missionaries to tell them about Jesus.

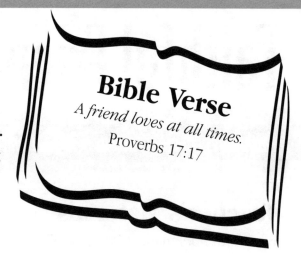

Bible Verse
A friend loves at all times.
Proverbs 17:17

Conclude

Read Proverbs 17:17 aloud. **Someone who is faithful shows friendship in good and bad times. How did David Zeisberger show faithfulness to his friends?** (He learned their language. He helped them build towns.) **Let's thank God for being faithful to us and loving us at all times.** Lead children in prayer. Talk with interested children about becoming members of God's family (refer to "Leading a Child to Christ" article on p. 8).

Discussion Questions

1. **Who has been a faithful friend to you? What has this person done to show friendship to you?**

2. **When is it hard to show friendship to others?**

3. **How can you be a good friend to someone who has a hard time learning at school or to someone who has a hard time getting along with others?**

4. **Why might kids your age have a hard time continuing to be a faithful friend to someone?** (When that person moves away. When he or she stops being nice. When we find new friends.) **What can we do to remember to be faithful friends, even when it's hard?** (Ask God's help. Remember the words of Proverbs 17:17.)

Additional Information for Older Children

David Zeisberger was such a good friend to the Native Americans that one tribe even adopted him into their tribe. This tribe called David Zeisberger their brother and gave him a Native-American name. (Optional: Print the name of the tribe, "Onandag," and the name they gave David Zeisberger, "Ganousaracherie," on a large sheet of paper. Show paper to children.) **Because David was adopted into this tribe, many other tribes also welcomed him as their friend.**

 The Really Big Book of Kid Sermons and Object Talks

Faithful Heroes

Remembering the actions of people in God's family encourages us to show our faith in God.

Teacher Materials

Bible with bookmark at 1 Corinthians 12:27, a variety of objects that remind us of other people (photo album, scrapbook, yearbook, postage stamp, locket, family Bible, coin, dollar bill, etc.).

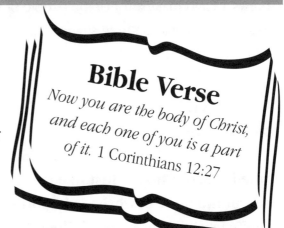

Bible Verse

Now you are the body of Christ, and each one of you is a part of it. 1 Corinthians 12:27

Introduce the Object Talk

Members of God's family have done many things that are important for us to remember. Their actions of faith encourage us to show our faith in God, too. Let's talk about ways to remember what other people have done.

Present the Object Talk

1. Who is an important person in your life? What is something you could do to always remember that person? Volunteers respond. Display objects one at a time and discuss with children. **What is this object? How does an object like this remind you about people?** (Photographs, lockets and family Bibles remind us of our family and friends. Postage stamps, coins and dollar bills remind us of famous people and our country's leaders.)

2. A long time ago, Christians chose one day on which they would remember the people in God's family who had been hurt or killed because of their faith in God and were already with Him in heaven. This special

day is called All Saints' Day. The Bible calls anyone who believes in God and loves and obeys Him a saint. What are people like who love and obey God? What kinds of things might they do? Volunteers tell ideas. **On All Saints' Day,**

we remember and celebrate all the members of God's family who have lived before us and who have showed their great faith in God—even people from Bible times! **Who are some Bible people you have heard about?** Children answer. (Optional: Older children read Hebrews 11 and make a list of the people of faith listed there. Children then share the list with the group.)

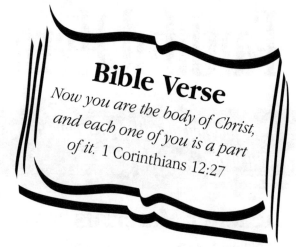

Bible Verse

Now you are the body of Christ, and each one of you is a part of it. 1 Corinthians 12:27

Conclude

We can celebrate and thank God that we are part of this family of faith! Read 1 Corinthians 12:27 aloud. **Another name for all the members of God's family is "the body of Christ." Just like every part of your body is important, every person in the body of Christ is important. Remembering how other people in God's family obeyed and followed Him helps us show our faith in God, too.** Pray, thanking God for all the members of His family and for the help of the Holy Spirit to obey God.

Discussion Questions

1. **What stories about Bible people help you want to love and obey God?**

2. **How can kids your age show faith in God?** (Do what God says in the Bible. Pray to God and ask His help in loving Him and others.)

3. **Who is someone you know who loves and obeys God? What can you learn about how to obey God from that person's example?** (Learn to tell the truth. Learn to be patient.)

4. **What are some ways kids your age can be examples of ways to love and obey God?**

Additional Information for Older Children

All Saints' Day is traditionally celebrated on November 1. The day before is called Halloween. The word "hallow" means holy or sacred. So "Hallow's Eve," or "Halloween," originally meant the evening of holy persons. Over the centuries, however, that meaning has been lost by many people.

Helicopter Project

> **When we show love for God by working together, good things can be accomplished.**

Teacher Materials

Bible with bookmark at Colossians 3:23, four ³⁄₄x6-inch (1.9x15-cm) paper strips, scissors, ruler, paper clips; optional—additional materials.

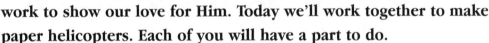

Bible Verse

Whatever you do, work at it with all your heart, as working for the Lord, not for men.

Colossians 3:23

Introduce the Object Talk

Whenever there is a big or small project to be done, it helps to have more than one good worker. God wants us to do good work to show our love for Him. Today we'll work together to make paper helicopters. Each of you will have a part to do.

Present the Object Talk

1. Select four volunteers. Volunteers stand in single-file line at a table. Give first volunteer the paper strips, scissors and ruler. Hand third volunteer the paper clips.

2. First volunteer cuts a 2-inch (5-cm) slit in the top of each paper strip (see sketch a). Second volunteer folds the lower corners of each strip to a point (see sketch b). Third volunteer attaches a paper clip to the folded part of the strip (see sketch c). Fourth volunteer folds one half of the cut portion of the strips in one direction and the other half in the opposite direction (see sketch d).

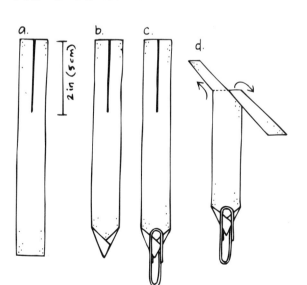

3. Volunteers fly helicopters by holding the paper clip and tossing the helicopters up in the air.

Small Group Option

Children form groups of four. Each group makes four helicopters.

Conclude

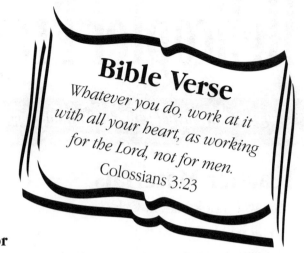

Bible Verse

Whatever you do, work at it with all your heart, as working for the Lord, not for men.
Colossians 3:23

Because each person did his or her part, we were able to make helicopters. Why does Colossians 3:23 say it's important to do our best work? Read verse aloud. **A good way to show love for God is by working together with other people.** Ask God's help in working with others to do the good things God wants us to do.

Discussion Questions

1. **What might have happened if someone didn't do careful work in making the helicopter?**

2. **What are some times kids need to do their best job when working with others to complete a project?** (School projects. Sports teams.)

3. **What are some examples of ways in which people who live together need to work together?** (Cleaning up after dinner. Decorating a Christmas tree. Cleaning the yard.)

4. **What's one way you can help someone else by doing your best work?**

Job Training

Show faithfulness by doing what God wants you to do.

Teacher's Materials

Bible with bookmark at Galatians 6:9, tablecloth, place setting (plate, utensils, glass or cup).

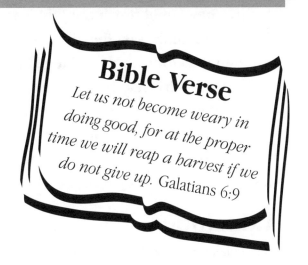

Bible Verse

Let us not become weary in doing good, for at the proper time we will reap a harvest if we do not give up. Galatians 6:9

Introduce the Object Talk

When we do what God wants us to, we show faithfulness to God. Let's find out about a woman who helped others learn to show faithfulness.

Present the Object Talk

1. Invite volunteers to use items you brought to show how to set a table. **For what kinds of jobs would you need to know how to set a table?** (Waiter.) **What are some other jobs you know of?** Volunteers answer. **In the early 1900s many African-Americans had a hard time finding good jobs. Mary McLeod Bethune was an African-American schoolteacher who wanted her students to be able to get good jobs.**

2. Mary started a school for African-American children. She taught her students how to read, how to study Bible stories and how to speak a language called Latin. She also taught practical skills like setting tables, cooking, gardening, sewing and cleaning. Mary wanted her students to have a good education, and she wanted them to have practical skills so that they could get good jobs.

One day some of the students had to wash white linen tablecloths. Mary told the girls to boil the tablecloths to get the tablecloths clean. But the girls didn't want to make a fire and wait for the water in the large kettle to boil before they could finish the job! Not much later, Mary saw the girls hanging up the tablecloths to dry. When Mary asked if the girls had boiled the tablecloths, they admitted that they had

Bible Verse

Let us not become weary in doing good, for at the proper time we will reap a harvest if we do not give up. Galatians 6:9

not. Mary insisted that the girls do the job again—the right way. Mary wanted her students to understand that being faithful and not giving up was important in every job they did, even washing tablecloths.

Conclude

Read Galatians 6:9 aloud. **When might kids today show faithfulness?** (Caring for a younger brother or sister. Doing a chore without being reminded.) **What is an example of a way Mary McLeod Bethune taught her students to show faithfulness?** (She made them boil the tablecloths in order to do a good job.) **Let's ask God to help us show faithfulness by doing what He wants.** Lead children in prayer.

Discussion Questions

1. **What does it mean to be faithful?** (To do what God wants consistently.)

2. **What are some things that God wants us to do faithfully?** (Be fair. Tell the truth.)

3. Read Galatians 6:9. **When might kids your age get tired, or grow weary, of obeying God?**

Additional Information for Older Children

Mary McLeod Bethune not only taught others to show faithfulness, but she also showed faithfulness to God herself! Mary attended Moody Bible Institute in Chicago and hoped to become a missionary to Africa. When she wasn't able to do that, she decided to stay in the United States and start a school for African-American children. The small school she started with five students in 1904 is now Bethune-Cookman College in Daytona, Florida. Because of Mary's faithfulness, thousands of students still learn about God each year!

Praise the Lord

God gives us abilities and wants us to be faithful in using them.

Teacher's Materials

Bible with bookmark at Colossians 3:23, marker, paper.

Introduce the Object Talk

God gives each of us abilities that we can be faithful to use. Let's listen to find out how one woman worked hard and was faithful to use her abilities, even when it was hard.

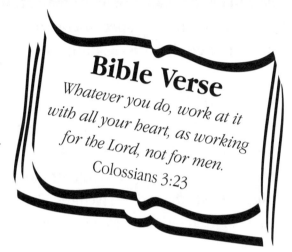

Bible Verse

Whatever you do, work at it with all your heart, as working for the Lord, not for men.
Colossians 3:23

Present the Object Talk

1. Ask a volunteer to put the marker in his or her mouth and try to draw a picture of a tree. **It's pretty hard to draw this way, but this is how a woman named Joni (JAHN-ee) Eareckson Tada learned to draw all her pictures!**

2. Joni didn't always draw this way. When Joni was a teenager, she had an accident. She dove into a lake at a place where the water was too shallow, and she broke her neck and became paralyzed. Joni could no longer use her arms or legs. But Joni was determined to be able to learn to do things again using her body parts that did work—like her mouth.

For two years, Joni worked hard to learn to draw by holding things like pencils and paintbrushes between her teeth. She began to draw beautiful pictures. Joni signed her pictures "PTL" for "Praise the Lord," reminding herself that God cared for her and thanking God for her ability to draw, even when

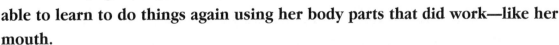

most of her body no longer worked. Her pictures were put onto cards and sold and displayed around the world. The pictures and the "PTL" reminded people to use whatever abilities they had to give praise to God. Joni and Friends is the name of an organization Joni started to give special encouragement to people with disabilities.

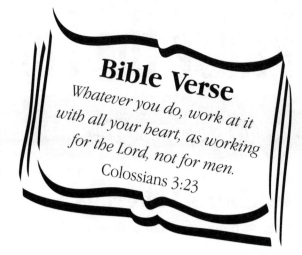

Bible Verse

Whatever you do, work at it with all your heart, as working for the Lord, not for men.
Colossians 3:23

Conclude

Read Colossians 3:23 aloud. **When we are "working for the Lord," it means we are trying to do our best work to show love for God. What did Joni Eareckson Tada do to obey this verse? How did she show that she was working to please God?** (Signed her pictures "Praise the Lord.") Lead children in prayer, thanking God for the abilities He has given us.

Discussion Questions

1. **What does it mean to be faithful?** (To keep doing something you said you would do. To keep your promises.)

2. **What are some of the things you like to do or are good at doing?** Encourage children to think beyond obvious talents such as reading well or playing sports to abilities such as being a good friend or listening well.

3. **What are some ways to be faithful in using the abilities God has given you?** (Practice using the abilities. Keep using them to help others. Have a good attitude while using the abilities.)

4. **How can you use those abilities to serve God or help others?** Answer this question with an example from your own life before asking children to respond.

Additional Information for Older Children

People were so amazed at Joni's story that they encouraged her to write a book about her life. Joni wrote an autobiography, and a movie was also made about her life. Now Joni has used her abilities to illustrate and write more books. (Optional: Bring a copy of her autobiography, *Joni,* to lend to an older child, or any of her children's books—*Tell Me the Truth, Tell Me the Promises, You've Got a Friend*—for children to borrow and read.)

Who's First?

We show our faithfulness to God by making good choices.

Teacher Materials

Bible with Psalm 119:30 marked with a bookmark, coin, two straws or paper strips of different lengths, baseball bat or stick.

Bible Verse

I have chosen the way of truth; I have set my heart on your laws. Psalm 119:30

Introduce the Object Talk

Every day we make many choices—what we're going to wear and what we're going to eat. Some choices, however, are more important than others and show our faithfulness to God. Let's talk about some of the ways we make choices.

Present the Object Talk

1. How do you and your friends choose who will take the first turn in a game? Volunteers answer.

2. Lead volunteers to take turns participating in one or more of these ways of choosing: *(a)* Toss a coin in the air. Two volunteers call heads or tails. *(b)* Hold straws or paper strips with lower end inside hand so that they appear to be the same length. Two volunteers choose straws or paper strips to see which is the longest. *(c)* Beginning at one end of a bat or stick, two volunteers alternate grasping hold of

the bat or stick to see whose hand is the last hand placed at the other end of the bat. *(d)* Choose a number between one and twenty. Two or more volunteers guess number. *(e)* Place hands behind back holding a coin in one hand. Two volunteers choose which hand they think holds the coin.

Conclude

These kinds of choices help us when we're playing games. But the Bible talks about the most important choice of all: whether or not we will be faithful to God. **What does Psalm 119:30 say about this important choice?** Read verse aloud. **Choosing the way of truth means to choose to believe in and obey God. When we make good choices, we show that we want to love and obey God.** Ask God for help in making good choices.

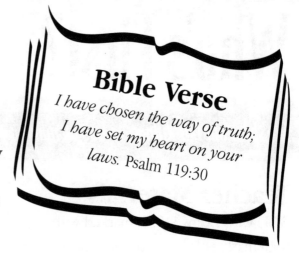

Bible Verse
I have chosen the way of truth; I have set my heart on your laws. Psalm 119:30

Discussion Questions

1. **Who is someone you think makes good choices? Why?**

2. **What are some good choices kids your age can make at school? At home? How do these choices show love and obedience to God?**

3. **What might make it hard to make a good choice?** (When you want to do something else. When others might make fun of you.) **Who does God provide to help you make good choices and show faithfulness to God?** (Family. Friends. The Holy Spirit.)

"Awe"some Forgiveness

God's forgiveness of our sins helps us forgive others, even when they don't deserve it.

Teacher Materials

Bible with bookmarks at Psalm 139:23-24 and Ephesians 4:32, large sheet of paper, marker.

Prepare the Object Talk

Print several misspelled words and incorrect math problems on large sheet of paper, adjusting the difficulty of the spelling and math according to the age of your children.

Bible Verse

Be kind and compassionate to one another, forgiving each other, just as in Christ God forgave you. Ephesians 4:32

Introduce the Object Talk

Because God forgives us when we ask, we can forgive others, even when they don't ask! In Old Testament times, there were 10 days during which God especially wanted His people to carefully think about the sins for which they needed to be forgiven. Let's find out about these 10 days and what it means to carefully look for something wrong.

Present the Object Talk

1. The 10 days between the Feast of Trumpets and the Day of Atonement are now called the Days of Awe. What do you think of when you hear the word "awe"? (Awesome. Things that are very good or beautiful.) **The word "awe" means those things, but it also means respect, admiration and amazement. During the Days of Awe, as God's people thought about how wonderful and perfect God is, they also thought about their own lives and realized the wrong things they had said and done.**

2. Show paper you prepared. Invite volunteers to correct the spelling and math. **In order to find what was wrong with these words and problems, we looked carefully for what was wrong. In the same way, during the Days of Awe, people examined their actions so that they knew what sins to ask forgiveness for.**

Bible Verse

Be kind and compassionate to one another, forgiving each other, just as in Christ God forgave you. Ephesians 4:32

3. **When we believe in Jesus and become members of God's family,** we are forgiven once and for all—forever! But the Bible says we should still look carefully at our lives and make sure they are pleasing to God. Read, or ask a child to read, Psalm 139:23-24.

Conclude

Knowing we are forgiven should make us want to please God more and more. Being forgiven makes us want to do something else. Read Ephesians 4:32 aloud. **What does God's forgiveness help us want to do?** (Forgive others.) Pray, thanking God that when we ask, He forgives our sins and helps us want to forgive others.

Discussion Questions

1. **When can kids your age forgive others?** (When others cheat you or lie to you.)

2. **What can we do to show forgiveness?** (Say I forgive you. Smile. Be friendly.)

3. **Why does God's forgiveness help us forgive others, even if they don't deserve it?** (God forgives us, even when we don't deserve it. To show our thankfulness to God, we show His love to others by forgiving them.)

Additional Information for Older Children

Invite several older children to take turns reading these verses that describe God's forgiveness and love: Psalm 103:1-4,8-13.

A Sweet New Year

God's forgiveness is for everyone who believes in Jesus.

Teacher Materials

Bible with bookmark at Acts 10:43, apples, knife, bowls, lemon juice, honey, napkins.

Prepare the Activity

Slice apples and place slices in bowls. Drizzle apple slices with lemon juice to prevent browning. Pour approximately ⅓ cup honey into bowls. (Prepare one bowl of slices and one bowl of honey for every six to eight children.)

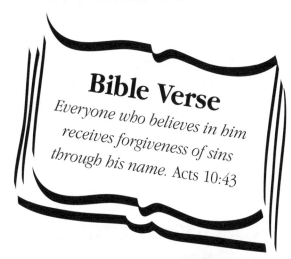

Bible Verse

Everyone who believes in him receives forgiveness of sins through his name. Acts 10:43

Introduce the Object Talk

No matter how old or young we are or how many good or bad things we've done, we can receive God's forgiveness when we believe in Jesus. Since Bible times, God's people (called Hebrews, or Jews) have celebrated a holiday that reminds them of their need for forgiveness. This holiday is called the Feast of Trumpets.

Present the Object Talk

1. The Feast of Trumpets got its name because it began with the sounds of a trumpet, called a *shofar* (SHOH-fahr) in Bible times. (Optional: Older children read Leviticus 23:23-24.) **This holiday was the beginning of a time of year when God wanted His people to turn away from their sins—the wrong things they had done. This was a time to realize that they needed God's forgiveness for their wrong actions.**

2. Rosh Hashanah (RAHSH huh-SHAH-nuh) is another name for this celebration; it means "new year." The Hebrew calendar started a new year in the fall. Rosh Hashanah reminds people to start the new year by celebrating God's loving forgiveness. To celebrate the new year, special foods are eaten. What are

some special foods you eat at parties or celebrations? (Birthday cake. Thanksgiving turkey.) **Apples dipped in honey are eaten at Rosh Hashanah to show that a sweet or good new year is hoped for.** Children dip apple slices into honey before eating.

Bible Verse

Everyone who believes in him receives forgiveness of sins through his name. Acts 10:43

Conclude

Apples and honey remind us that God gives us many good things. God's greatest gift is that when people believe in Jesus and admit their sin, God forgives them. Read Acts 10:43 aloud. Thank God for His forgiveness. Talk with interested children about becoming members of God's family (see "Leading a Child to Christ" on p. 8).

Discussion Questions

1. What are some things people might think they have to do to be forgiven? (Go to church. Read their Bibles.) **Those are all good things to do, but who does Acts 10:43 say can have their sins forgiven?** (Anyone who asks God for forgiveness of sin and who believes in Jesus.)

2. What does it mean to believe in Jesus? (To believe that Jesus is God's Son and that He died to take the punishment for our sins.)

3. How can we be sure our sins are forgiven? (God always keeps His promises.)

Additional Information for Older Children

In the Old Testament book of Micah we can read about God's forgiveness of sin. Ask a volunteer to read Micah 7:18-19. **How do these verses describe God's forgiveness of sin? As a reminder that God takes away all sin, on Rosh Hashanah Jewish people throw bread crumbs into the ocean or a river and watch the crumbs disappear.**

At One with God

Jesus' death on the cross made it possible for us to be saved through the forgiveness of our sins.

Teacher Materials

Bible with bookmark at 1 Timothy 2:3-4, variety of objects used to cover things (tablecloths, blankets, slipcovers, hats, coats, canopy, box or pan lids, umbrellas, etc.).

Bible Verse

God our Savior . . . wants all men to be saved and to come to a knowledge of the truth.
1 Timothy 2:3-4

Introduce the Object Talk

God loves us so much that He planned a way for our sins to be forgiven. In Bible times, on a special day called the Day of Atonement, the priests followed God's instructions for forgiveness. Let's find out what happened on the Day of Atonement and how we can be sure that our sins are forgiven.

Present the Object Talk

1. Show each object you brought. **What is this object used for?** After all objects have been shown, ask, **What do all of these objects have in common?** (They are all used to cover something.) Ask children to name other coverings.

2. The Hebrew name for the Day of Atonement is Yom Kippur (YAHM kih-POOR) **which means "day of covering." When something is completely covered up, you can't see it. It's like the object doesn't exist. That's how it can be with our sins—the wrong things we have done. Even though the first people who celebrated the Day of Atonement didn't know about Jesus, today we can believe that Jesus is God's Son and that He died on the cross to take the punishment for our sins. Then we become**

members of God's family. When God looks at us, He doesn't see our sins—they are not only covered up by Jesus' death, but our sins are also removed. God forgives us and our sins are gone! God promises that He will NEVER remember them again!

Bible Verse

God our Savior . . . wants all men to be saved and to come to a knowledge of the truth.
1 Timothy 2:3-4

Conclude

Because Jesus took the punishment for our sins by dying on the cross, we say that Jesus atoned for our sins. Instead of being separated from God by our sins, our sins are removed. Now we can be "at one" with Him. So no matter what name you call this holiday, Day of Atonement, or Yom Kippur, the good news for everyone everywhere is that our sins are forgiven. Read 1 Timothy 2:3-4 aloud. Pray, thanking God for sending Jesus to die on the cross so that our sins can be forgiven. Talk with interested children about becoming members of God's family (see "Leading a Child to Christ" on p. 8).

Discussion Questions

1. How can we stop doing wrong things? (Ask God to forgive our sin and to help us do what's right.)

2. How do we know that our sin is forgiven? (The Bible tells us that if we ask God for forgiveness for the wrong things we have done, we will be forgiven.)

3. What are some ways we can learn the right things God wants us to do? (Read God's Word. Follow the instructions of people who love God. Pray.)

Additional Information for Older Children

A scapegoat is something or someone blamed when things go wrong. That word comes from something that happened on the Day of Atonement. Ask a child to read Leviticus 16:10. **On the Day of Atonement the high priest would ask God to put all the blame for everyone's sins onto a goat. Then the goat was chased away into the desert never to be seen again to show that God had removed the guilt of the people's sins for another year.**

Debt Free

When we realize how much we have been forgiven, we become more willing to forgive others.

Teacher Materials

Bible with bookmark at Luke 6:37, a variety of household bills.

Bible Verse

Forgive, and you will be forgiven. Luke 6:37

Introduce the Object Talk

Because God has forgiven us, we are to forgive others, too! In Bible times, God's people celebrated a holiday that reminds us how important it is to forgive others. This holiday, called the Year of Jubilee, was celebrated once every 50 years! Let's find out what happened in this holiday.

Present the Object Talk

1. Show children the bills you brought and make a comment such as, **When I get bills like these, it means I have to pay someone for the gasoline I've put in my car and for the electricity and water I've used in my house. Until I've paid these bills, I'm in debt, which means I owe money. How do you think I would feel if someone told me I didn't have to pay these bills?** (Excited. Happy. Glad.)

2. During the Year of Jubilee if you owed someone money, your debt was taken away, or forgiven. Slaves were set free! And if you had sold land to someone, that land would be returned to you. God wanted His people to celebrate the Year of Jubilee so that poor people would receive the help they needed. The word "jubilee" means liberty or freedom. This holiday was celebrated the whole year long! (Optional: Older children read Leviticus 25:10; 27:24.)

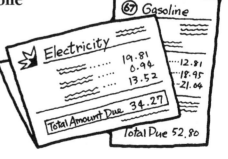

Conclude

God thinks forgiving others is so important that He doesn't want us to do it only once every 50 years. Read Luke 6:37 aloud. **The Bible teaches us that because God has forgiven us, He wants us to forgive others every day.** Pray, thanking God for His forgiveness and asking His help in forgiving others.

Bible Verse

Forgive, and you will be forgiven. Luke 6:37

Discussion Questions

1. In what ways do people today show that they forgive others? (Treat the person kindly. Be friendly. Say "I forgive you.")

2. When has someone forgiven you? How did you know you were forgiven?

Additional Information for Older Children

Jesus made it very clear that He places a high priority on forgiveness of others. Read Jesus' story of a forgiving king in Matthew 18:21-35.

Fast and Slow

God is eager to love and forgive us.

Teacher Materials

Bible with bookmark at Psalm 145:8, scratch paper, pencil, coin, crackers; optional— stopwatch or watch with second hand.

Bible Verse
The Lord is gracious and compassionate, slow to anger and rich in love.
Psalm 145:8

Introduce the Object Talk

God's love and forgiveness are so amazing that the Bible talks about them in many different ways. Let's do some actions that help us understand the ways in which God treats us.

Present the Object Talk

1. Invite volunteers to take turns seeing how slowly and then how quickly they can complete a variety of tasks: do three jumping jacks, write his or her name, crumple

up four pieces of paper, flip a coin five times, eat a cracker. Select different volunteers for each fast and slow action. (Optional: Time children using watch, limiting the slow actions to about 30 seconds.) If time is short, ask more than one volunteer to complete tasks at the same time.

2. Your actions were good examples of what it means to do things slowly and what it means to do things quickly. Psalm 145:8 tells us something God is slow to do and something God is quick to do. Read verse aloud. **What does this verse say God is slow to do?** (Be angry.) **What does this verse say God is eager to give us a lot of?** (His love.) **God cares for each of us so much that He is eager and glad to show His love to us. He is quick to forgive us when we've done wrong things.**

Small Group Option

Ask all children to complete the tasks.

Conclude

Lead children in prayer, thanking God for His love and forgiveness.

Bible Verse

The Lord is gracious and compassionate, slow to anger and rich in love.
Psalm 145:8

Discussion Questions

1. What are some ways in which God has shown His love to us? (Hears and answers prayer. Gives us courage. Gives what we need every day. Provided a way for us to become members of His family.)

2. When might kids your age feel as though God doesn't love them? (When they've done wrong. When they have problems. When prayers aren't answered right away.)

3. What words can you think of that describe God's love and forgiveness?

Feelings Masks

When we're sorry for the wrong things we've done, God is always ready to forgive us.

Teacher Materials

Bible with bookmarks at Psalm 51:10 and 1 Corinthians 13:7, six large paper plates, marker; optional—paper plates, markers.

Prepare the Object Talk

Prepare paper plate masks as shown in sketch.

Bible Verse

[Love] always protects, always trusts, always hopes, always perseveres. 1 Corinthians 13:7

Introduce the Object Talk

God will always forgive us for the wrong things we do, if we feel truly sorry and ask for His forgiveness. Let's look at some ways people show how they are feeling.

Present the Object Talk

1. One at a time, ask volunteers to hold over their faces the masks you prepared. As each mask is shown, ask children to describe how the person might be feeling. Children imitate the expressions. (Optional: Children make their own masks.)

2. Show the mask with sad expression. **During the 40 days before Easter, many Christians think about the sad or wrong things they have done and ask God to help them love and obey Him. This time of year is called Lent.** Ask a volunteer to read Psalm 51:10 as an example of a prayer people often pray during Lent. **On the first day of Lent, called Ash Wednesday, some people have a cross drawn with ashes on their foreheads. This cross shows that they believe and remember that Jesus died on a cross so that their sins can be forgiven.**

Also during Lent, some people choose to give up eating favorite foods or doing certain things they like.

Giving up things they like reminds them of how Jesus had to give up His life to show His love for them.

3. Thinking about Jesus' death on the cross does make us feel sad, but it also helps us get ready to celebrate the exciting, good news of Easter Sunday when Jesus was alive again. Show face with happy and/or excited expression.

Bible Verse

[Love] always protects, always trusts, always hopes, always perseveres. 1 Corinthians 13:7

Conclude

Read 1 Corinthians 13:7 aloud. **The word "persevere" means to keep doing something that is hard. It must have been very hard for Jesus to keep loving us and to give up His life on the cross, but He was willing to die so that we can have forgiveness of sins.** Pray, thanking God that He always forgives us when we're sorry for our sin.

Discussion Questions

1. When might kids your age want to ask God's forgiveness? (When they've been unkind to others. When they've told lies.)

2. When is a good time to ask God to forgive us? (Whenever we realize we have sinned, are sorry for the wrong things we have done and want to start doing right things.)

3. How do we know that God will forgive us? (God always keeps His promises. Jesus died on the cross to pay for our sins.)

4. What are some ways to celebrate God's forgiveness of our sins? (Sing songs to thank Him. Thank Him in our prayers. Forgive others. Tell others about God's forgiveness.)

Additional Information for Older Children

During Bible times, people wore an itchy shirt, called sackcloth, and covered themselves with dust or ashes to show that they were sorry for the wrong things they'd done. Read Jonah 3:4-10 to learn how the people of Nineveh not only gave up eating food but also wore sackcloth and ashes to show God they were sorry for their sin.

Have a Seat!

God's patience and forgiveness show us how to be patient with others.

Teacher's Materials

Bible with bookmark at 1 Corinthians 13:7, newspaper.

Introduce the Object Talk

God shows patience by forgiving us and loving us, even when we don't deserve it. When we realize God's patience with us, it helps us be patient with others. Let's find out how some people showed patience.

Bible Verse

[Love] always protects, always trusts, always hopes, always perseveres. 1 Corinthians 13:7

Present the Object Talk

1. Give each child a sheet of newspaper. **What can you do with a newspaper?** Children demonstrate ideas. **In China, some people used newspapers in an unusual way.**

2. Pastor Li was the leader of a church in China that met in a house. It was against the law for this church to meet and for Pastor Li to preach about Jesus. But he didn't stop. Because of his preaching, Pastor Li was arrested and severely beaten many times.

    One day the police came to the church meeting and not only took every Bible they found, but they also took all the chairs! Still, the people didn't give up meeting together. They patiently folded up newspapers to sit on instead of chairs and kept right on meeting together and worshiping God. (Optional: Children fold newspapers, place them on the floor and sit on them.) **The people even prayed for the police and thanked God for the opportunity to talk about Jesus.**

Conclude

Read 1 Corinthians 13:7 aloud. **What word in this verse means the same thing as "patient"?** ("Perseveres.") **To persevere means to keep on doing something, even when it's hard. When we remember God's patience toward us, it helps us keep on showing patience to others. How did Pastor Li and the people in his church show patience?** (They kept on worshiping God and praying for others, even when the police made it hard.) Pray, thanking God for His patience and asking His help in showing patience toward others.

Bible Verse

[Love] always protects, always trusts, always hopes, always perseveres. 1 Corinthians 13:7

Discussion Questions

1. **How does God show patience toward us?** (He forgives us when we're sorry. He takes care of us, even when we don't thank Him.)

2. **When is a time you need to keep on showing patience toward others?** (When others make fun of me. When others don't keep their promises.)

3. **What are some ways you could show patience with others?** (Not yelling back when someone starts yelling. Waiting to take a turn without complaining. Praying every day for a friend who is sick, even if he or she doesn't get well right away.)

4. **What can help you show patience when it's hard?** (Remembering God's love for me.)

Additional Information for Older Children

One night as Pastor Li was preaching, the police came and arrested him. Instead of fighting with them, Pastor Li and his people simply prayed for the police. As the police took Pastor Li to their car, they noticed he was carrying a bag with him. They asked him what was in the bag. Pastor Li explained that the bag had a blanket and some clothes in it. Three years earlier, the police had threatened to arrest him, so Pastor Li had packed a bag that he kept for three years in case the police came back to arrest him.

Laundry Day

God's great love in sending Jesus to die for our sins is shown to others when we forgive them.

Teacher's Materials

Bible with bookmark at Colossians 3:13, laundry basket and/or detergent.

Bible Verse

Bear with each other and forgive whatever grievances you may have against one another. Forgive as the Lord forgave you.
Colossians 3:13

Introduce the Object Talk

When we have been forgiven by God, we can show His love to other people by forgiving them. Let's find out how a woman helped some people forgive each other and show God's love.

Present the Object Talk

1. Show laundry basket and/or detergent. **What are these things used for?** Children respond. **Before washing machines had been invented, it took people many hours to wash and iron their clothes. People often hired others to do their laundry.**

2. Amanda Smith was a former slave who earned money by doing laundry for others. After her husband died, she had to work hard to earn enough money to care for her family. Amanda also worked hard so that she could spend time telling others about God's love and forgiveness.

One day after hearing Amanda speak, a young man asked for help. The man had fought with a friend several years before. Amanda's teaching helped the young man see that he needed to forgive his friend, but he was afraid to speak to him. Amanda prayed for him and said that God would help him.

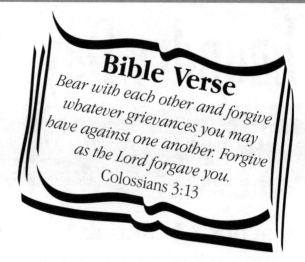

Bible Verse
Bear with each other and forgive whatever grievances you may have against one another. Forgive as the Lord forgave you.
Colossians 3:13

The next day, the young man saw the man he had fought with. Even though he was afraid, the young man walked up to him and started to speak. The other man said, "I'm so glad you came to talk to me. I wanted to say something, but I was afraid you wouldn't speak to me!" The two men quickly forgave each other and became good friends again. Amanda felt that seeing those two men forgive each other was worth all the clothes she had to wash in order to have time to tell others about God and His love.

Conclude

Read Colossians 3:13 aloud. **How did Amanda Smith help the two friends obey this verse?** Children respond. **Let's thank God for forgiving us and ask God to help us have courage to obey this verse and forgive others.** Lead children in prayer.

Discussion Questions

1. When have you needed to forgive a friend? What happened when you forgave your friend?

2. Why is forgiveness important? What do you think might happen to friendships if neither friend is willing to forgive the other one?

3. How does forgiveness help people get along with each other better?

Additional Information for Older Children

Amanda Smith was a friend to people all over the world! She traveled to countries all over the world to tell others about Jesus. She also started a home for orphaned African-American girls in Harvey, Illinois. The school was called the Amanda Smith Orphans Home. Amanda also wrote her autobiography, which tells about her faith in God and her missionary travels in America, England, Ireland, Scotland, India and Africa.

Road Signs

Admit when you've done wrong, and ask God's help to change your actions.

Teacher Materials

Bible with bookmark at Psalm 119:59, separate sheets of paper on which you have drawn road signs (see sketch).

Introduce the Object Talk

God wants us to think carefully about His commands and how we can obey them. Let's talk about what we can do when we have disobeyed God.

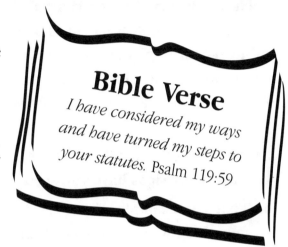

Bible Verse

I have considered my ways and have turned my steps to your statutes. Psalm 119:59

Present the Object Talk

1. One at a time, show each of the road signs you drew. **What would the driver of a car need to do to obey this sign?** Volunteers answer. Explain road signs as needed.

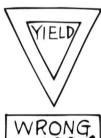   

2. Which of these signs help us know what to do when we realize we have disobeyed God? Children tell ideas. **The stop sign reminds us that we should stop doing what's wrong. The U-turn sign tells us we should turn away from doing wrong and start doing what God says is right.**

The Really Big Book of Kid Sermons and Object Talks

Conclude

Read Psalm 119:59 aloud. **What word in this verse means the same as "commands"?** ("Statutes.") **Psalm 119:59 reminds us to choose to obey God's commands. None of us is perfect; but when we disobey God, we can tell God we're sorry and ask His help in making a U-turn—turning away from our wrong actions and doing what's right.** Pray, asking God for help in obeying Him and thanking Him for forgiving us when we sin.

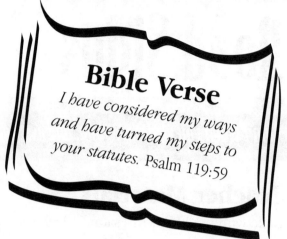

Bible Verse
I have considered my ways and have turned my steps to your statutes. Psalm 119:59

Discussion Questions

1. What other signs have you seen on the road?

2. What's an example of a time a kid your age might choose to stop doing something wrong and start doing something right?

3. When are times you are tempted to disobey God?

4. Who can help you obey God instead of disobeying Him? (God promises to help us obey. God gives us parents, teachers and friends to help us obey.)

Shofar Sounds

God's forgiveness helps us make a new start.

Teacher Materials

Bible with marker at 2 Corinthians 5:17;
optional—*shofar*, trumpet, horn, or prerecorded trumpet sounds (see pattern below)
and player; rhythm instruments.

> ## Bible Verse
> Therefore, if anyone is in Christ, he is a new creation; the old has gone, the new has come! 2 Corinthians 5:17

Introduce the Object Talk

When we believe in Jesus, God's forgiveness helps us make a brand-new start. God
forgives the wrong things we have done. In the
Old Testament the sound of a trumpet reminded the people of their need
for forgiveness. Let's find out what happened.

Present the Object Talk

1. (Optional: Play blasts of *shofar* or trumpet.) **When do you hear trumpets blow?**
(Parades. Concerts. Church.) **In Bible times, God's people played trumpets as signals. On the holiday called Feast of Trumpets, the sound of a trumpet called a**
shofar **signaled the people to remember their
need for God's forgiveness.** *Shofars* **were
made from the horns of rams.**

**2. At the Feast of Trumpets, also called
Rosh Hashanah** (RAHSH huh-SHAH-nuh),
the *shofar* is played in a special way. Clap
hands in this pattern: one clap followed by a long pause,
three claps, nine fast and short claps, one clap. Invite children to clap hands in this same pattern, repeating the pattern several times. (Optional: Blow pattern on shofar or any
single note of trumpet or horn or play prerecorded trumpet
sounds. Children play pattern with rhythm instruments.)

Conclude

In Bible times at the Feast of Trumpets, God's people would think about the wrong things they had done. When we think about our sins, we can ask God to forgive us, and He will! Jesus' death on the cross makes it possible for our sins to be forgiven. Read 2 Corinthians 5:17 aloud. Lead children in prayer, thanking God for forgiving our sins.

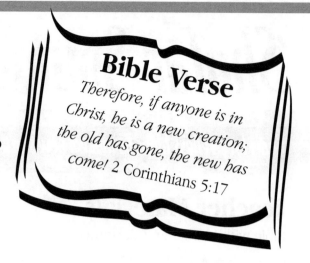

Bible Verse

Therefore, if anyone is in Christ, he is a new creation; the old has gone, the new has come! 2 Corinthians 5:17

Discussion Questions

1. **According to 2 Corinthians 5:17, "the old has gone and the new has come"; what does this mean?** (When you become a member of God's family, you don't have to feel guilty for the wrong things you have done. You have a new chance to obey God and do right things without worrying about the past.)

2. **When are some times that kids your age need to ask forgiveness?**

3. **How do we know God forgives us?** (He sent Jesus to take the punishment for our sin. God promises to forgive us when we are sorry for what we have done and ask for His forgiveness.)

Additional Information for Older Children

The sound of the trumpets not only signaled a time to get ready for the forgiveness of their sins but also signaled a new year was beginning. (In Bible times, the people didn't have calendars to keep track of what day of the week or year it was.) The words "Rosh Hashanah" actually mean "new year." When do we celebrate the beginning of the new year? (New Year's Eve in the month of December.) **Find out the season of the year in which the Hebrew people in Bible times celebrated their new year.** Children read Leviticus 23:23-25 to find information: the Hebrew people's seventh month which is the fall of our year—the months of September or October.

Take It Away

God's love is bigger than our sin.

Teacher Materials

Bible with bookmark at Psalm 130:7, clear glass, measuring cup, water, blue food coloring, bleach, spoon; optional—markers, white construction paper.

Bible Verse

Put your hope in the Lord, for with the Lord is unfailing love and with him is full redemption. Psalm 130:7

Introduce the Object Talk

When we sin, we might feel like God can't love us anymore and that our sin can't be taken away. Watch to see if anything gets taken away in this experiment.

Present the Object Talk

1. Place one cup water in a clear glass. Add three drops of blue food coloring. **How can we take the color out of the water? Can we pour it out?** Volunteers tell ideas.

2. Add a half cup of bleach to glass. Stir and let stand. The water will become clear. NOTE: Keep bleach away from children. (Optional: Draw on white construction paper with markers. Use spoon to add several drops of bleach onto the drawings. Drawings will disappear.)

Conclude

This experiment is an example of a way color can be taken away even when it seems impossible. It reminds me that our sin can be taken away, too. God's love and forgiveness are bigger than our sin. When we ask His forgiveness, He takes away our sin.

Bible Verse

Put your hope in the Lord, for with the Lord is unfailing love and with him is full redemption. Psalm 130:7

Listen for the last word in this verse: it means something wonderful God does for us. Read Psalm 130:7 aloud. When something is redeemed, it becomes useful or valuable. This verse reminds us that because God's love for us never ends, we can depend on Him to always treat us as valuable. Thank God for His unfailing love.

Discussion Questions

1. How does doing wrong often make us feel?

2. Who in your family has forgiven you? How did you feel?

3. When are times kids need to remember God's forgiveness?

4. Why can we depend on God to forgive us? (Because God loves us.)

Action Words

God's words are valuable because they show us the best ways to live.

Teacher Materials

Bible with Psalm 119:127 marked with a bookmark.

Introduce the Object Talk

The words we say can't be seen, but they can be powerful. Let's talk about why words—especially God's words—can be so powerful.

Bible Verse

I love your commands more than gold, more than pure gold. Psalm 119:127

Present the Object Talk

1. Whisper "fire!" to a volunteer who then acts out his or her response to the word. Other children in the group try to identify the word. Give clues as needed to help children guess. After the word is guessed ask, **Why is the word "fire" powerful?** (Gives us important information. Knowing about a fire can save our lives.)

2. Repeat activity with other volunteers and these words or phrases: "stop," "free candy," "home run," "goal," "I'm not it," "dinner's ready," "on your mark—get set—go," "foul ball."

Conclude

Why do you think God's words or commands are so powerful? (They help us know the best way to live. They tell us how to obey God instead of sinning.) **Because God's commands help us in so many ways, the Bible says they are very valuable.** Read Psalm 119:127 aloud. **If this verse were written today, what words might be substituted for the word "gold"?** Pray, thanking God for His commands and asking His help to obey them.

Bible Verse

I love your commands more than gold, more than pure gold. Psalm 119:127

Discussion Questions

1. **What are some other powerful things that can't be seen?** (Wind. Thunder.)

2. **What are some ways kids your age can show they think God's commands are valuable?**

3. **How has one of God's commands helped you know what to do or say?** Tell children about a time one of God's commands has helped you.

Bibles and Books

God's Word tells us the good news about Jesus and helps us grow in God's family.

Teacher Materials

Bible with bookmark at Psalm 32:8, examples of instruction books (computer book, cookbook, appliance manual, textbook, etiquette book, etc.), one sheet of paper for each child.

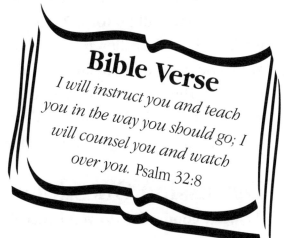

Bible Verse

I will instruct you and teach you in the way you should go; I will counsel you and watch over you. Psalm 32:8

Introduce the Object Talk

The Bible is a collection of books that tells us the good news about Jesus and helps us grow in God's family. Let's compare God's Word with other books that help us.

Present the Object Talk

1. Display examples of instruction books one at a time, and ask questions such as, **What kind of book is this? What does it help us do?** Volunteers respond. **What do all of these books have in common?** (Help people learn to do something.)

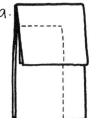

2. All of these books help us learn how to do things. Show Bible. **What makes this book different from all these other books?** (God's messages to us.) **God's Word helps us learn much more important information than how to (work a computer). The instructions in God's Word help us know the right way to live so that we can show our love to God and others.**

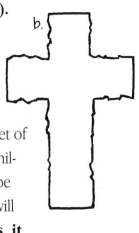

3. Let's follow instructions and make something to remind us that God's Word tells us the good news about Jesus and helps us grow in God's family. Give each child a sheet of paper. Instruct children to fold paper in half lengthwise. Then tell children to fold the top third down. Children tear out a rectangular shape from the nonfolded edges (see sketch a). When unfolded, children will have made a torn-paper cross (see sketch b). **When we see a cross, it**

reminds us of the way in which Jesus died to take the punishment for our sins. Jesus' death and resurrection are the good news the Bible tells us about.

Bible Verse

I will instruct you and teach you in the way you should go; I will counsel you and watch over you. Psalm 32:8

Conclude

Read Psalm 32:8 aloud. **What does Psalm 32:8 say God will do for us?** (Instruct and teach us about the right way to live.) **What are some ways God teaches us?** (Through His Word. Through parents and teachers.) **God's instructions show us how to grow as members of God's family. This is a great reason to celebrate!** Pray, praising God and thanking Him for His help in learning the right way to live.

Discussion Questions

1. **What good news do you learn about Jesus from reading the Bible?** (Jesus died on the cross to pay for our sins. He rose from the dead. Jesus healed and cared for many people.)

2. **How does the Bible help us grow in God's family?** (The Bible tells us how to become a part of God's family: believe that Jesus died for our sins and ask for forgiveness. When we read the Bible, we can learn the good things God wants His family members to do.)

3. **When can you read or hear about God's Word?** (At school. Playing a game during recess. At home with family.)

4. **What are some of the ways the Bible tells us to live?** (Love God. Love our neighbors. Be kind and help others. Tell the truth. Obey our parents. Tell about God.)

Additional Information for Older Children

In some Bibles, two phrases are written under the title of Psalm 32: "Of David" and "A maskil." What does "of David" mean? (David wrote the psalm.) **David wrote this psalm as a conversation between himself and God.** Volunteers read verse 5 as an example of David's words and verse 8 as an example of God's Words. ***Maskil* is a Hebrew word which means "any who understand." That means that the psalm was written for anyone who would follow the instructions in it.**

Follow the Light

We can learn the very best way to live from God's Word.

Teacher Materials

Bible with bookmark at Psalm 119:105, flashlight, index card on which you have written Psalm 119:105; optional—laser penlight.

Bible Verse

Your word is a lamp to my feet and a light for my path.
Psalm 119:105

Introduce the Object Talk

God's Word helps us learn to live in the very best way. Because God's Word is so important, it is sometimes compared to a light. Let's use this flashlight to find out how light helps us.

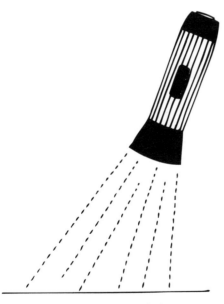

Present the Object Talk

1. While a volunteer covers his or her eyes, hide index card nearby. Volunteer uncovers eyes.

2. Use flashlight to slowly trace on the floor a path which the volunteer follows, eventually leading the volunteer to the location of the hidden card. (Optional: Use laser penlight instead of flashlight.) Volunteer reads verse aloud.

3. Repeat activity with other volunteers as time permits, inviting children to take turns hiding card and using the flashlight. (If you have a large group, use the flashlight to direct volunteer's attention around the room, stopping the light on the location where the card is hidden. Volunteer comes forward to find the card and read it aloud.)

4. Discuss the activity by asking, **How did the flashlight help you? Where did the flashlight lead you?**

Conclude

God's Word, the Bible, is like a light because it shows us the path to follow and the very best way to live. The things we learn in the Bible help us know how to love and obey God. Read Psalm 119:105 aloud. Lead the children in prayer, thanking God for His Word.

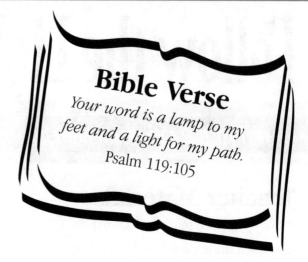

Bible Verse

Your word is a lamp to my feet and a light for my path.

Psalm 119:105

Discussion Questions

1. When might you need a flashlight or other kind of light to help you find your way?

2. When do kids your age need help to know how to love and obey God? (When someone wants to start an argument. When someone is being unkind.)

How can God's Word help us in those situations? (Helps us know what to say and do. Gives us commands to follow.)

God's Word in English

Patiently keep doing what God wants you to do.

Teacher's Materials

Bible with bookmark at 1 Kings 8:61, several different versions of the Bible and/or several written in different languages.

Bible Verse

Your hearts must be fully committed to the Lord our God, to live by his decrees and obey his commands. 1 Kings 8:61

Introduce the Object Talk

God wants us to keep showing our love of and obedience to Him. Let's find out about one man who had to patiently keep doing what God wanted him to do.

Present the Object Talk

1. Invite volunteers to examine the Bibles you collected. **In what ways are these books alike? How are they different?** Children respond. **Today the Bible has been written in many different languages so that people all over the world can read God's Word. But a long time ago in the 1500s, the Bible was only written in Latin. Because only a few people could understand Latin, most people couldn't read God's Word for themselves.**

2. One man named William Tyndale, however, wanted people to have Bibles they could read. William was a teacher who lived in England. But the leaders in England didn't want people to be able to read the Bible for themselves! William didn't let that stop him. He understood Latin, so he carefully translated the New Testament into English. Soon people all over England were buying and reading this English New Testament.

The leaders, however, were so angry they bought all the English New Testaments they could find and burned them! William was very discouraged. But then he heard some good news. The money William had earned from selling the English New Testaments to the angry leaders was enough to print even more New Testaments than before! William Tyndale patiently worked to print the English New Testaments over again so that people once again could read God's Word!

Bible Verse

Your hearts must be fully committed to the Lord our God, to live by his decrees and obey his commands. 1 Kings 8:61

Conclude

Read 1 Kings 8:61 aloud. **When we are "committed to the Lord," it means we patiently keep doing what's right, even when it's hard. What did William Tyndale do, even though it was hard?** (He translated the New Testament into English. He sold copies of the New Testament so that he could print more.) **God promises to help us.** Lead children in prayer, asking God to help children patiently continue to obey Him.

Discussion Questions

1. **What do you think it means to commit our hearts to God?** (To love God more than anyone or anything.) **How will this help us to do the right thing?** (When we are committed to God, we want to please Him in everything we do.)

2. **What are some of the things we know God wants us to do?** (Show love to others. Speak kind words to others. Tell the truth. Pray to Him.) **When would kids your age need patience to keep doing those good things?** (When they don't feel like being kind. When people aren't being kind to them. When people make fun of them.)

3. **What is another word for doing what God wants you to do?** ("Obeying.") **When is a time it might be hard to patiently keep obeying God?** (When friends ask you to do something you know is wrong, or they don't care if you do the right thing or not.)

4. **What are some things you can do to keep doing what God wants you to do?** (Pray to God for His help. Talk with others who love God.)

Additional Information for Older Children

William Tyndale's first New Testament was printed in 1526. About 10 years later, William was killed because he translated the Bible. Then within five years of his death, the king of England approved another English Bible (based on William's translation) and required every church to make copies available to the people!

Stronger Than Sin

Knowing God's Word will help us when we are tempted.

Teacher Materials

Bible with bookmark at Psalm 119:11, one or more bottles of vitamins (if you have very young children, you might want to bring empty vitamin bottles, child-proof bottles or empty bottles).

Bible Verse

I have hidden your word in my heart that I might not sin against you. Psalm 119:11

Introduce the Object Talk

One of the best ways God's Word helps us is when we're tempted to sin—to disobey God. God's Word helps us be strong and obey God. Let's talk about some things that can help us grow stronger.

Present the Object Talk

1. Show bottle(s) of vitamins. Invite volunteers to read aloud the name(s) of the vitamins. **Why do people take vitamins? How might taking vitamins or eating foods with lots of vitamins help us?** (Helps us stay healthy. Helps our bodies grow strong.)

2. One at a time, pantomime (or ask an older child to pantomime) these actions: lifting weights, jogging, getting enough rest, drinking water. Children guess each action. **All these actions can help us become healthier and stronger.**

Conclude

The Bible tells us about something we can do to help us be strong in our desire to obey God when we feel like doing wrong. Read Psalm 119:11 aloud. **What does this verse say we should do to keep from sinning? What do you think it means to hide God's Word in our hearts?** (Read and think about God's Word. Memorize it.) Lead children in prayer, thanking God for His Word and asking His help in obeying it.

Bible Verse

I have hidden your word in my heart that I might not sin against you. Psalm 119:11

Discussion Questions

1. When are some times kids your age might be tempted to do something wrong?

2. What can we do when we feel like disobeying God? (Remember the right things God's Word says to do. Ask God for help in obeying Him.)

3. What are some other ways God helps us obey Him? (Gives us parents and teachers to help us learn about Him. Promises to answer our prayers. Promises to always be with us. Helps us remember verses from His Word.)

The Shelter

God's Word helps us learn how to have self-control and live wisely.

Teacher's Materials

Bible with bookmark at Psalm 119:133, umbrella.

Introduce the Object Talk

God's Word helps us learn how to have self-control and live wisely. Listen to find out about one man and his family who helped others learn about God's Word, too!

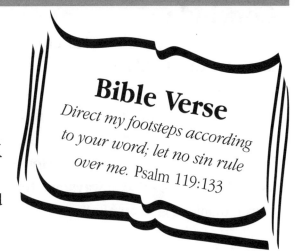

Bible Verse
Direct my footsteps according to your word; let no sin rule over me. Psalm 119:133

Present the Object Talk

1. Show umbrella. **When do people use this? Why?** Children respond. **People use an umbrella for shelter from rain and snow. A man named Francis Schaeffer and his family named their home in Switzerland L'Abri** (lah-BREE)**, the French word for "shelter." Why might you call a home a shelter?** (Keeps you safe.)

2. Francis Schaeffer and his family moved from America to Switzerland because they wanted to help people in Europe learn about God. They knew that many Europeans had questions about God and the Bible. Francis and his family wanted to help people discover the answers to their questions by teaching them about God's Word.

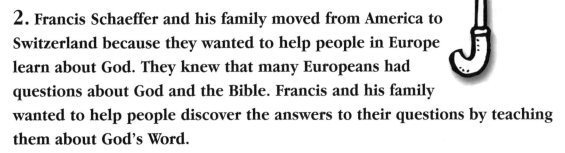

The Schaeffer family made their house, L'Abri, a place where people from around the world could come and study God's Word. They prayed that God would send to L'Abri people who had questions about God. While the Schaeffers' guests lived at L'Abri, they saw how people who loved God lived each day. The Schaeffers helped their guests learn wisdom from the Bible. Many of these guests became convinced that God is real and that His Word tells the best way to live.

Bible Verse

Direct my footsteps according to your word; let no sin rule over me. Psalm 119:133

Conclude

Read Psalm 119:133 aloud. **What does it mean for God to "direct [your] footsteps according to [His] word"?** (He will help you obey the Bible.) **What did the Schaeffer family do that showed they obeyed God's Word?** (They opened their home to teach others about God.) **God's Word teaches us wise ways to live, and as we follow these wise ways, we learn to have self-control.** Lead children in prayer, thanking God for His Word that tells us wise ways to live.

Discussion Questions

1. **What are some of the ways God's Word tells us to live?** (Love and forgive others. Ask Jesus to forgive our sins. Pray to God and ask for help with our problems. Tell the good news about Jesus to other people.)

2. **What is one way you can obey God's Word this week?** Share your own answer with your children before asking children to respond.

Additional Information for Older Children

When Francis Schaeffer was a teenager, he decided that he didn't know if God really existed or not. Francis began to read the Bible to find out if God is real or not. Francis started reading in the book of Genesis. After reading the Bible, Francis became convinced that God is real. Francis also believed that the Bible is God's Word. Francis became a Christian when he was 18 years old, and for the rest of his life he helped others learn to believe in God.

Weeks of Celebration

God's Word tells us the best way to live.

Teacher Materials

Bible with bookmarks at Leviticus 23:17 and Psalm 119:66, two loaves of bread, honey, softened cream cheese (8 oz.), small bowl, plastic knives, napkins.

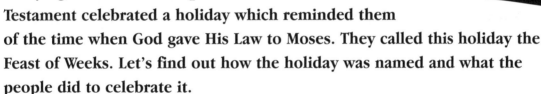

Bible Verse

Teach me knowledge and good judgment, for I believe in your commands. Psalm 119:66

Introduce the Object Talk

We can learn the best way to live by studying God's Word. People in the Old Testament celebrated a holiday which reminded them of the time when God gave His Law to Moses. They called this holiday the Feast of Weeks. Let's find out how the holiday was named and what the people did to celebrate it.

Present the Object Talk

1. The Feast of Weeks is celebrated seven weeks plus one day after the Passover celebration. Another name for this holiday is Shavuot (shah-voo-OHT) **which is the Hebrew word for "weeks."**

2. At this celebration, God told His people that two loaves of bread were to be waved as an offering, or gift, to God. Wave loaves of bread in the air as a demonstration. Read, or ask an older child to read, Leviticus 23:17. **At this time of the year, the harvest of grains used to make bread had just been completed, and the people were glad to thank God for the food they would make from the grains.**

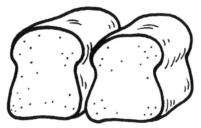

3. Today the two loaves of bread remind us of the two tablets on which God wrote the Ten Commandments He gave to Moses. God gave the Ten

Commandments so that His people would have His Word to help them. During the Feast of Weeks, Jewish people read the Ten Commandments aloud.

4. During the Feast of Weeks, it is also traditional to eat dairy products as reminders of God's Word, which is "sweet" because it gives us what we need to grow in our knowledge of God. Mix small amounts of honey with cream cheese to form a spread. Spread mixture on bread. Cut bread into quarters and serve.

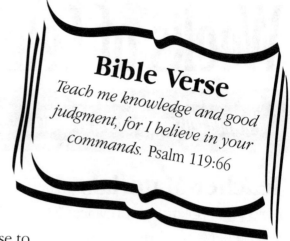

Bible Verse

Teach me knowledge and good judgment, for I believe in your commands. Psalm 119:66

Conclude

Now we have more than the Ten Commandments to help us learn the best way to live. We have the whole Bible to help us! Read Psalm 119:66 aloud. **To have good judgment means to be wise and know the right things to do and say. We know that we can depend on God to help us be wise and make good choices.** Pray, asking God's help in doing what's right.

Discussion Questions

1. **What are some of the commands God gives us in the Bible?** (Love God more than anything. Love your neighbor. Forgive each other. Do not lie. Do not steal. Honor your parents. Treat others fairly. Say kind words.)

2. **What is one way you can follow these commands this week?** Volunteers respond.

3. **When you need help following God's commands, what can you do?** (Ask God for help to obey. Talk to your mom or dad about what to do.)

Additional Information for Older Children

The Bible uses word pictures to describe God's Word and the ways in which it helps us. Children find and read these verses in their Bibles: Psalms 12:6; 19:9-10; 119:103,105.

You've Got Mail!

The Bible is God's true story and reading it helps us know and love Him.

Teacher Materials

Bag into which you have placed a Bible with bookmark at John 20:31 and a variety of mail (bill, letter, greeting card, advertisement, catalog, e-mail, magazine, etc.).

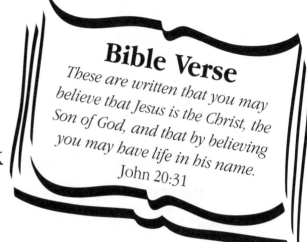

Bible Verse

These are written that you may believe that Jesus is the Christ, the Son of God, and that by believing you may have life in his name.
John 20:31

Introduce the Object Talk

The Bible is like a letter from God—written just to me and you. In this bag I've got a sample of some of the mail I received this week. As I take the mail out of the bag, let's talk about how God's letter is different from the rest of the mail.

Present the Object Talk

1. One at a time, hold up each piece of mail (keeping the Bible until the last) and ask volunteers to describe it. Discuss mail by asking questions such as, **Who is this mail from? What is this mail trying to get me to do? What message does this mail tell me? Why might I be excited to get this mail?**

2. Hold up the Bible. **How would you describe this letter? How is God's letter to us different from the rest of the mail I've received?** (It was written long ago. Its message is for everyone.) **What makes God's Word better than any other message to us?** (It's true. It tells the good news about Jesus.)

Conclude

Read John 20:31 aloud. **The words in the Bible help each person learn that when we believe Jesus is God's Son, we can be part of God's family.** Talk with interested children about becoming Christians. (Follow guidelines in "Leading a Child to Christ," p. 8.) Thank God for sending His letter to each of us and ask His help in getting to know more about Him as we read the Bible.

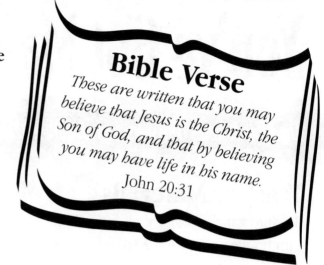

Bible Verse

These are written that you may believe that Jesus is the Christ, the Son of God, and that by believing you may have life in his name.
John 20:31

Discussion Questions

1. What's your favorite kind of mail?

2. What's the best thing you've ever received in the mail?

3. When are some times you read God's letter—the Bible?

Bible Translators

Have a gentle attitude so that you can learn wisdom from God and others who love Him.

Teacher's Materials

Bible with bookmark at Proverbs 19:20, object representing something a friend has taught you or helped you with (golf club, crocheted blanket, paintbrush, pie tin, etc.).

Bible Verse

Listen to advice and accept instruction, and in the end you will be wise. Proverbs 19:20

Introduce the Object Talk

Having a gentle attitude helps us learn wisdom from God and others who love Him. Let's listen to find out how one man's gentle attitude helped him learn something that helped people all over the world.

Present the Object Talk

1. Show and describe object. **I brought this (golf club) because my friend (Sam) helped me learn how to (play golf). What is something a friend has helped you learn?** Children respond. **A man named Cameron Townsend went to Guatemala as a missionary. He was very glad to find a friend there to help him out!**

2. When Cameron first went to Guatemala, whenever he met people with whom he wanted to talk about God, he'd ask, "Do you know the Lord Jesus?" But when he asked this question in Spanish, it translated as, "Do you know Mr. Jesus (hay-SOOS)**?" Because Jesus is a common Hispanic name, the people he was talking to did not know Cameron was talking about Jesus the Son of God. He also discovered that many of the people he talked to did not even know Spanish but spoke other languages. There were hundreds of different languages in that area!**

Cameron wondered how he would be able to talk to these people about

Jesus, so he prayed for God's help. Soon Cameron met an Indian named Francisco Diaz (FRAHN-sees-koh DEE-ahz) who loved God, too. Francisco taught Cameron his language and helped him translate the New Testament into that language. Cameron was so excited about this idea of translating the Scriptures into everyone's own language that he began an organization called Wycliffe Bible Translators. Today Wycliffe missionaries help people all over the world learn about God in their own language, all because of God's help and Cameron Townsend's willingness to learn from Francisco Diaz.

Bible Verse

Listen to advice and accept instruction, and in the end you will be wise. Proverbs 19:20

Conclude

Read Proverbs 19:20 aloud. **This verse describes what someone who has a gentle attitude is like. What did Cameron Townsend learn because he had a gentle attitude and accepted instruction?** (He learned to speak the language of the people he wanted to help.) Lead children in prayer, asking God's help in learning from others.

Discussion Questions

1. **What other words can you use to describe someone who has a gentle attitude?** ("Listens." "Humble." "Peaceful." "Respectful." "Unselfish.")

2. **Why does having a gentle attitude lead to wisdom?** (Listening to others is a way to learn from them.) Ask a volunteer to read Proverbs 19:20 aloud.

3. **Who are some good people to learn from?** (Parents. People who love God. Teachers. Pastors.) **What can you learn from (teachers) when you have a gentle attitude?** (How to love God and others. Right choices and ways to obey God.)

4. **What are some ways you can get instructions from God?** (Read God's Word. Pray to Him. Talk to other people who love God.)

Additional Information for Older Children

Wycliffe Bible missionaries have translated the New Testament into over 500 languages, and they work in over 70 countries. The average translation job takes 10 to 20 years! (Optional: Invite someone who has served with Wycliffe to talk to your children, or find additional information at www.wycliffe.org.)

Birthday Candles

God gives us the Holy Spirit to guide us and to help us tell others about Jesus.

Teacher Materials

Bible with bookmark at Acts 28:31, birthday candles; optional—small cake or cupcake, matches.

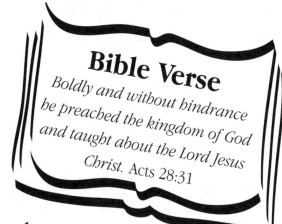

Bible Verse

Boldly and without hindrance he preached the kingdom of God and taught about the Lord Jesus Christ. Acts 28:31

Introduce the Object Talk

The Holy Spirit was given to us by God in order to guide us and help us tell others about Jesus. Let's look at a way to remember the special day the Holy Spirit came to the disciples.

Present the Object Talk

1. Display candles you brought. **How are candles used on birthdays? What do the number of candles on a birthday cake often show?** Volunteers tell. (Optional: Place candles in small cake or cupcake. Light candles and allow children to blow them out.)

2. On one day every year, the birthday of God's Church is celebrated. This day is called Pentecost. The word "pentecost" means 50. Pentecost takes place 50 days after the Passover celebration. In Bible times, Jesus' disciples had come to Jerusalem after Jesus had gone to heaven. While they were there, God sent His Holy Spirit to the disciples. This day is celebrated as the beginning of God's Church.

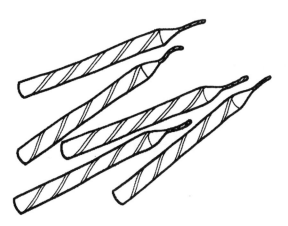

Conclude

The Holy Spirit is still with us, helping us to love and obey God. Read Acts 28:31 aloud. **What does it mean to do something "boldly and without hindrance"?** (To not be afraid. To be brave and confident.) **This verse is talking about Paul. The Holy Spirit helped Paul tell others about Jesus. The Holy Spirit will help us, too! All we have to do is ask.** Pray, thanking God for His gift of the Holy Spirit and asking for His guidance and help as we tell others about Jesus.

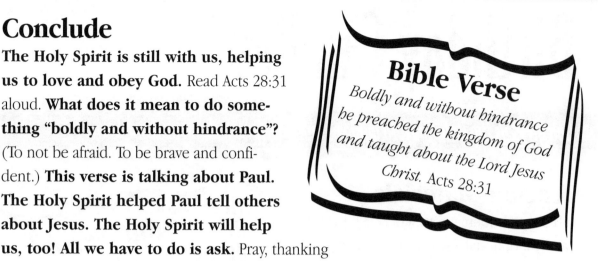

Bible Verse

Boldly and without hindrance he preached the kingdom of God and taught about the Lord Jesus Christ. Acts 28:31

Discussion Questions

1. **What happened when God first sent the Holy Spirit?** (The disciples spoke in different languages. Jesus' followers formed the first church.)

2. **Why did God send the Holy Spirit?** (To help members of His family love and obey Him.)

3. **What are some ways the Holy Spirit can help us?** (Guides us in knowing the right things to do. Reminds us of and helps us follow God's commands in the Bible. Helps us know the words to say when we tell others about Jesus.)

Additional Information for Older Children

The first Sunday after Pentecost is called Trinity Sunday. On this day, some churches celebrate the Holy Trinity, the fact that God is made up of three persons: God the Father, God the Son and God the Holy Spirit. One of the objects used to stand for the Holy Trinity is the candle, because a candle is made up of three parts: the wax, the wick and the flame. Children read Jesus' words about the Holy Spirit in John 15:26.

Gifts to Honor

God gives us people to guide and care for us.

Teacher Materials

Bible with bookmarks at Exodus 20:12 and Proverbs 3:5-6, several gifts traditionally given on Mother's Day (candy, flowers, cards, etc.).

Bible Verse

Trust in the Lord with all your heart and lean not on your own understanding; in all your ways acknowledge him, and he will make your paths straight. Proverbs 3:5-6

Introduce the Object Talk

One of the ways God cares for us is by giving us people to guide and care for us. Let's look at ways we can honor these people who are gifts from God.

Present the Object Talk

1. One at a time, display the gifts you brought. **Who might you give this gift to? Why would you give this gift?** Repeat for each of the gifts you brought.

2. On Mother's Day, we give gifts like these to mothers and other people who care for us. Read Exodus 20:12 aloud. **Giving gifts is one way to honor people who care for us and let them know we appreciate all that they do for us. There are lots of types of mothers—grandmothers, stepmothers, foster mothers and people who act like mothers! They are all given to us by God to guide and care for us. Who are some other people God has given to care for you?**

(Fathers. Aunts. Older brothers or sisters. Teachers.) Invite volunteers to tell ways people care for them.

3. This year on Mother's Day, you can honor your mother or anyone else who guides you and cares for you. What are some special or unusual ways to honor this person? (Say, "I love you." Give a back massage. Water flowers. Clean your room and bathroom. Cook dinner.)

Bible Verse

Trust in the Lord with all your heart and lean not on your own understanding; in all your ways acknowledge him, and he will make your paths straight. Proverbs 3:5-6

Conclude

Read Proverbs 3:5-6 aloud. **According to these verses, whose directions should we follow?** (God's directions.) **How can we know what God wants us to do?** (By reading God's Word. By listening to parents and other people who guide and care for us.) Pray, thanking God that He gives us people to guide and care for us.

Discussion Questions

1. Who are the people you want to honor today? How do they guide and care for you?

2. What are some ways we need to be cared for? What are some good reasons to have people to guide us? (To help us know what to do in our lives. To teach us good ways to live.)

3. Who are some people who teach you about God? What can you do to thank God for giving you people to guide you in knowing Him?

Additional Information for Older Children

Mother's Day in the United States was first suggested by Julia Ward Howe (who wrote the words to the "Battle Hymn of the Republic") in 1872; the holiday was first celebrated nationally in 1914. Other countries around the world (such as France and Yugoslavia) have also established spring days to honor mothers. England observes Mothering Sunday, a custom dating back to the Middle Ages when worshipers returned to their "mother" churches for special services.

It Is Well

Rely on God's wisdom and show patience, even when bad things that we don't understand happen.

Teacher's Materials

Bible with bookmark at Proverbs 3:5, sheet of paper, pencil; optional—hymnbook with "It Is Well with My Soul," a musician to lead children in singing the hymn.

Bible Verse

Trust in the Lord with all your heart and lean not on your own understanding.
Proverbs 3:5

Introduce the Object Talk

When bad things happen that we don't understand, sometimes the hardest thing to do is trust God's wisdom and show patience. But that is actually the best thing to do! Let's find out how one man trusted God's wisdom when something terrible happened to his family.

Present the Object Talk

1. Hold up paper and pencil. **What do you usually do with these two objects?** Children respond. **A man named Horatio Spafford used a pencil and paper to write a poem to express how he was feeling.**

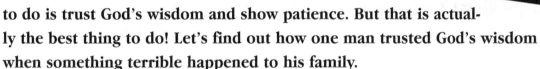

2. In 1873, Horatio Spafford sent his wife and four daughters ahead of him on a ship to Europe while he completed some unexpected business. Soon he got a message from his wife that the ship had sunk and all of their daughters died. Only his wife was saved. Horatio quickly got on a ship and sailed to meet his wife. As his ship was passing the spot where his daughters had drowned, Horatio went out on the deck and wrote these words: "When sorrows like sea billows roll—Whatever my lot, Thou hast taught me to say, It is well, it is well with my soul." (Optional: Read entire first verse of the hymn aloud.)

3. What do you think he meant by writing "it is well with my soul"? Children respond. **Horatio wrote that whether he felt peace or sorrow, he trusted God. People were so impressed with the words of Horatio's poem that they put the poem to music and it became a popular hymn which people still sing today.** (Optional: Musician leads children in singing hymn.)

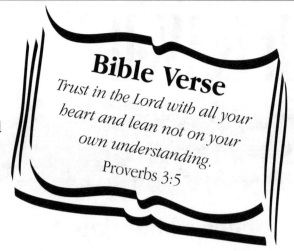

Bible Verse

Trust in the Lord with all your heart and lean not on your own understanding.
Proverbs 3:5

Conclude

Read Proverbs 3:5 aloud. **How did Horatio Spafford show he trusted in God, even when bad things happened to him?** (He wrote a song about loving and trusting God.) Lead children in prayer, thanking God that we can trust Him with our problems, no matter how bad the problems are.

Discussion Questions

1. **What might help you show patience during hard times?** (Talking to God about the situation. Praying and asking God for patience. Reading the Bible to find out how God helped people in all kinds of hard situations.)

2. **How does knowing that God is wise make it easier to be patient in hard times?** (God knows what we need and will give it to us at just the right time. He plans everything for our good. He has a reason for everything.)

3. **What are some things you can do to remember God's wisdom in order to help you show patience?** (Talk to God. Read about how God helped people in the Bible. Talk to others about times they relied on God's wisdom.)

Additional Information for Older Children

After the accident, the Spaffords moved to Israel and had more children. Mrs. Spafford decided to do everything she could to save other children. One day a Muslim man whose wife had died came and asked Mrs. Spafford to raise his newborn baby. Soon many people were bringing her children whose parents had left them, and Spafford's Children's Home began. God helped the Spaffords raise as many as 60 children at a time!

Quick Change

Listen to God your whole life.

Teacher Materials

Bible with bookmark at Exodus 15:26, stopwatch or watch with second hand.

Bible Verse

Listen carefully to the voice of the Lord your God and do what is right in his eyes.

Exodus 15:26

Introduce the Object Talk

Sometimes you might think that only grown-ups need to listen to God. But God wants everyone—for their whole lives—to listen to Him. When you listen to someone, it's important to pay careful attention to what the person says and does. Let's find out how good we are at paying attention.

Present the Object Talk

1. Ask children to look at you for 10 seconds, paying attention to the details of how you are dressed.

2. Ask children to close their eyes (or you may briefly step out of the room). Quickly change one detail about how you are dressed (remove glasses, take off a sweater, roll up sleeves, etc.).

3. Ask children to carefully look at you again, trying to identify the change you made. After change is identified or after 30 seconds, repeat activity with yourself or with volunteers. Vary the difficulty of changes made according to the age of children. As children are guessing changes, comment occasionally about the way in which they are paying careful attention.

Conclude

What does this verse say about listening and paying careful attention? Read Exodus 15:26 aloud. **Listening to God's voice helps us know how to love and obey Him. We can listen to God's voice as we read and hear Bible stories and as we pray to Him.** Lead children in prayer, asking God's help in listening to Him and doing what's right in His eyes.

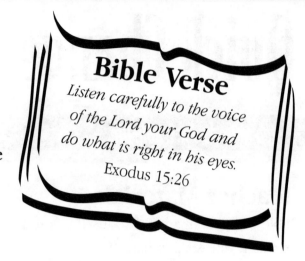

Bible Verse

Listen carefully to the voice of the Lord your God and do what is right in his eyes.

Exodus 15:26

Discussion Questions

1. **Who are some people you listen to?**

2. **When might it be hard to remember to listen to God?** (When someone wants you to do wrong.)

3. **Who are some people who help you listen to God?**

4. **How can you help others listen to God?** (Pray for them. Talk with them about what you read in God's Word.)

Shoe Talk

God chooses all kinds of people to learn from Him.

Teacher Materials

Bible with bookmark at Isaiah 48:17, one shoe from a variety of pairs of shoes (tennis, dress, sandal, slipper, boot, cleats, etc.) in a bag.

Introduce the Object Talk

Even though God has made each person different, He wants each of us to learn about Him. Look at the things in this bag that remind us of the different ways in which God has made us and what He wants us to do.

Bible Verse

I am the Lord your God, who teaches you what is best for you, who directs you in the way you should go. Isaiah 48:17

Present the Object Talk

1. Invite volunteers to take turns removing shoes, one at a time, from the bag. As each shoe is shown ask, **What kind of shoe is this? How is it different from other kinds of shoes? How is it the same? When might someone wear this shoe? What makes this shoe useful?**

2. When all the shoes have been shown and discussed say, **Even though these are all shoes, they are all different from each other. In the same way, we're all people made by God, but we are different from each other, too. All these different kinds of shoes remind me that God has chosen many different kinds of people to learn from Him.**

Conclude

These shoes also remind me of walking down a path or a street. **Listen to Isaiah 48:17 to find out who will help us know the right ways to act.** Read Isaiah 48:17 aloud. **Who does this verse say will teach us and help us learn the best way to live?** Lead children in prayer, thanking God for inviting each of us to learn from Him and for teaching us about Him.

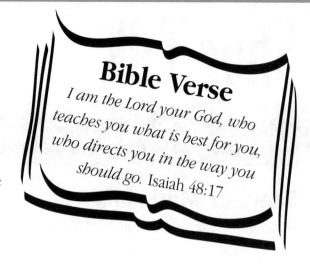

Bible Verse

I am the Lord your God, who teaches you what is best for you, who directs you in the way you should go. Isaiah 48:17

Discussion Questions

1. **What are some other kinds of shoes you wear? How are they alike or different?**

2. **How did God make people alike? How did He make them different?**

3. **What are some of the ways people today can learn more about God?** (Hear Bible stories. Talk to others who love and obey God.)

4. **What can you do this week to learn about God?**

What's Dependable?

Teacher Materials

Bible with bookmark at Jeremiah 17:7, a variety of familiar objects (alarm clock, ruler, pen, flashlight, dictionary, measuring cup, TV remote, etc.).

Bible Verse

Blessed is the man who trusts in the Lord, whose confidence is in him. Jeremiah 17:7

Introduce the Object Talk

We all need help when we have problems, feel worried or don't know what to do. God's Word tells us that in any situation we can be confident that God will help us. Let's find out why we can depend on God more than any object or person.

Present the Object Talk

Show each object one at a time. Invite volunteers to answer these questions about each object: **What is this object used for? When have you used this object? How did this object help you? Why can you depend on this item to help you? When can't you depend on this item to help you?**

Conclude

Even though these items can help us and give us true information in many situations, sometimes they can't help us. Listen to this Bible verse to find out whom we can depend on in ANY situation, no matter how bad things look. Read Jeremiah 17:7 aloud. **Why can we be confident in God's help?** (He is more powerful than anything in the world. He loves us and promises to be with us.) Lead children in prayer, thanking God for His help and that He is always with us.

Bible Verse

Blessed is the man who trusts in the Lord, whose confidence is in him. Jeremiah 17:7

Discussion Questions

1. **What are some other objects that you depend on?** (Car. Bike. Computer.) **Why might these items not always be dependable?** (Cars break down. Bikes get flat tires. Computers "crash.")

2. **What are some times when kids your age need to depend on God's help? People older than you? Younger than you?**

3. **What can you do when you need to remember God's help?** (Pray to Him. Remember a Bible verse about His power and help.)

Wise Ways

God's gift of wisdom helps us know the best way to live.

Teacher Materials

Bible with bookmark at Proverbs 2:6, variety of lists (grocery list, phone book, chore list, encyclopedia, dictionary, etc.); optional— large sheet of paper, marker.

Bible Verse

For the Lord gives wisdom, and from his mouth come knowledge and understanding.
Proverbs 2:6

Introduce the Object Talk

If we ask God, He will give us wisdom to know the best way to live. When people celebrate the coming of a new year, they often think about better ways to live. Let's talk about how some people remind themselves of wise ways to live.

Present the Object Talk

1. Give each list you brought to a volunteer to describe. **What kind of list is this? How does this list help the person who wrote it or who is reading it? What kinds of lists do you or the people in your family make?** Volunteers respond.

2. As part of their New Year's Day celebrations, some people make lists called New Year's resolutions. A resolution is something you plan or promise to do. When people write New Year's resolutions, they usually list wise ways of living. (Optional: Ask children to tell items often listed as New Year's resolutions.)

3. We can always think of good ways to live, such as eating healthy food or getting enough sleep, but because God loves us so much, He gives us the help we need to live the very best way. What are

some ways we can find out the very best ways to live? (Ask God for wisdom. Read God's Word. Listen to advice from people who love and obey God.) Volunteers read Proverbs 10:8; 10:12; 12:18; 15:1 and 17:17 for additional ideas. (Optional: On large sheet of paper, children list wise ways to live that each begin with one of the letters in the words "Happy New Year.")

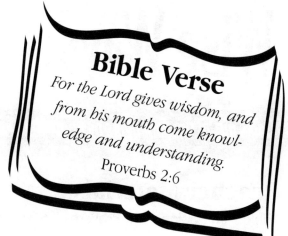

Bible Verse
For the Lord gives wisdom, and from his mouth come knowledge and understanding.
Proverbs 2:6

Conclude

Read Proverbs 2:6 aloud. **What are some wise actions God will help us learn?** (How to show His love to others. How to be a good friend.) Pray, praising God for His gift of wisdom and asking for His help to live in wise ways.

Discussion Questions

1. **What are some times kids your age need to be wise?** (When tempted to do something wrong. When making a choice about how to treat others.)

2. **The Bible tells us that God gives us wisdom. How can we get wisdom from God?** (Ask God to help us make wise decisions, and then trust Him to answer our prayers. Think about what God's Word says to do and how to obey it.)

3. **What does the Bible say are some wise ways to live?** (Love others. Be kind. Tell the truth. Be generous to others.) **Why is it wise to live those ways?**

Additional Information for Older Children

King Solomon was known throughout the world for his wisdom. He wrote several books in the Bible, including Ecclesiastes. Ecclesiastes 3:1-13 is a list of different things that may happen to people. These verses are sometimes read at New Year's services. A volunteer reads Ecclesiastes 3:1-13 aloud.

Anger Control

God can help us control angry feelings so that we can treat others in ways that please Him.

Teacher's Materials

Bible with bookmark at Proverbs 29:11, month-by-month calendar; optional—copy of "I Have a Dream" speech by Dr. Martin Luther King, Jr. (available from library or on the Internet).

Bible Verse

A fool gives full vent to his anger, but a wise man keeps himself under control.

Proverbs 29:11

Introduce the Object Talk

With God's help, we can treat others in ways that please Him, even when we're angry. Let's find out what one man did to control angry feelings.

Present the Object Talk

1. Show calendar. Invite several volunteers to find favorite holidays listed on the calendar. **What or whom do these holidays help us to remember?** Children tell. **Martin Luther King, Jr., is a man whose actions are remembered each year by many people.**

2. Martin Luther King, Jr., Day is celebrated each year on the third Monday of January. What do you know about Dr. King? Volunteers respond. Supplement children's information as needed with the following information: **In 1954, Dr. King became the pastor of a church in Alabama. At this time many African-American people felt very angry, because they weren't being treated fairly. Dr. King was angry, too. Dr. King believed that because God loves everyone the same, all people should be treated fairly.**

Even though he was angry, Martin Luther King, Jr., didn't let his angry feelings cause him to treat others in unkind ways. Instead, he led marches to call attention to unfairness. He gave speeches and preached sermons, telling people to treat each other fairly. Dr. King asked government leaders to pass laws so that African-Americans would be treated fairly. He also warned people to do what was right at all times and to treat others in ways that pleased God. (Optional: Read aloud part of Dr. King's "I Have a Dream" speech.)

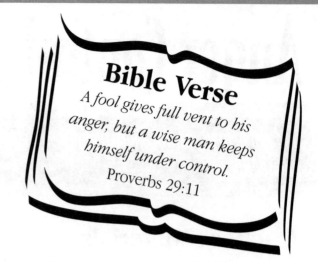

Bible Verse
A fool gives full vent to his anger, but a wise man keeps himself under control.
Proverbs 29:11

Conclude

Read Proverbs 29:11 aloud. **What does Proverbs 29:11 say a wise man does?** Volunteer answers. **When we keep our words and actions under control, it means we think about and plan our words and actions so that they show love and obedience to God. What is a way Martin Luther King, Jr., showed he had self-control?** (He didn't treat others in unkind ways, even when he was angry. He taught others to do right and please God.) Lead children in prayer, asking God to help them show self-control.

Discussion Questions

1. When are some times it is hard for kids your age to control their anger?

2. What are some things people do to help control their anger? (Count to 10. Take a deep breath. Walk away. Tell God about their anger. Ask God's help in being kind.)

3. Why do you think it is wise to control your anger?

Additional Information for Older Children

In 1964, Martin Luther King, Jr., won the Nobel Peace Prize. Every year, beginning in 1901, money set aside by a Swedish inventor, Alfred Nobel, is divided; and five prizes are given away to people who have worked hard to help others. There are awards for the most important discovery or invention in physics, chemistry and medicine as well as awards for literature and working for international peace. Martin Luther King, Jr., won the prize for peace because he taught others to live peacefully with each other.

Animal Talk

God is big enough to care for us in all situations.

Teacher Materials

Bible with a bookmark at Nahum 1:7, large sheet of paper, marker; optional—pictures of the animals discussed below.

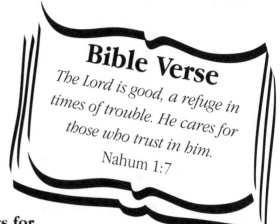

Bible Verse

The Lord is good, a refuge in times of trouble. He cares for those who trust in him.

Nahum 1:7

Introduce the Object Talk

A refuge is a place of safety. Because God is so great, He is like a refuge for us. He also cares for His creation by making ways for them to be safe. Let's discover some ways in which God made refuges for animals.

Present the Object Talk

1. On large sheet of paper, draw nine blank lines, one for each letter of the word "porcupine." Volunteers guess letters of the alphabet. As each correct letter is guessed, write it on the appropriate blank line. When an incorrect letter is guessed, write it to the side of the blank lines. Volunteers keep guessing letters until the word is identified. **What did God give a porcupine to help keep it safe?** (Quills that stand up when a porcupine is afraid.)

2. Repeat game with other animals: chameleon—able to change skin color, so it is less noticeable; gorilla—usually peaceful and shy but beats chest and screams when afraid; ostrich—the largest bird in the world and can protect itself with a very powerful kick; snowshoe hare—grows white coat in winter to help it hide from attackers; alpine marmot—hides in rocks and whistles to other marmots when danger is present; mountain goat—special pads on hoofs stop it from slipping on steep rocks; sea otter—two layers of fur give warmth in cold ocean water.

_ _ r _ u _ _ _ E

z T s A

Conclude

God made these animals in special ways to help them stay safe when they are in danger. God is like a refuge for us, too. Read Nahum 1:7 aloud. **What does God do for the people who believe and trust in Him?** (Promises to answer prayers. Gives courage.) Thank God for His loving care and for helping us when we are in danger or feel afraid.

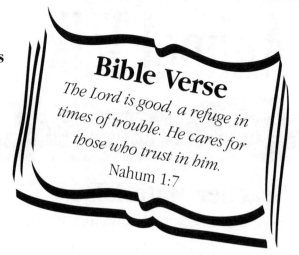

Bible Verse

The Lord is good, a refuge in times of trouble. He cares for those who trust in him.
Nahum 1:7

Discussion Questions

1. What are some other ways in which God made animals so that they are protected from danger?

2. When are some times people need God's help to keep them safe?

3. Who are some people God has given you to help you stay safe?

4. What are some other ways God shows His care for you?

Choosing Self-Control

Depending on God for self-control helps us make good choices.

Teacher's Materials

Bible with bookmark at 1 Corinthians 16:13, one or more ears of corn (if possible, bring corn still in its husk).

Bible Verse
Be on your guard; stand firm in the faith; be men of courage; be strong. 1 Corinthians 16:13

Introduce the Object Talk

Asking God for help with self-control can help us make good choices. Let's find out about someone who depended on God's help and made good choices.

Present the Object Talk

1. Show ear(s) of corn. **We usually eat the corn and throw the husk and the cob away. One man, Peter Cartwright, used an entire corn- stalk to show self-control and to help another person do the same thing.**

2. In the early part of the 1800s, many fami- lies in America lived far away from each other. One of the few times these families would get together was when a traveling preacher, like Peter Cartwright, came to visit. Each time Peter came to an area where several families lived, he led church meetings and talked with the families about God.

After one of these church meetings, Peter was invited to dinner at a nearby home. One of the men at the dinner was angry with Peter, be- cause he thought that Peter had treated the man's son unfairly. The man challenged Peter to a duel to the death!

Peter could have gotten angry with the man. Instead he just said, "According to the rules of honor, I have the right to choose the weapon. Isn't that right?" The man nodded. Peter smiled and said, "Let's go outside and grab a couple of cornstalks to fight with. I think that ought to settle things. Don't you?" The other man started to laugh and realized that he didn't need to be so angry. Soon the argument ended. At the next church meeting, the man became a member of God's family.

Bible Verse

Be on your guard; stand firm in the faith; be men of courage; be strong. 1 Corinthians 16:13

Conclude

Read 1 Corinthians 16:13 aloud. **How did Peter Cartwright obey this verse?** (Peter didn't get angry. He helped the other man do what was right.) **How did his self-control help to avoid trouble?** Children respond. Lead children in prayer, asking for God's help to have self-control and make good choices. **One good choice we can all make is to become members of God's family.** Talk with interested children about becoming members of God's family (see "Leading a Child to Christ" on p. 8).

Discussion Questions

1. When do you think a kid your age needs self-control?

2. When were some times you needed to have self-control? How did your self-control help the situation? What might have happened if you didn't have self-control?

3. What can you do when you need self-control and the ability to make good choices? (Pray to God and ask for His help. Remember Bible verses that tell about God's help.)

Additional Information for Older Children

Peter Cartwright hated slavery and in 1824, he moved his family to the state of Illinois. In Illinois, it was against the law to own slaves. Peter Cartwright decided to become a government leader and won many elections. His only defeat was in 1846 when he lost an election for the Unites States Congress to Abraham Lincoln! Peter Cartwright wrote the story of his life in the book *Autobiography of Peter Cartwright, The Backwoods Preacher.*

Delicious Decorations

Remembering God's goodness throughout our lives makes us want to celebrate the ways He cares for us.

Teacher Materials

Bible with bookmark at Romans 8:28, several types of fruits and vegetables, large bag, one or more blindfolds, knife.

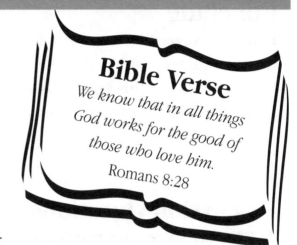

Bible Verse

We know that in all things God works for the good of those who love him.

Romans 8:28

Prepare the Activity

Place fruits and vegetables in large bag.

Introduce the Object Talk

When we remember God's goodness throughout our lives, we want to celebrate His care. During Old Testament times God's people celebrated the Feast of Tabernacles, called Sukkot (suh-KOHT) **in Hebrew, as a reminder of the good things God provides for His people. Let's discover some of the things they used in their celebration.**

Present the Object Talk

1. What did the people build during the Feast of Tabernacles? Why? (God's people built booths to remind them of God's care for their ancestors while they traveled in the desert on their way to the Promised Land.) **Try to discover what items people in our city might use to decorate a booth during the Feast of Tabernacles.**

2. Blindfold one or more volunteers. Take out one fruit or vegetable from bag. Volunteer(s) tries to identify the food only by touching it. If volunteer(s) cannot identify food by touching it, suggest volunteer(s) smell and then taste bite-size pieces of the food. As time allows, repeat with new volunteers for each fruit and vegetable. **During Sukkot, the booths are decorated with fruits and vegetables as a reminder of the good things God provides for His people.** (Optional: Read Deuteronomy 16:13-15 aloud.)

Bible Verse
We know that in all things God works for the good of those who love him.
Romans 8:28

Conclude

Fruits and vegetables are only a few of the good things God has given to His people. Read Romans 8:28 aloud. **This verse tells us that God always cares for us no matter what happens. What are some of the ways God has cared for you?** Pray, thanking God for the things mentioned in student responses. Close prayer by praising God for His goodness to us.

Discussion Questions

1. **What are some ways to celebrate God's goodness?** (Thank Him when you pray. Treat others with the same goodness God shows to you. Tell people about God's goodness. Sing songs of praise to Him.)

2. **What does God show us about Himself by caring for us?** (He loves us. He is good.)

3. **How does God show His goodness to us in hard times?** (Keeps His promises to us.)

4. **What are some of the ways people today celebrate God's care?** (Thank Him in prayer. Make banners or write prayers about God's care.)

Additional Information for Older Children

The Feast of Tabernacles was one of three important holidays God instructed His people to celebrate. In Bible times, God's people (called Hebrews, or Israelites) traveled to Jerusalem for these three celebrations. As they traveled, they sang songs from the book of Psalms. Psalms 120—134 are called the Psalms of Ascent. The word "ascent" means to be rising or climbing up toward something. Invite volunteers to read aloud the first verse of Psalms 120, 121, 122 and 123.

Games to Go

We can trust in God's promises to guide and protect us.

Teacher Materials

Bible with bookmarks at Psalm 121 and Jeremiah 17:7, example(s) of travel games (travel-size board games, magnetic checker and chess sets, etc.).

Bible Verse

Blessed is the man who trusts in the Lord, whose confidence is in him. Jeremiah 17:7

Introduce the Object Talk

Wherever we go, we can trust God's promises to guide and protect us. Let's talk about some things we often do when we travel and discover how God's promises can help us all the time, not just when we travel.

Present the Object Talk

1. Show example(s) of travel games. **When might you play a game like this?** Volunteers respond. **What games do you play on trips with your family?** (Twenty Questions, the Alphabet Game, etc.) **What songs might you sing when you travel?** ("Bingo," "Old MacDonald," etc.) (Optional: Sing songs or play games children suggest.)

2. In Old Testament times, the people sang songs when they traveled, just like we do. Many of these songs are written for us in the book of Psalms. Ask a volunteer to read the first phrase written under Psalm 121: "A song of ascents." **The word "ascent" means to go or move upwards. This phrase means that the psalm was sung during a yearly trip, called a pilgrimage, to Jerusalem. Jerusalem and the Temple were located higher up on a mountain than most of the other towns in Israel, so the people would travel up to Jerusalem in order to worship God**

in the Temple. As they traveled, there must have been times when God's people were scared or worried. Singing this song reminded them of God's promises to love, guide and protect them. Read, or ask an older child to read, Psalm 121.

Bible Verse

Blessed is the man who trusts in the Lord, whose confidence is in him. Jeremiah 17:7

Conclude

Wherever we go, we can remember God's promises to guide and protect us, too. Read Jeremiah 17:7 aloud. **Who does this verse tell us is blessed?** (Anyone who trusts God.) **Who can give us confidence?** (The Lord.) Pray, praising God for His guidance and protection and thanking Him that we can trust in Him to keep us safe wherever we go.

Discussion Questions

1. **How do your parents or teachers give you guidance or instruction?** (Tell what to do. Write lists. Show how to do things.)

2. **When are some times kids your age need to pray and trust God for His guidance and protection?** (When there are hard jobs to do at home or at school. When others do mean things.)

3. **In what ways does God guide us?** (By His instructions in the Bible. By giving us people who tell us the right ways to love God and others. By answering our prayers.)

4. **What are some ways to show we trust God to be our guide?** (Ask His help when making choices. Read God's Word to discover His commands.)

Additional Information for Older Children

Just as we have different songs for different holidays and other occasions, people in Old Testament times had many different kinds of songs. The word "psalms" means "praises." The book of Psalms is actually 150 songs. Many of them are songs of praise to God. Psalms 120—134 are all Psalms of Ascent and are also known as the pilgrimage psalms because people sang them while going from one place to another.

House Afire

Wait patiently and depend on God to keep His promises.

Teacher's Materials

Bible with bookmark at Psalm 33:20, an item from your home you would want to save in the event of a house fire; optional—copy of "Upon the Burning of Our House" by Anne Bradstreet (available on the Internet and in most American literature anthologies).

Bible Verse
We wait in hope for the Lord; he is our help and our shield.
Psalm 33:20

Introduce the Object Talk

Because we know that God will always keep His promises, we can be patient and depend on Him. Let's find out how one person showed hope and trust in God's promises.

Present the Object Talk

1. What would you try to save if your house caught on fire? Volunteers respond. Show item that you brought. **This is something I would not want to lose in a fire.** Explain why the item is important to you. **A woman named Anne Bradstreet realized that something else was important when her house burned down.**

2. Anne Bradstreet, her husband and her parents sailed on a boat from England to America in 1630. They began living in the Massachusetts Bay Colony. One night, Anne woke up to the sounds of a fire. Anne and her family escaped the blaze, but they couldn't save anything at all in their house. The entire house and everything in it were destroyed!

Anne wrote a poem about her feelings when her home burned. In the poem, Anne said that she would miss the many things that were destroyed, but the things most important to her—God's promises—could not be burned. Anne believed that God's promises were her most important treasures. Through her poem, Anne showed that she trusted God to care for her family and that she chose to hope and trust in God's promises. (Optional: Read "Upon the Burning of Our House" aloud.)

Bible Verse

We wait in hope for the Lord; he is our help and our shield.
Psalm 33:20

Conclude

Read Psalm 33:20 aloud. **How did Anne Bradstreet show hope in God? Why do you think Anne chose to respond the way she did?** Children respond. **Let's ask God to help us remember to depend on His promises and be patient.** Lead children in prayer.

Discussion Questions

1. **What are some promises you know God has made? What do you know about God that would make you trust Him to keep His promises?**

2. **What might help us wait patiently for God to keep His promises?** (Remembering the times He has helped us in the past. Thanking Him for His love for us. Praying and asking Him for patience.)

3. **What are some of God's promises for which we never have to wait?** (God's promise to always be with us. God's promise to give us courage.)

Additional Information for Older Children

During the time when Anne Bradstreet lived, few women could read or write, let alone write poems! But when she was growing up, Anne's father had worked for an important man in England. Because her father had such an important job, he was able to pay people to teach Anne how to play music and how to speak and write several languages. Later on, after she had moved to America, Anne used her talent for writing to describe her love for her husband, her children and, most of all, her love for God.

Joy in the Pit

Joyfully celebrate God's help and protection.

Teacher's Materials

Bible with bookmark at Psalm 92:4; shovel.

Introduce the Object Talk

We can joyfully celebrate God's help and protection! Let's find out about a man who celebrated God at every opportunity he had!

Bible Verse

You make me glad by your deeds, O Lord; I sing for joy at the works of your hands.
Psalm 92:4

Present the Object Talk

1. Ask a volunteer to demonstrate how to use a shovel. **What are some hard jobs people have to do with shovels?** (Dig ditches. Dig in fields. Dig big holes.) **A man named George Chen had to dig with a shovel every day for more than five years doing a job no one else wanted!**

2. **George Chen lived in China and was sent to prison because he was a Christian and came from a wealthy family. In that prison, no one was allowed to talk about God, read a Bible or pray.**

Each person in the prison had a job to do. George's job was to shovel out the huge hole in the ground where all of the waste from the prison was put. Each day the guards lowered George and his shovel into the pit. All day long George worked hard.

Most people would have hated such a smelly, dirty job! But George soon discovered that because the pit was so dirty and smelly, no guards came to check on him while he worked. Every day George was free to sing songs of praise to God, to pray out loud and to recite Bible verses he had memorized. If he had worked inside the prison in a cleaner place, he would not have

been able to sing and pray aloud!
George joyfully thanked God—even
when it was hard!

Conclude

Read Psalm 92:4 aloud. **When was George
Chen able to sing to God and praise
Him? We don't have to wait to be alone
or in a smelly pit to sing and praise
God! We can praise Him anytime!** Lead
children in prayer, praising God for specific actions He has done (created the world, forgiven our sins, answered our prayers).

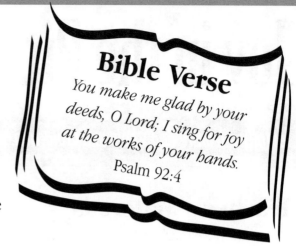

Bible Verse
You make me glad by your deeds, O Lord; I sing for joy at the works of your hands.
Psalm 92:4

Discussion Questions

1. When has God helped or protected you or someone you know? Share an age-appropriate example of your own before asking children to answer.

2. When are some times a kid your age might need God's help and protection? (During a thunderstorm. When going to a new school. When standing up for what's right.)

3. What are some ways to show your joy and celebrate God's help and protection? (Sing songs of praise to God. Pray to God, thanking Him for all He has done. Tell others about how God helps and protects His people.)

4. Why do you think praising God brings us joy? (We are happy that He has cared for us and promises always to care for us. It pleases God when we praise Him. It reminds us of His love and faithfulness. It makes us love Him more.)

Additional Information for Older Children

George Chen spent 18 years in the prison. When he was set free, he helped Chinese Christians start new churches and tell other people about Jesus. During the years George was in prison, the government killed many Chinese Christians who were not in prison. George thanked God that because he was in prison for so long, he was kept alive, and he could continue to obey God after he was set free.

More Than Enough!

God's wisdom helps us know what's best to do.

Teacher Materials

Bible with bookmark at James 1:5, table, one or more of the following: room freshener spray; electric fan with several settings; pitcher of water, small cup and plastic dishpan; snack divided into both bite-size and larger portions.

Bible Verse

If any of you lacks wisdom, he should ask God, who gives generously to all without finding fault, and it will be given to him.
James 1:5

Introduce the Object Talk

We're talking today about wisdom—knowing what's best to do and say. God promises to give us wisdom if we ask Him. Watch what I do to discover a word that describes the way in which God gives us wisdom.

Present the Object Talk

1. One at a time complete one or more of these demonstrations to illustrate what it means to do something generously: *(a)* Ask children what they smell as you first spray a small amount of room freshener and then spray a larger amount. *(b)* Ask children what they feel as you first turn on fan at lowest speed and then turn fan to highest speed. *(c)* Ask children what they see as you first pour a tiny amount of water into cup and then pour water into cup until it overflows into the dishpan. *(d)* Ask children what they taste as you first serve bite-size portions of snack to children and then serve larger portions to children.

2. Of the actions I just did, which one(s) would you describe as generous? Which one(s) were not? Why? How do you know if someone is generous or not?

Conclude

Listen to what the Bible says about God's promise of wisdom. Read James 1:5 aloud. **What should we do if we need wisdom, being able to understand what happens and know the right thing to do?** Pray, asking God for wisdom and thanking Him for giving wisdom generously.

Bible Verse

If any of you lacks wisdom, he should ask God, who gives generously to all without finding fault, and it will be given to him.
James 1:5

Discussion Questions

1. **Who are some wise people you know? What do you think makes them wise?**

2. **When is a time a kid your age needs to be wise?** (To understand what God want us to do.) **Why?**

3. **Why can we be sure God will give us wisdom if we ask for it?** (God's Word tells us.)

4. **How can you be wise today?** (Follow God's Word. Listen to our parents.)

Passover Power

Whenever we need help, we can depend on God's power.

Teacher Materials

Bible with bookmark at Exodus 12:24-27 and Psalm 46:1, bite-size pieces of unleavened bread (or *matzo* crackers) and bread prepared with yeast, two paper plates.

Bible Verse
God is our refuge and strength, an ever-present help in trouble. Psalm 46:1

Prepare the Activity

Put each type of bread on a different plate.

Introduce the Object Talk

We can depend on God's power whenever we need help. Long ago in Old Testament times, God helped the Israelites escape from slavery in Egypt. Let's find out how God told His people to remember and celebrate His great power and help.

Present the Object Talk

1. As part of this celebration God told His people to eat a special kind of bread. Children eat samples of each type of bread. **What are the differences you can find by touching and tasting the two different kinds of bread?** Volunteers respond. Identify which is unleavened bread. **Because unleavened bread does not have yeast in it, it doesn't rise or puff up into a loaf shape when it is baked, and it can be made very quickly. Why do you think the Israelites only had time to make unleavened bread?** (They were in a hurry to escape from Egypt.)

2. What else do you remember about the Israelites' escape from Egypt? (God sent 10 plagues to convince Pharaoh, the Egyptian ruler, to let the people leave.) **The name of this holiday, Passover, comes from the last plague. God had given the Israelites special instructions to paint on their doorposts the blood of a lamb.**

On the night the Israelites escaped from Egypt, in any house that did not have the lamb's blood painted on its doorposts, the oldest son would die. Because death passed over the Israelite homes, the holiday is called Passover. The lamb killed at this celebration was called the Passover Lamb. Jesus is called our Passover Lamb because He gave His life to rescue us from sin.

Bible Verse
God is our refuge and strength, an ever-present help in trouble. Psalm 46:1

3. The Passover celebration helps people remember God's power.
Read, or ask an older child to read, Exodus 12:24-27.

Conclude

God's power helps us today, too. Read Psalm 46:1 aloud. **What do you learn about God from Psalm 46:1?** Pray, thanking God that we can depend on His power.

Discussion Questions

1. **When are some times kids your age need God's help?**

2. **When are some times God has helped you?** Tell your own answer before volunteers respond.

3. **What can we do to receive God's help?** (Pray to God and ask for His help. Read what God tells us to do in the Bible.)

4. **Why can we depend on God's power and help?** (He loves us. He keeps His promises.)

Additional Information for Older Children

Yeast spreads through dough and causes the bread to rise, or get bigger. How does yeast remind us of sin? (When a person sins, it can spread through his or her life.) **Throughout Scripture, yeast is compared to sin. Read 1 Corinthians 5:6-8 to find what the apostle Paul wrote about sin and how Jesus' death on the cross takes away our sin.**

Sending Portions

God's power helps us accomplish His plans.

Teacher Materials

Bible with bookmarks at Esther 9 and Psalm 33:11, basket; optional—canned foods.

Introduce the Object Talk

God has many good things He wants us to do and with His power, He helps us to do them. Queen Esther, who lived long ago in Old Testament times, rescued her people to keep them safe as God had planned. Her brave and good actions are remembered with a special holiday called Purim (POO-rihm). **Let's find out how this holiday is celebrated.**

Bible Verse

The plans of the Lord stand firm forever, the purposes of his heart through all generations.
Psalm 33:11

Present the Object Talk

1. Display the basket you brought. **If you were to fill this basket with food for a friend, what would you put in it?** Volunteers answer. Repeat with gifts for a neighbor, a teacher and a grandparent. (Optional: Put canned foods in basket to make a gift for a needy person.) **Giving gifts to others, especially those in need, is one of the ways Purim is celebrated.**

2. Purim is also celebrated by reading aloud the whole book of Esther. As the story is read, children in costumes act out the story of how God's people were saved. The audience cheers the good characters and boos the bad characters in the story. Purim is a day for celebrating God's power and doing good things to help others. The custom of giving gifts to friends and to the poor is written about in the book of Esther. Read Esther 9:22 aloud. **This custom is called *Shalach Manot*** (shah-LAHK muh-NOHT).

(In English *Shalach Manot* means "sending portions.")

Bible Verse

The plans of the Lord stand firm forever, the purposes of his heart through all generations.
Psalm 33:11

Conclude

When we do things that show our love and obedience to God, we are following God's plans for us. Read Psalm 33:11 aloud. **This verse helps us learn that God's power is so strong that nothing can keep His plans from taking place. What are some of the good things God wants us to do?** (Receive His love. Become a member of God's family. Talk to God in prayer.) Pray, asking for God's help to do the good things He wants us to do.

Discussion Questions

1. **What did Esther and her people celebrate on Purim?** (Esther's brave actions. The defeat of Haman. God's power and care for them.)

2. **What are some of the good things God has helped you do?** (Be kind to a brother or sister. Tell others about Him. Help someone who was in danger.)

3. **What are some ways to learn more of the good things God has planned for you to do?** (Read God's commands in the Bible. Ask teachers or older Christians. Pray to God.)

Additional Information for Older Children

The word "Purim" is the plural form of a Hebrew word that means "lots." The name refers to the way in which the evil Haman decided which day to destroy the Jews. Haman cast lots, a phrase that means to choose something by chance—like drawing straws or participating in a lottery. Another way in which Purim is celebrated is by eating a special pastry called *hamantaschen*. This pastry is shaped like a triangle to remind people of the shape of Haman's hat.

Thundering Sounds

Because God's power is greater than anything, He can help us when we're afraid.

Teacher Materials

Bible with bookmarks at Psalm 29 and John 14:27; optional—picture of a storm, objects to make sound effects for rain and thunder (cookie sheet, drum, rain stick).

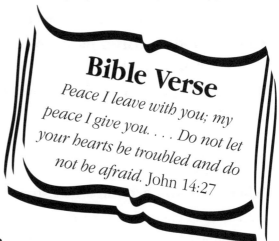

Bible Verse

Peace I leave with you; my peace I give you. . . . Do not let your hearts be troubled and do not be afraid. John 14:27

Introduce the Object Talk

When we're afraid, God can help us because His power is the greatest thing there is. Let's look at some of the ways we can see God's power in nature.

Present the Object Talk

1. **What kinds of sounds do you hear during a thunderstorm? How do you think we could make the sounds of a thunderstorm? Volunteers respond.**

(Optional: Display picture of a storm.)

2. Children suggest and practice three sounds which can be used to represent a thunderstorm (rubbing palms together, snapping fingers, patting legs, stomping feet, etc.).

After practicing sounds, divide children into three groups and assign an order in which to make sounds. (Optional: Ask an older child to lead each group.) Direct children to make sounds as in a round. The first group begins a sound, followed in five to eight seconds by the second group and then the third group. When the first group begins a different sound, the other groups continue with the old sound until

directed to change. (Optional: Children use objects to make sound effects for rain and thunder.)

3. The sound of thunder is one way the Bible describes God's power. Read or ask older children to read Psalm 29:3-4,7 aloud. **These verses help us discover what God's power is like. How is the voice of God described in this psalm?** (Majestic. Powerful. Like thunder and lightning.) **God's power is greater than anything He has made.**

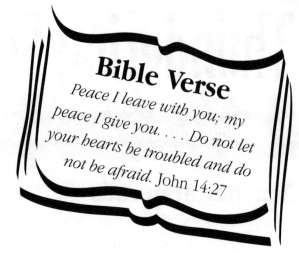

Bible Verse
Peace I leave with you; my peace I give you. . . . Do not let your hearts be troubled and do not be afraid. John 14:27

Conclude

When have you been in a bad storm? How did you feel when you heard thunder? Volunteers respond. Read John 14:27 aloud. **What does this verse tell us about being afraid?** (When we feel afraid, God promises to help us feel peaceful.) Pray, praising God for His great power and thanking Him for His help when we're afraid.

Discussion Questions

1. What are some powerful things that kids your age might be afraid of? (Storms. Earthquakes. Tornadoes.)

2. Why can God help us when we are afraid of these things? (Because He is the one true God. God created everything. He is more powerful than anything He created. He loves us and wants to help us.)

3. How does God help us when we are afraid? (Answers our prayers. Gives us adults to help us feel safe. Helps us remember His power. Gives us courage and peace.)

Additional Information for Older Children

Psalm 29 is a psalm of praise to God. This psalm has been called "The Psalm of the Seven Thunders" because it refers to the voice of God seven times. Many books of the Bible show God's power by comparing His voice to thunder. Children read the following Scriptures that compare God's voice to thunder: Job 37:5, Psalm 68:32-33, Jeremiah 10:12-13.

Balloon Pop

Because Jesus is alive, we know He will keep His promise to be with us now and forever.

Teacher Materials

Bible with bookmark at Matthew 28:20, two large balloons, transparent tape, sewing needle; optional—additional balloons.

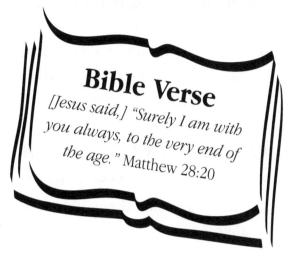

Bible Verse

[Jesus said,] "Surely I am with you always, to the very end of the age." Matthew 28:20

Prepare the Object Talk

Inflate (a little less than full) and tie the balloons. Place a 2-inch (5-cm) strip of tape at end of one balloon. Smooth over the tape to remove all air bubbles. Before class, practice Step 2 below.

Introduce the Object Talk

All through our lives we need help—especially when things happen that make us afraid. Because Jesus is alive, He can protect and help us. Look at these balloons to find out what protects them.

Present the Object Talk

1. Hold up the needle and the balloon without the tape. **What will happen when I poke the balloon with the needle? The balloon doesn't have any protection**

against the sharp needle, so it will pop. Use the needle to pop the balloon.

2. Hold up the second balloon. Firmly push the needle through the tape, keeping a good grasp on the needle. Then smoothly remove the needle. **Why didn't this balloon pop?** Volunteers tell ideas. **This balloon didn't pop when I poked it with the needle because it had something helping it to stay strong and not pop.** Show children the tape on the balloon. (Optional: Depending on the number of children in your group and their ages, invite children to blow up balloons and attempt to pop them with and without tape.)

Conclude

Jesus promises to help us. Because Jesus is alive, we know He will keep His promises to us. Listen to Jesus' promise. Read Matthew 28:20 aloud. **Jesus promises to be with us now and forever, helping us and caring for us.** Lead children in prayer, thanking Jesus for His promise to be with us.

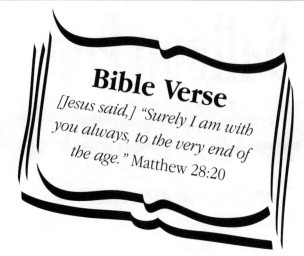

Bible Verse

[Jesus said,] "Surely I am with you always, to the very end of the age." Matthew 28:20

Discussion Questions

1. **When do people need to know of Jesus' help?**

2. **When are some times kids your age need to remember that Jesus is with them?**

3. **What are some other promises Jesus makes to His followers?** (To hear and answer their prayers. To forgive sins.)

Believe It or Not

Believe that Jesus is alive, and accept His love for you!

Teacher Materials

Bible with bookmarks at John 3:16 and John 20:29; objects for children to describe (unusual stuffed animal, kitchen utensil, tool, etc.), placed in a bag.

Bible Verse

For God so loved the world that he gave his one and only Son, that whoever believes in him shall not perish but have eternal life.

John 3:16

Introduce the Object Talk

We accept Jesus' love for us and believe that He is alive, even though we didn't see Him for ourselves! Let's try an experiment to discover why it sometimes might be hard to believe what other people tell us about something we didn't see for ourselves.

Present the Object Talk

1. Several volunteers leave the room (or close eyes). Show one of the objects and give children several moments to look at it. **When the volunteers return, describe the object to them, but don't use the words ("stuffed" or "animal").** Volunteers return and try to guess what the object is based on children's descriptions. Repeat for each object you brought, reminding children not to use obvious words that would give away the object's identity.

2. What made it difficult to figure out what the object was? Volunteers respond. **Sometimes it's hard to believe something is true if you haven't seen it yourself. When Jesus rose from the dead, Thomas, one of His disciples, didn't believe Jesus was really alive**

because he hadn't seen Jesus with his own eyes.

Even though we didn't see what Jesus did or hear what He said when He lived on earth and even though we didn't see Him after He rose from the dead, we believe all these things happened. That's why we celebrate Easter! We can read God's Word that tells us exactly what the disciples saw and that they believed Jesus was alive! What did Jesus say about people who believe in Him without seeing Him? Read John 20:29.

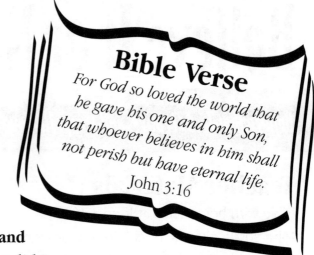

Bible Verse

For God so loved the world that he gave his one and only Son, that whoever believes in him shall not perish but have eternal life. John 3:16

3. Thinking about Jesus' death on the cross does make us feel sad, but it also helps us get ready to celebrate the exciting, good news of Easter Sunday when Jesus was alive again. Ask children to demonstrate a face with happy and/or excited expression.

Conclude

Because we know Jesus is alive, we can also have eternal life—life that lasts forever with God in heaven. Read John 3:16 aloud. Pray, thanking God that Jesus is alive and that He loves us.

Discussion Questions

1. **What are some of the things you believe about Jesus?** (He loves me. He forgives the wrong things I do. He makes it possible for me to be part of God's family.)

2. **Who has helped you learn to believe in Jesus?** (Sunday School teacher. Parent.)

3. **In what ways do kids your age show they believe that Jesus is alive?** (Pray to Him. Obey His commands. Read the Bible to learn more about Him.)

Additional Information for Older Children

Jesus appeared several times to many different people in the days immediately following his resurrection. You can read about Jesus' appearance to two men traveling on the road to Emmaus in Luke 24:13-35.

Dead or Alive?

Jesus' death and resurrection were the fulfillment of God's promise of salvation.

Teacher Materials

Bible with bookmark at Romans 6:4, two each of several examples of fruits with pits (avocados, peaches, olives, dates, plums), knife.

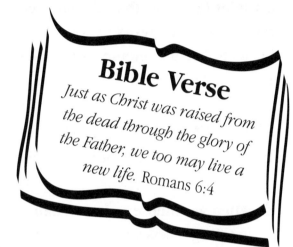

Bible Verse

Just as Christ was raised from the dead through the glory of the Father, we too may live a new life. Romans 6:4

Prepare the Object Talk

Before children arrive, cut open one of each kind of fruit and remove the pit.

Introduce the Object Talk

All through the Old Testament, we read about God's promise to send a Savior. God kept His promise through Jesus' death and resurrection. Let's look at these reminders of how something that looks dead can grow new life.

Present the Object Talk

1. One at a time, show each fruit pit. **What fruit do you think this pit is from? Does the pit look dead or alive? Why? What would happen if this pit were planted in good soil and watered?**

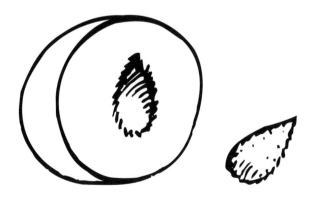

2. Show each fruit. Invite children to match fruit with their pits. After each fruit and pit are matched correctly, comment, **Even though the pits, or seeds, look like they are dead, new plants are able to grow from them.**

Conclude

When Jesus died, His friends thought they would never see Him again. But God's power made Jesus come back to life again. Read Romans 6:4 aloud. **What does this verse say we may have because of Jesus' death and resurrection?** (A new life.) **Jesus made it possible for us to become members of God's family.** Thank God in prayer for His gift of salvation.

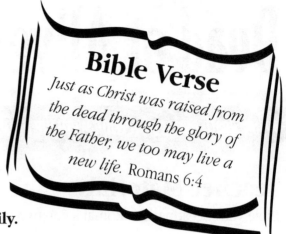

Bible Verse

Just as Christ was raised from the dead through the glory of the Father, we too may live a new life. Romans 6:4

Discussion Questions

1. Why was Jesus the only One who could take the punishment for our sins? (Jesus is the only person who never sinned. He is the One God promised to send.)

2. When we choose to become members of God's family, what does He give us? (Forgiveness for our sins. Eternal life.)

3. What are some other things in nature that remind us of new life? (Flowers. Baby animals. Butterflies.)

God's Smuggler

Growing the fruit of the Spirit in our lives begins when we believe Jesus is God's Son, ask forgiveness for our sins and become part of God's family.

Teacher's Materials

Bible with bookmark at Galatians 5:22-23, suitcase packed with clothes and several Bibles; optional—hide Bibles in room.

Bible Verse

The fruit of the Spirit is love, joy, peace, patience, kindness, goodness, faithfulness, gentleness and self-control. Against such things there is no law. Galatians 5:22-23

Introduce the Object Talk

When we're growing God's good fruit in our lives, we show that we are members of God's family by the things we do. Let's find out how someone showed love for God.

Present the Object Talk

1. A man called Brother Andrew didn't grow up loving God. In fact, when he was a young man, he loved doing dangerous things and didn't care if other people got hurt because of his actions.

But one day Brother Andrew began to read the Bible and realized that God loved him and forgave him for his wrong actions. His love for God and others began to grow. As he learned more about loving God, Brother Andrew worked hard to show love to other people and find ways to tell them about Jesus.

2. Show suitcase. **What do you think is in this suitcase?** Invite a volunteer to look through the suitcase to find Bibles. (Optional: Children find Bibles hidden in room.) **Brother Andrew heard of some countries where the government did not allow Bibles. So he hid Bibles in his suitcases and car and took them to Christians in these countries. If the hidden Bibles had been discovered, Brother Andrew**

could have been put in jail. God helped Brother Andrew, and he was able to safely deliver many, many Bibles. The actions of Brother Andrew showed how much he loved God and how much he wanted others to love God.

Bible Verse

The fruit of the Spirit is love, joy, peace, patience, kindness, goodness, faithfulness, gentleness and self-control. Against such things there is no law. Galatians 5:22-23

Conclude

Read Galatians 5:22-23 aloud. **These verses tell us the good ways in which God's Holy Spirit helps each member of His family live. Which of these characteristics have you seen someone show? How?** Children respond. **Which of these characteristics did Brother Andrew show?** (Love. Kindness. Faithfulness.) Pray, asking God to help children show love for God in their actions and words. Talk with interested children about becoming members of God's family (see "Leading a Child to Christ" on p. 8).

Discussion Questions

1. **Which of the fruit of the Spirit in Galatians 5:22-23 are hardest for kids your age to show?**

2. **When might a kid your age show love? Patience? Joy?** Repeat with other fruit of the Spirit, as time allows.

3. **How can others know that we are part of God's family and that we love Him?** (We can tell others about our love for God. They can see the fruit of the Spirit in our lives.)

Additional Information for Older Children

The name Brother Andrew was like a nickname. Because some countries didn't want Brother Andrew to bring Bibles to their people, he didn't want everyone to know his real name. Another nickname Brother Andrew had was "God's Smuggler." *God's Smuggler* was also the name of a book that Brother Andrew wrote about the exciting ways that God helped him show love to others.

Here's Jesus!

Jesus' baptism and John's announcement help everyone know that Jesus is the Savior.

Teacher Materials

Bible with bookmark at John 1:29, a variety of newspaper and/or magazine ads and announcements (classified ad, product advertisement, notice of sale at a store, announcement of a coming event, etc.).

Bible Verse

John saw Jesus coming toward him and said, "Look, the Lamb of God, who takes away the sin of the world!" John 1:29

Introduce the Object Talk

In the Bible, the good news about Jesus was announced by John the Baptist. Today we hear about good news in lots of different ways. Look at these announcements to find what news is being told.

Present the Object Talk

1. One at a time show the ads and announcements you collected. Ask a volunteer to describe the message of each ad or announcement. **What are some other ways in which announcements are made?** (Birth or graduation announcements. Billboards. TV or radio commercials.)

2. All of these announcements tell things that will soon happen. But after a few weeks—after the sale is over or after the event has happened—we don't

really need to remember the announcement any more. The announcement John made about Jesus, however, is something people have needed to know about and will remember for a long time! The words John said about Jesus are so important that EVERYONE still needs to hear them. Read John 1:29 aloud.

Conclude

What kind of ad or billboard would you make to announce this good news about Jesus? Volunteers tell ideas. Lead children in prayer, thanking God for the good news that Jesus is His Son.

Bible Verse

John saw Jesus coming toward him and said, "Look, the Lamb of God, who takes away the sin of the world!" John 1:29

Discussion Questions

1. Why was Jesus called the "Lamb of God"?

("Lamb of God" is a name for Jesus that tells us that He died to take away our sins. Jewish people used to offer a lamb as a sacrifice to God for their sins; Jesus became like one of those lambs when He died.)

2. What other news about Jesus would you like to announce to others?

3. How would you announce the good news about Jesus?

Hidden Picture

We can worship Jesus as the Savior whom God sent for everyone in the world.

Teacher Materials

Bible with bookmark at John 8:12, a large picture (picture of wise men, nature scene, children or family scene, etc.), large Post-it Notes.

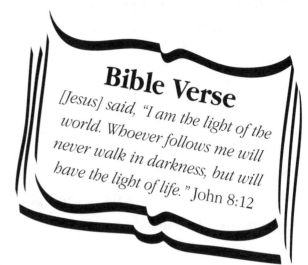

Bible Verse

[Jesus] said, "I am the light of the world. Whoever follows me will never walk in darkness, but will have the light of life." John 8:12

Prepare the Activity

Completely cover large picture with rows of Post-it Notes.

Introduce the Object Talk

One of the best reasons to worship Jesus is because He is the Savior God sent for all the people of the world. In the Bible we read of some ways that people found out about this good news. Let's find out who these people were and how they learned and celebrated the fact that Jesus is the Savior for everyone!

Present the Object Talk

1. Display picture covered with Post-it Notes. **What picture might be hidden behind these Post-it Notes?** Invite one volunteer at a time to remove a Post-it Note, asking each to guess what the picture is. Continue until all Post-it Notes are removed.

2. It's always exciting to discover something that has been hidden. A long time ago in Bible times, some men traveled a long way to discover a new King. Who were these men and who did they find? (The wise men who found and worshiped Jesus.) **The wise men were glad to have the Savior of the world shown to them when they came to Bethlehem. This discovery of the wise men is celebrated around the world at a special holiday on January 6 called Epiphany. Epiphany comes from a Greek word that means to show or reveal.**

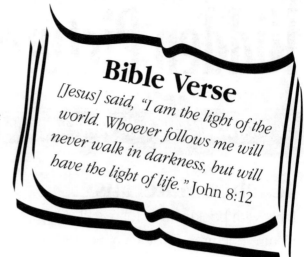

Bible Verse

[Jesus] said, "I am the light of the world. Whoever follows me will never walk in darkness, but will have the light of life." John 8:12

Conclude

Removing the papers helped you reveal and see what the picture was. The wise men helped show everyone in the whole world that Jesus is God's Son and that He came to be the Savior of everyone in the world! Read John 8:12 aloud. When Jesus said He is the light of the world, He meant that He shows people of all countries how to know God. Pray, thanking Jesus for being the Savior of the world.

Discussion Questions

1. **What does it mean to worship Jesus?** (To show how much we love Him. To thank and praise Him.)

2. **What can we thank Jesus for doing?** (Loving us. Hearing and answering our prayers.)

3. **What are some other gifts we can give Jesus?** (Bring offering to church. Obey Jesus and show His love by caring for others. Thank Jesus when we pray.)

Additional Information for Older Children

The Bible tells us the wise men came from the East. (See Matthew 2:1.) **Many Bible students believe they came from the area around Babylon. The Jewish people had lived as captives for 70 years in Babylon. One of these captives was Daniel, the Old Testament prophet. The wise men may have learned about the promise of the Messiah from the writings of Daniel. Read some of Daniel's writings about the Messiah in Daniel 7:13-14.** Invite children to find and read these verses.

Jungle Fever

We learn what love is like by looking at Jesus' life.

Teacher's Materials

Bible with bookmark at 1 John 3:16, jungle item (fern, picture of jungle animals from a nature magazine, tape of jungle sounds, rainstick or other artifact, video of jungle scenery, etc.).

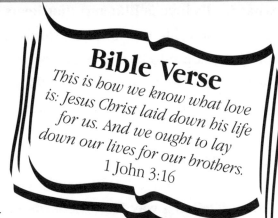

Bible Verse

This is how we know what love is: Jesus Christ laid down his life for us. And we ought to lay down our lives for our brothers.
1 John 3:16

Introduce the Object Talk

Jesus' words and actions when He lived on Earth showed us what love is like. Let's find out how some people who lived in a jungle learned about Jesus' life and His love for them.

Present the Object Talk

1. Show and describe the jungle item you brought. **What would you like about living in a jungle? What do you think might be difficult about living there?** Children respond. **One tribe of people who lived in a jungle in New Guinea had a difficult time, because they often fought with another tribe. New Guinea is near Australia.**

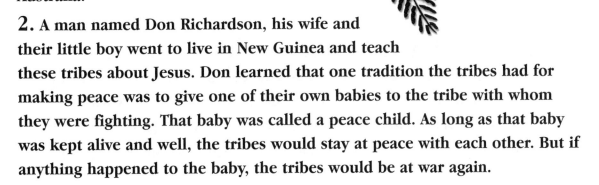

2. A man named Don Richardson, his wife and their little boy went to live in New Guinea and teach these tribes about Jesus. Don learned that one tradition the tribes had for making peace was to give one of their own babies to the tribe with whom they were fighting. That baby was called a peace child. As long as that baby was kept alive and well, the tribes would stay at peace with each other. But if anything happened to the baby, the tribes would be at war again.

Don told the people about Jesus by describing Jesus as God's peace child. He told them that God gave Jesus to all people to make peace between God and people forever. After hearing Don's words, the people understood what God's love is like and that Jesus made it possible for sin to be forgiven and for people to live in peace with each other. The people in the village never had to give one of their own children as a peace child again.

Bible Verse

This is how we know what love is: Jesus Christ laid down his life for us. And we ought to lay down our lives for our brothers.
1 John 3:16

Conclude

Read 1 John 3:16 aloud. **How would you describe Jesus' love for us?** Children respond. **What is a way Don Richardson showed that he loved Jesus?** (He helped other people learn about Jesus.) Lead children in prayer, thanking God for Jesus and for His love for them.

Discussion Questions

1. **What are some ways Jesus showed love to people?** (Cared for people's needs. Helped them get well. Gave them food. Was kind to them. Taught them.)

2. **What is one way to show love like Jesus did when you are at school? In your neighborhood?** (Forgive someone when he or she says something rude or mean. Invite kids whom other people usually ignore to play a game.)

3. **What might happen if we were to show love in some of the ways that Jesus showed love?**

4. **What are some ways we can show God's love to others?** (Be kind to younger kids. Help people who are hungry or sick. Tell others about Jesus and how to become members of God's family. Be kind and show love to brothers and sisters.)

Additional Information for Older Children

Don Richardson has written several books. One of his books, *Peace Child*, tells about the Sawi people and how their lives changed as a result of learning about Jesus. *Eternity in Their Hearts* has many short stories about groups of people from around the world and how they learned about Jesus. (Optional: Bring to class one or more of Don Richardson's books and invite interested children to borrow books.)

Music Man

Knowing that Jesus is God's Son and that Jesus makes it possible for us to be part of God's family gives us joy.

Teacher's Materials

Bible with bookmark at Psalm 95:1, keyboard or other musical instrument; optional—CD or cassette of Keith Green's music and player.

Bible Verse

Come, let us sing for joy to the Lord; let us shout aloud to the Rock of our salvation.

Psalm 95:1

Introduce the Object Talk

We can have joy because we know that Jesus is God's Son and that He makes it possible for us to be part of God's family. Let's find out how one person was joyful because of what he knew about Jesus.

Present the Object Talk

1. Show and/or play keyboard or other musical instrument. **What musical instrument do any of you play? How often do you practice your instrument? What do you like most about playing your instrument?** Volunteers answer.

2. **Keith Green started playing instruments when he was only three years old. It didn't take him long to learn to play the piano and write songs. In fact, Keith's songs were recorded and sold when he was still a teenager. He loved music!**

When Keith grew up, he became a Christian. Knowing about Jesus' love made Keith so joyful that he wanted to love and obey God and to tell everyone he could about Jesus. Keith and his wife, Melody, spent almost every night leading Bible studies for people who had no homes, drug addicts and other people who needed help. But then, because of his love for God, Keith decided to write and sing songs to tell people about Jesus and how to follow Him.

Bible Verse

Come, let us sing for joy to the Lord; let us shout aloud to the Rock of our salvation.

Psalm 95:1

When Keith was 28 years old, he died in a plane crash. Many of the songs he wrote are still sung today because they tell the truth about what it means to love and obey Jesus. (Optional: Play one or more of Keith Green's songs.) **It's sad to know that Keith Green died, but as Christians we can have joy because we know that Keith is in heaven with a living Jesus.**

Conclude

Read Psalm 95:1 aloud. **What are some ways Keith Green showed he felt joyful because of what he knew about Jesus?** Children respond. **Let's thank God for Jesus.** Lead children in prayer. Talk with interested children about becoming members of God's family (refer to "Leading a Child to Christ" article on p. 8).

Discussion Questions

1. **Psalm 95:1 tells us to "sing for joy to the Lord." When have you sung for joy? How is singing for joy different from singing because you have to?**

2. **What do you know about Jesus that makes you joyful?**

3. **What are some other ways to show that we are joyful because Jesus is God's Son and makes it possible for us to be part of God's family?**

Additional Information for Older Children

When Keith and Melody Green first became Christians, they lived in a small house. Many people came to their house to hear about Jesus and learn about Jesus' love for them. Pretty soon their small house was overflowing with people and they were running out of space! So Keith and Melody bought the house next door, and when that house became too crowded, they rented five more houses on nearby streets!

Out of Sight

Jesus promises to care for the members of His family now and in the future.

Teacher Materials

Bible with bookmarks at John 14:3 and Acts 1:11.

Introduce the Object Talk

Both now and in the future, Jesus will care for the members of His family. He promised to always be with us. Jesus gave this promise when He lived on earth. Let's find out what happened.

Bible Verse

If I go and prepare a place for you, I will come back and take you to be with me that you also may be where I am. John 14:3

Present the Object Talk

1. Take children outside (or ask several volunteers to stand near a window). **Look at something near your feet. What do you see?** Volunteers describe what they see. **Look at something a few feet away. What do you see?** Continue a few more times until children identify the farthest things they can see.

2. On the day when Jesus promised to be with us, His disciples looked as far up into the sky as they could see. Why were they looking up into the sky? (Jesus had left the earth to return to heaven.) **Jesus' return to heaven is sometimes called the ascension. The word "ascend" means to go up. The day of Jesus' return to heaven and the promise He made just before He left is so important that many Christians celebrate this special day every year. On this day, called Ascension Sunday, we remember**

that Jesus went up to heaven where He rules the whole world. We also remember that He's coming back again some day! Read, or ask an older child to read, Acts 1:11.

Bible Verse

If I go and prepare a place for you, I will come back and take you to be with me that you also may be where I am. John 14:3

Conclude

Jesus promised to take care of the members of His family for all time. Read John 14:3 aloud. **What does this verse tell us Jesus is doing to care for us in heaven?** (He's preparing a place for us so that we can be with Him forever.) Pray, thanking God for His loving care and that we can always depend on Him to care for us.

Discussion Questions

1. **How can we be sure that Jesus will keep His promise to care for us?** (Jesus always keeps His promises. He's cared for us and others in the past. The Bible tells us about Jesus' care for us.)

2. **What does Jesus do to care for us?** (Answers our prayers. Forgives our sins. Helps us obey Him.)

3. **When do you or someone in your family need to remember that Jesus is always with you?** (When we need courage to do what's right. When we need help in stopping an argument with friends. When we want to tell others about Jesus.)

Additional Information for Older Children

Before He died on the cross, Jesus told His disciples that even though He was going away, He would not leave them alone. His ascension did not mean that He was leaving His friends but that He would be with them in a whole new way. Read in John 14:15-21 about Jesus' promise to ask God to send the Holy Spirit to be with His believers.

Ready Wreaths

Get ready to celebrate the birth of the promised Savior.

Teacher Materials

Bible with bookmark at Isaiah 9:6, Advent wreath and candles; optional—picture of Advent wreath, matches.

Bible Verse

For to us a child is born, to us a son is given, and the government will be on his shoulders. And he will be called Wonderful Counselor, Mighty God, Everlasting Father, Prince of Peace. Isaiah 9:6

Introduce the Object Talk

At this time of year, we're getting ready to celebrate the birthday of Jesus, the Savior sent by God. One word that describes this time of year means the same as "arrival" or "coming." Let's find out what this celebration is.

Present the Object Talk

1. **What are some ways your family gets ready to celebrate Jesus' birth?** Volunteers answer. **A word that some people use when they talk about getting ready to celebrate Jesus' birth is the word "Advent." Advent not only describes the season of the year in which we celebrate Jesus' birth, but it also describes four Sundays before Christmas when we can especially look forward or get ready to celebrate Christmas.**

2. Show Advent wreath. (Optional: Show picture of Advent wreath.) **On the first Sunday of Advent only the first candle is lit.** (Optional: Light candles as you describe them.) **The first candle is called the Hope candle. It reminds us of Old Testament times when God's people hoped and waited for the Savior God had promised to send. On each of the following Sundays, another candle is lit. The second, or Peace candle, reminds us of the peace Jesus gives us. The third, or Joy**

candle, reminds us of the joy we feel at Jesus' birth. The fourth, or Love candle, reminds us of God's love for us and our love for God. Sometimes a fifth candle, called the Christ candle, is placed in the center of the Advent wreath. It is lit Christmas Eve or Christmas Day to remind us of Jesus' birth. (Optional: As each candle is explained, invite volunteers to suggest a motion for the name of each candle. Ask children to describe other objects used at Advent—calendars, daily Advent candle, etc.)

Bible Verse

For to us a child is born, to us a son is given, and the government will be on his shoulders. And he will be called Wonderful Counselor, Mighty God, Everlasting Father, Prince of Peace. Isaiah 9:6

Conclude

The prophet Isaiah looked forward to the coming of God's promised Savior. Listen to what Isaiah wrote. Read Isaiah 9:6 aloud. **This verse reminds us that Jesus is the reason we celebrate!** Pray, thanking God for His love and for sending His Son, Jesus.

Discussion Questions

1. **Who was the promised Savior the Old Testament prophets told about?** (Jesus.)

2. **What do you do to get ready for school? To go on a trip? To celebrate Christmas? What do you do that especially reminds you of Jesus' birth?**

3. **Because Jesus came to live on earth, what do we learn about God?** (God loves all people. God made a way for our sins to be forgiven.)

4. **Who has helped you learn about the coming of Jesus as our Savior?**

Additional Information for Older Children

What colors of candles have you seen in Advent wreaths? Children tell. **Three purple candles are sometimes used in Advent wreaths to remind us of God's royalty. A pink or rose candle may be used for the Joy candle. The Christ candle is usually white and reminds us that Jesus is the light of the world.**

Advent not only celebrates Jesus' birth and the first time He came to earth, but it's also a time to look forward to His return! (Optional: Read Acts 1:9-11.)

Washed Clean

Because God announced that Jesus is His Son, we can celebrate who Jesus is and become part of God's family.

Teacher Materials

Bible with bookmark at 1 John 5:20, objects used for baptism in your church; optional— dirty drinking glass, bowl of soapy water, towel.

Bible Verse
The Son of God has come and has given us understanding, so that we may know him who is true. 1 John 5:20

Introduce the Object Talk

God announced that Jesus is His Son. When we believe that Jesus is God's Son, we show that we want to love and obey God with our actions. Let's look at some objects that remind us of one way of showing what we believe about Jesus.

Present the Object Talk

1. Display objects you brought that are used in your church for baptism. If children are familiar with objects, invite volunteers to tell about them. Explain how each object is used and the baptismal method your church uses. (Optional: Explain baptism in the following way: Show dirty glass. **Would you want to drink from this glass?** Wash glass and offer volunteer a drink. **We use water for cleaning. The Bible often compares washing with water to how God cleans the sin from our lives. Baptism is a special way to show that God washes us clean from sin and makes us ready to love and obey Him.**) You may wish to invite your pastor or another church leader to come and explain the baptismal method used by your church.

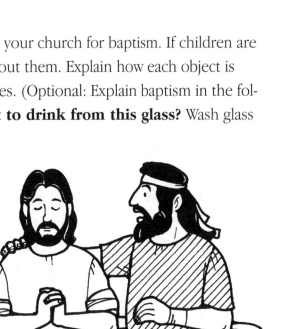

2. Jesus was baptized when He lived on earth to show that He was ready to completely obey God. (Optional: Ask a volunteer to read Matthew 3:13-17 aloud.) **What are some ways we show love for God and obey Him?** (Treat others in ways that please God. Tell others about Jesus.)

Bible Verse

The Son of God has come and has given us understanding, so that we may know him who is true. 1 John 5:20

Conclude

When Jesus was baptized, God was pleased and told the whole world that Jesus was His Son. When we are baptized, we are telling the world that we believe in Jesus as our Savior. Read 1 John 5:20 aloud. **This verse tells us that we can get to know who Jesus is. What are some ways we can get to know Jesus?** (Learn about Jesus at church. Study God's Word. Pray to Jesus.) Pray, asking for God's help to know more about Jesus.

Discussion Questions

1. God spoke from heaven to tell everyone that Jesus is His Son. What are some ways people make announcements today? (By e-mail or on a web page. Sending a letter or flyer. Telling the news on the radio or TV.)

2. What did Jesus do as God's Son? (Died to save all people from their sins. Healed people. Cared for the sick and the poor. Taught people how to love others.)

3. How can we help people today learn that Jesus is God's Son? (Invite them to church. Tell them stories about Jesus.)

Additional Information for Older Children

The Old Testament contains many prophecies about Jesus. The Old Testament prophet Isaiah wrote some words that describe the Savior God promised to send the world. Ask older children to find, read and compare Isaiah 42:1 and Matthew 3:17. **The words God spoke at Jesus' baptism let everyone know that Jesus was the Savior written about in the Old Testament.**

Worldwide Praise

The birth of God's Son, Jesus, the Savior, is reason for the whole world to celebrate.

Teacher Materials

Bible with bookmark at 1 John 4:9, nativity scene; optional—Christmas object from your cultural heritage.

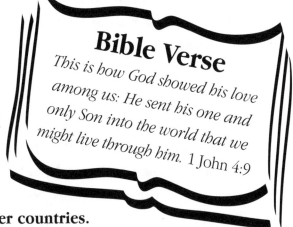

Bible Verse

This is how God showed his love among us: He sent his one and only Son into the world that we might live through him. 1 John 4:9

Introduce the Object Talk

The birth of God's Son, Jesus, is reason for everyone to celebrate. Many of our Christmas traditions, or the ways we celebrate Jesus' birth, actually began in other countries. Let's find out how one Christmas tradition began.

Present the Object Talk

1. What do you know about the place where Jesus was born? Volunteers respond. Display nativity scene. **One of the objects we often see at Christmastime is a nativity scene like this one. People all over the world put up nativity scenes at Christmas to remind them of Jesus' birth.**

2. Nativity scenes were first made in Italy about 800 years ago. Since then, people in countries all over the world make nativity scenes. In France, the nativity scene is used in place of a Christmas tree. In South America, a whole room is often decorated as a nativity scene, including drawings of hills, shepherds, the wise men crossing the desert and even sailboats on the sea! (Optional: Show object from your

cultural heritage and explain its history and the customs surrounding it.)

Conclude

Nativity scenes are just one of the objects people all over the world use to celebrate the birth of God's Son, Jesus. Read 1 John 4:9 aloud. **What does this verse tell us is the reason God sent His Son to earth?** (God loves us.) Pray, thanking God for the gift of His Son, Jesus, and that we can celebrate Jesus' birth with people all over the world.

Bible Verse

This is how God showed his love among us: He sent his one and only Son into the world that we might live through him. 1 John 4:9

Discussion Questions

1. **Why should the whole world celebrate Jesus' birth?** (He came as the Savior for all people. God showed His love for the whole world when He sent Jesus.)

2. **What are some ways you've seen or heard the Christmas story?**

3. **What are some ways you, your family or our church tell other people that Jesus has been born?**

4. **What are some ways we can help others celebrate Jesus' birth?** (Send Christmas cards picturing events from the story of Jesus' birth. Sing praise songs about Jesus.)

Additional Information for Older Children

Most nativity scenes show the wise men worshiping Jesus at the stable. However, many people who study the Bible believe that the wise men actually arrived in Bethlehem when Jesus was between one and two years old. There are two reasons for this belief. First, it probably took the wise men a while to research the meaning of the star they saw, then to organize for their journey and then to travel a long distance. Second, when they arrived in Bethlehem, the Bible says they found Jesus in a house, not a stable. Read Matthew 2:11.

Worldwide Singing

We can celebrate with people all over the world the birth of God's Son, sent by God to keep His promise of a Savior.

Teacher Materials

Bible with bookmark at Luke 2:11, world map or globe; optional—a player and recording of "Silent Night" in a foreign language.

Bible Verse

Today in the town of David a Savior has been born to you; he is Christ the Lord. Luke 2:11

Introduce the Object Talk

The angels' message about Jesus' birth was such good news that people all over the world celebrate Jesus' birthday. Let's look at some of the places where people believe in Jesus and sing songs about His birth.

Present the Object Talk

1. Show map or globe and point out the area where your church is located. (Optional: Older children may find locations.)

2. Read Luke 2:11. **Another name for the town of David is Bethlehem.** Locate Bethlehem on map or globe. **In the Old Testament part of the Bible, prophets told about God's promise to send His Son to be born in Bethlehem.**

3. What are the names of some Christmas carols you remember? Volunteers tell answers. **"Silent Night" is one of the most famous Christmas carols. This carol was first written in Germany.** Locate Germany on map or globe. **A pastor of a church wrote a poem about Jesus' birth in Bethlehem. He gave the poem as a Christmas gift to his friend Franz Gruber. Later that same night, Mr. Gruber wrote a melody to go with the words. Everyone who heard the carol liked the words so much that the carol**

spread all over the world. (Optional: Sing "Silent Night" with children, play recording of the carol in a foreign language or ask someone to sing the carol in another language.)

Conclude

When we sing carols like "Silent Night," we can think about the thousands and thousands of people all over the world who sing this song in their own languages. Let's thank God for sending His Son to be born. Lead children in prayer.

Bible Verse

Today in the town of David a Savior has been born to you; he is Christ the Lord. Luke 2:11

Discussion Questions

1. **What are some of the ways that people in our country celebrate Jesus' birth?**

2. **What are the ways that people in other countries remember Jesus' birth?** (People in Mexico act out the story of Joseph and Mary looking for a place to stay. Christians in Israel plant seeds in front of nativity scenes; the growing seeds remind people of new life.)

3. **What is your favorite song to sing about Jesus' birth?**

A Ship in Danger

Because we've experienced God's great love for us, we can show compassion to others.

Teacher's Materials

Bible with bookmark at Luke 10:27, toy boat or picture of a boat.

Introduce the Object Talk

God's love and compassion for us are great! Because we know about God's love, we can show compassion to other people. Let's find out how someone showed compassion to people on a boat.

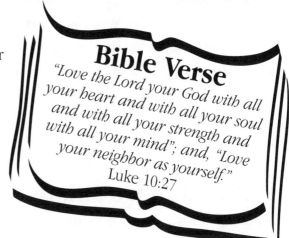

Bible Verse

"Love the Lord your God with all your heart and with all your soul and with all your strength and with all your mind"; and, "Love your neighbor as yourself."
Luke 10:27

Present the Object Talk

1. Show toy boat or picture of boat. **When have you sailed on a boat? What was the weather like?** Children respond. **Sailing on a boat is fun when the weather is nice, but in cold and stormy weather, boats are dangerous places to be!**

2. **One cold winter day in a sea near the country of Holland, the passengers on a boat were in big trouble. The weather was so cold that the water was beginning to freeze. The boat was getting stuck, and the people couldn't get to shore.**

To make matters worse, the rescue crew from the nearest city would not help the passengers on the boat because the passengers were all members of a church the rescue crew hated. The passengers were stranded at sea!

But one man, Menno Simons, heard about the passengers on the boat. Menno belonged to a different church from the passengers, too—but he didn't

let that stop him from showing God's love. Menno and some of his friends from his church decided to help the stranded passengers. Menno and his friends risked their lives in the icy water and rescued all the passengers!

Bible Verse
"Love the Lord your God with all your heart and with all your soul and with all your strength and with all your mind"; and, "Love your neighbor as yourself."
Luke 10:27

Conclude

Read Luke 10:27 aloud. **What is another way to describe how this verse says we are to love God?** (We are to love God with everything we have and in every way we can.) **How did Menno Simons and his friends obey Luke 10:27?** Lead children in prayer, thanking God for His love and asking Him to help children show His love to others.

Discussion Questions

1. **What does it mean to show compassion to others?** (To care about others and do what you can to help them.)

2. **How has God shown compassion to us?** (He sent Jesus so that we could be forgiven. He promised to help us and be with us.)

3. **When is a time you can show compassion to someone in your family? To your friends? When you are at school?**

Additional Information for Older Children

Many government leaders in the country of the Netherlands didn't like Menno Simons and the other members of his church. They wanted to stop people from becoming members of Menno's church. The government leaders thought if they could stop Menno from telling others about God, they could stop his church from growing. They offered a reward of 100 gold coins to anyone who would tell them where Menno was. But God protected Menno. No one ever turned him in to collect the reward!

Balloon Drop

Loving God means loving all kinds of people.

Teacher Materials

Bible with bookmark at Ephesians 4:2, balloons; optional—balls.

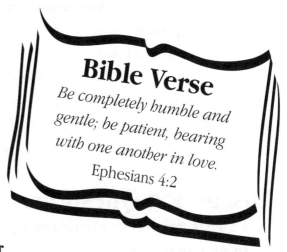

Bible Verse

Be completely humble and gentle; be patient, bearing with one another in love.
Ephesians 4:2

Introduce the Object Talk

The Bible is full of stories about what it means to love God. One way to love God is to show His love to all kinds of people by caring about their needs. Let's watch someone in our group try to help another person.

Present the Object Talk

1. Invite a volunteer to stand next to you. **Let's see how many balloons (Kaitlyn) can hold.** Ask other volunteers to blow up balloons and give them to volunteer to hold. (Optional: To save time, blow up balloons beforehand or use balls instead of balloons.)

2. When volunteer cannot hold any more balloons, ask him or her to help you with a task (open or shut a door, find verse in Bible, etc.). After volunteer expresses difficulty in helping you while still holding onto the balloons, ask, **What would you have to do in order to help me?** (Drop the balloons.) **When others need our help, sometimes we need to drop what we're doing or put aside until later something we're doing so that we can help them.**

Conclude

Listen to Ephesians 4:2 to find the word that describes someone who thinks about what others need instead of always thinking about him- or herself. Read Ephesians 4:2 aloud. **Someone who is humble cares about other people and wants to help them. What else does this verse say we should do?** (Be patient with others as a way of showing love.) **Ephesians 4:2 doesn't say to care only about people we like or who like us. When we say we love God, it means we want to show His love to all kinds of people.** Lead children in prayer, asking God's help in showing love for Him by caring for others.

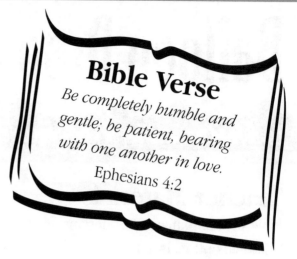

Bible Verse

Be completely humble and gentle; be patient, bearing with one another in love.
Ephesians 4:2

Discussion Questions

1. **In what way has someone been patient with you? Helped you with something you needed?**

2. **When might you need to stop doing something in order to help someone who needs help?** (Stop watching TV when parent needs help setting the table. Stop playing a game at recess when a friend gets hurt.)

3. **When might it be hard to do what Jesus wants you to do? What can we do when we need help loving and obeying Jesus?**

Birthdays Around the World

God created us as unique people who can know Him and love one another.

Teacher Materials

Bible with bookmark at Psalm 100:3, one or more objects used to celebrate birthdays (choose from those listed below).

Bible Verse

Know that the Lord is God. It is he who made us, and we are his. Psalm 100:3

Introduce the Object Talk

God created all the people in the world so that we would know Him and love one another. One way we show love to others is by celebrating their birthdays. Let's look at some ways birthdays are celebrated around the world!

Present the Object Talk

1. What do you like to do to celebrate your birthday? Volunteers tell. **Birthdays are good times to show love to people and to celebrate the unique ways in which God made them.**

2. Display and discuss objects you brought that are associated with some of the following birthday traditions: *China*—friends and relatives join in a lunch of noodles to wish the birthday child a long life; *Denmark*—a flag is flown outside a window to show someone in the house is having a birthday; *Japan*—the birthday child wears all new clothes; *Mexico*—the birthday child uses a bat to break open a piñata which is stuffed with candy and small toys to be shared; *Philippines*—blinking lights decorate the home of the birthday child; *Russia*—the birthday child receives a birthday pie with a greeting carved in the crust; *United States*—the birthday child receives a birthday cake with one candle for each year of the child's age. (Optional: Children reenact one or more of the traditions.)

Conclude

Read Psalm 100:3 aloud. **According to this verse, to whom do we belong? Why?** (God. Because He made us.) **God created us and wants us to know and love Him. God also wants us to show His love to others. No matter what the tradition, birthdays are a time to celebrate and show love to people we care about.** Pray, thanking God for creating us and asking His help in loving each other.

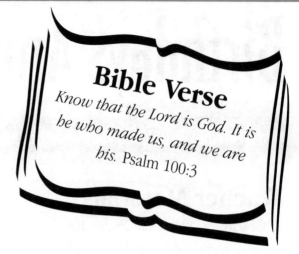

Bible Verse

Know that the Lord is God. It is he who made us, and we are his. Psalm 100:3

Discussion Questions

1. How did God show His love in the ways we are created? (Made our bodies in amazing ways. Gave us minds to think.)

2. What are some ways we can get to know God? (Read the Bible. Listen to older people who love God talk about Him. Ask your parents, pastor or teacher questions about God.)

3. Why should we show love to other people? (To show God's love. Jesus tells us that loving God and loving others are the most important things to do.)

4. What are some ways to show love to other people? (Be kind to them. Help them with tasks they are doing. Care for them when they are upset. Be patient with people who sometimes annoy you.)

Additional Information for Older Children

The most important birthday ever was the day Jesus Christ was born. How did the shepherds celebrate the birth of the baby Jesus? Volunteers answer or children may read Luke 2:16-20. **Who else came to celebrate the birth of Jesus?** (The wise men.) **How did they worship Jesus?** Children tell about the gifts given by wise men or read Matthew 2:9-11.

Circle Attraction

Giving to others doesn't depend on our wealth because Jesus helps us give more than money.

Teacher Materials

Bible with bookmark at Ephesians 5:2, hole punch, tissue paper, small round balloon.

Prepare the Object Talk

Use the hole punch to make 20 to 30 tissue-paper circles. Inflate and tie the balloon.

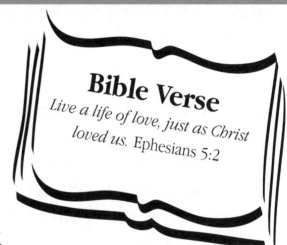

Bible Verse
Live a life of love, just as Christ loved us. Ephesians 5:2

Introduce the Object Talk

Jesus helps us give more than money to others. Our gifts of love can make a big difference. Watch the different actions that take place in this experiment.

Present the Object Talk

1. Place the tissue-paper circles on a table.

2. Rub the balloon against your hair (or a carpet) at least 10 times. Then hold the rubbed side of the balloon several inches (cm) above the paper circles. The paper circles will be attracted to the balloon and jump off the table onto the balloon.

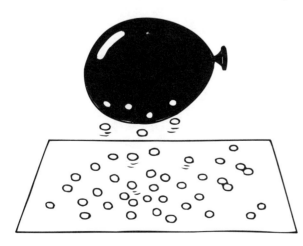

3. As time permits, invite volunteers to take turns creating the attraction between the balloon and the paper circles. (Optional: Provide additional balloons and circles so that more volunteers can participate at once.) **Rubbing the balloon makes an electric charge that attracts, or pulls, the paper circles.**

The Really Big Book of Kid Sermons and Object Talks

Conclude

When we show Jesus' love to others, it attracts them to Jesus and helps them want to learn about Jesus. Read Ephesians 5:2. **How does this verse describe the way Jesus' followers should live? What should we be like?** Volunteers tell ideas. Lead children in prayer, asking His help in giving and showing love to others.

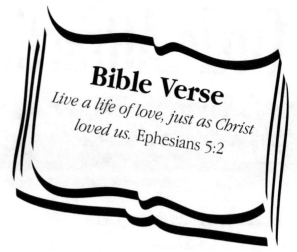

Bible Verse

Live a life of love, just as Christ loved us. Ephesians 5:2

Discussion Questions

1. **What other kinds of things attract each other?** (Magnets attract many metal items. Flowers attract bees. Gravity attracts, or pulls, falling objects.)

2. **How does showing Jesus' love help others learn about Him?** (Helps others discover what the people who love Jesus are like. Helps them understand how much Jesus loves them.)

3. **How has someone shown Jesus' love to you and your family?**

4. **How can you show Jesus' love to someone else?**

Double Trouble

We can show God's love through attitudes and words that are gentle and respectful.

Teacher's Materials

Bible with bookmark at 2 Timothy 2:24-25, photograph of a newborn or young baby.

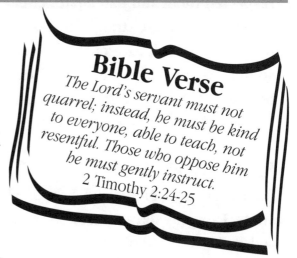

Bible Verse
The Lord's servant must not quarrel; instead, he must be kind to everyone, able to teach, not resentful. Those who oppose him he must gently instruct.
2 Timothy 2:24-25

Introduce the Object Talk

Our gentle and respectful words and attitudes show God's love to others. Let's find out about a woman who was gentle and respectful, even though she didn't agree with what others were doing.

Present the Object Talk

1. Show photograph of baby. **How do people usually treat a newborn or young baby?** Children respond. **Many years ago, people in a village in Africa felt afraid when they saw babies who were twins. These people believed that twin babies were evil and should be killed. The people wouldn't even walk on a road on which a mother of twins had walked!**

2. In 1876, a woman named Mary Slessor lived near this village. Mary wanted to help the people there learn about God's love. One day, Mary heard that twins had been born in the village. Mary quickly ran through the jungle to the village, hoping to save the lives of the babies. When Mary arrived, one of the babies was already dead, but the other one was alive. Mary gently took the baby and started walking back with the baby's mother to Mary's house.

As she was walking on the road, however, Mary realized that if the mother walked on the road, the people wouldn't walk on that road again. They would have to work hard to cut a new road through the jungle. So instead of ignoring the people's beliefs, Mary respected them and had a path cut through the jungle straight to her house. Mary took care of the baby, and soon many people in the village learned to love the baby, too. And best of all, because of Mary's gentle actions, the people kept coming to her house and learned about God's love for them!

Bible Verse
The Lord's servant must not quarrel; instead, he must be kind to everyone, able to teach, not resentful. Those who oppose him he must gently instruct.
2 Timothy 2:24-25

Conclude

Read 2 Timothy 2:24-25 aloud. **People who love God are sometimes called servants. How did Mary Slessor show that she was God's servant?** (She was gentle and kind and helped others learn about Jesus.) **Let's ask God to help us remember to use words and attitudes that are gentle and respectful.** Lead children in prayer.

Discussion Questions

1. **When has someone treated you gently and respectfully? What did they do? What did you do?**

2. **Why do you think God wants us to treat others gently and respectfully?** (Because He loves all people.)

3. **What are some gentle and kind words you like to hear?** ("Thank you." "Sorry." "You can have the first turn." Words that are encouraging instead of bossy. Words that show we care about the other person.) **When is it hard to use kind and gentle words?**

Additional Information for Older Children

One time when Mary Slessor needed to build a new building to use in teaching people in the village about God, she asked the chief of the village for help. Though the chief agreed to send people to help her, several days passed and no one showed up. Instead of yelling and complaining, Mary simply started doing the work herself! Mary chose to be gentle and kind, even when it was hard.

In Sickness and in Health

Because Jesus loves and accepts us, we can show His love to all kinds of people.

Teacher's Materials

Bible with bookmark at Romans 15:7, one or more Hawaiian items (lei, shirt, pictures of Hawaii, etc.).

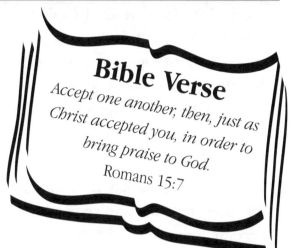

Bible Verse

Accept one another, then, just as Christ accepted you, in order to bring praise to God.
Romans 15:7

Introduce the Object Talk

Because of Jesus' love for and acceptance of us, we can show His love to other people, no matter who they are or where they live. Let's find out about some people who were difficult to accept and care for.

Present the Object Talk

1. Show Hawaiian item(s). **What do you think of when you hear someone talk about Hawaii?** Children tell ideas. **We usually think that because Hawaii is so beautiful, everyone who lives there must be happy! But a long time ago, in the 1800s, there were some people living in Hawaii who weren't happy because they were sick with leprosy (a disease now called Hansen's disease).**

2. At that time there was no treatment for leprosy, so everyone in Hawaii with leprosy was sent away to live on the Hawaiian island of Molokai (MOH-loh-ki). **Ships came to bring food and medicine, but no healthy person lived on Molokai to help the sick people living there.**

Then a man named Father Damien heard about the people who were sick with leprosy. Even though Father Damien lived far away from Hawaii in the country of Belgium and even though he knew that he could get sick, too, he moved to Molokai.

Father Damien was a friend to the people with leprosy. He taught them to grow crops and take better care of themselves. He gave the people medicine and helped them bandage their sores. Father Damien stayed with the people he cared about until he got sick and died from leprosy himself.

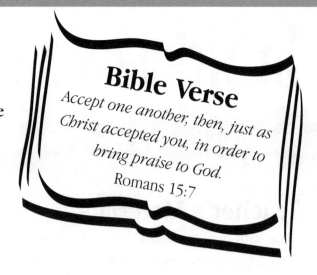

Bible Verse

Accept one another, then, just as Christ accepted you, in order to bring praise to God.
Romans 15:7

Conclude

Read Romans 15:7 aloud. **How did Father Damien show that he accepted others?** Volunteers respond. **God showed His care for us by sending Jesus so that we can become members of God's family.** Pray, asking God to help children accept and care for others. Talk with interested children about becoming members of God's family (refer to "Leading a Child to Christ" article on p. 8).

Discussion Questions

1. **When are some times that it is hard to accept others or treat them like friends?**

2. **What are some good reasons to accept others?** (Christ accepts us and loves us.)

3. **How can you show friendship and acceptance this week to someone who hasn't been a friend before?**

Additional Information for Older Children

Father Damien's love and acceptance of the lepers in Hawaii helped them live better lives and even caused people in other countries to help people with leprosy. In 1889, when Father Damien died from leprosy, the news of his death spread quickly around the world. Many people started working harder than ever before to find a cure for leprosy. Today, taking medicines can cure most people who become sick with leprosy.

Love Songs

The fruit of the Spirit is shown through our love for God and others.

Teacher's Materials

Bible with bookmark at Colossians 3:14; optional—hymnal containing "Take My Life, and Let It Be" by Frances Havergal.

Introduce the Object Talk

The fruit of the Spirit is shown through our love for God and others. Let's learn how one woman showed her love for God through her whole life!

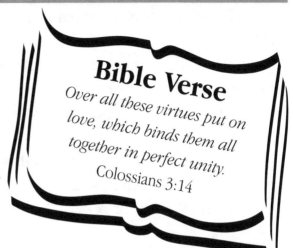

> ## Bible Verse
> Over all these virtues put on love, which binds them all together in perfect unity.
> Colossians 3:14

Present the Object Talk

1. Hold out your hand. **What do you use your hands to do?** Repeat question with feet and voice. **Frances Havergal is a woman who wrote a song about how she wanted to use her hands, her mouth, her money—her whole life! Frances said she wanted to use everything in her life to show her love for God and obedience to Him.** (Optional: Read the words of "Take My Life, and Let It Be" or sing the hymn together.)

2. The words that Frances wrote were not just nice-sounding words to her. She actually gave away most of her money to help others. And she often studied the Bible. In fact, Frances memorized the entire New Testament and several books in the Old Testament.

Frances spent her whole life loving God. She started writing poems about her love for God when she was only seven years old. Before she would do anything or write any songs or poems, Frances would pray. In fact, the words of "Take My Life, and Let It Be" are a prayer to God. Frances only lived to be 42 years old, but she wrote many books and poems, including over 60 songs that still help people tell about their love for God.

Bible Verse

Over all these virtues put on love, which binds them all together in perfect unity.

Colossians 3:14

Conclude

Read Colossians 3:14 aloud. **What does this verse say we are to "put on," or show? How did Frances Havergal show her love for God?** (She memorized portions of the Bible. She prayed. She wrote poems and songs about God.) Lead children in prayer, expressing their love for God. (Optional: Read or sing hymn again as a prayer.) **A great way to show our love for God is to become members of His family.** Talk with interested children about becoming members of God's family (refer to "Leading a Child to Christ" article on p. 8).

Discussion Questions

1. How can you show love for God with your hands? Your feet? Your voice?

2. What are some actions that show love for God? (Singing songs of praise to God. Telling others about Jesus. Praying. Helping someone in need. Obeying God's commands. Giving an offering.)

3. What are some actions that show love for others? (Helping someone who is hurt. Being honest. Saying kind words.)

4. What is a way you can show love for God this week? Show love for others?

Additional Information for Older Children

One of the songs Frances wrote is "Who Is on the Lord's Side?" The title for this song is taken from Exodus 32:26 when Moses asks God's people to choose if they will love and obey God. Ask a volunteer to read the verse aloud. Then ask a volunteer to read the words of the first stanza of the song, "Who Is on the Lord's Side?" **How did Frances describe what it means to be on the Lord's side? How might kids your age show that they want to love and obey God?**

Music of Courage

God can give us courage to love our enemies.

Teacher Materials

Bible with bookmarks at Psalm 57:8, Psalm 150:3-6 and Luke 6:27; variety of musical instruments (tambourine, cymbals, guitar, autoharp, keyboard, rhythm instruments, etc.); optional—music cassette/CD and player.

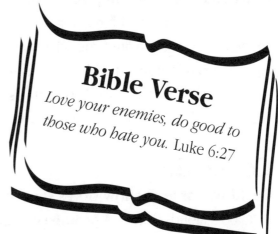

Bible Verse

Love your enemies, do good to those who hate you. Luke 6:27

Introduce the Object Talk

If we pray and ask, God gives us courage to show love to our enemies. In Bible times, people often sang and played instruments to pray for courage or other things. Let's find out about some of the instruments they used.

Present the Object Talk

1. Read, or ask an older child to read, Psalm 150:3-6 while other children count the number of instruments mentioned. **Lyres are like small harps. The way instruments sound often helps us express the feelings of the words we are saying or singing. What kind of feeling would a cymbal make you think of?** Volunteers respond.

2. Psalm 57 is a song written by David at a time when he needed God's courage to love his enemy Saul. Read Psalm 57:8 aloud. **David talked about harps and waking up in the morning. What instruments would remind you of waking up?** Volunteers tell.

3. Distribute instruments to volunteers. **Use these instruments or your hands to make sounds for other phrases in Psalm 57: people chasing someone** (see verse 3), **lions or spears and arrows** (see verse 4), **people falling in a pit** (see verse 6), **a heart constantly beating** (see verse 7). Children experiment with making different sounds. (Optional: Invite a musician to make sounds on an instrument such as an electric guitar or synthesizer.) **At the end of this psalm, David praised God for His love.** (Optional: Play a song for children to accompany with instruments.)

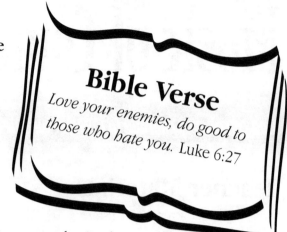

Bible Verse

Love your enemies, do good to those who hate you. Luke 6:27

Conclude

David was able to show God's love, even when Saul didn't deserve it. Read Luke 6:27 aloud. **God has promised that He will give us the courage to do what is right. All we have to do is ask.** Pray, thanking God for His love and asking Him for courage to love everyone, even our enemies.

Discussion Questions

1. What are some ways to show love, and do good things for people you might think of as enemies? (Don't be mean back to them. Don't say mean things about them to others. Smile and be friendly to them.)

2. In what ways can we obey Luke 6:27? (Be kind to others who are mean to us. Pray for people who don't like us. Be kind even when others aren't.)

3. What can you do when it seems too hard to show God's love to an enemy? (Ask God for courage to do what's right. Ask a parent or teacher for advice on how to show love.)

Additional Information for Older Children

Psalm 57 is one of a group of psalms known as the psalms of the history of Israel. Psalms 42 through 72 are about the great deeds God has done for His people, especially those recorded in the book of Exodus. (Optional: Children find and read Psalms 44:1 and 47:1-3 aloud.)

Prison Reform

We can follow Jesus' example of showing love to people others might ignore.

Teacher's Materials

Bible with bookmark at John 15:12, bag containing six to eight school supplies (pencil, notebook, eraser, ruler, pencil sharpener, crayons, folder, book, etc.).

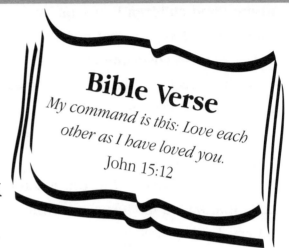

Bible Verse

My command is this: Love each other as I have loved you.
John 15:12

Introduce the Object Talk

Jesus showed love to people whom other people ignored. Let's find out how one person followed Jesus' example and how we can follow His example, too.

Present the Object Talk

1. Show bag. **This bag is full of things you might need for school.** Invite volunteers to guess items in the bag. Show items that children correctly guess and then identify items not guessed. **A long time ago in England, some children didn't have any of these things. They didn't even have a school to go to, because they lived with their mothers in a prison. The children hadn't done anything wrong; but at that time, children had to go to prison with their mothers if they didn't have other family members to care for them.**

2. **Even though most people didn't care about prisoners, a woman named Elizabeth Fry visited this prison. She was shocked by the horrible conditions in which the women and their children lived. Within a few years, Elizabeth helped to organize a school for the children and collected the school supplies they needed. Then she set up a room where the women prisoners could learn to sew.**

Elizabeth also wanted the prisoners to know about Jesus' love for them. She talked about Jesus to the women and children and read from her Bible about Jesus' love and forgiveness. Elizabeth's work to help women and children in prison became so well known that people in the English government and even the queen of England, Queen Victoria, gave money to support her work.

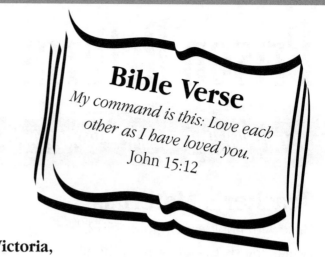

Bible Verse

My command is this: Love each other as I have loved you.

John 15:12

Conclude

Read John 15:12 aloud. **How did Elizabeth Fry obey this verse?** Children respond. **Let's thank God for Jesus' example and ask Him to help us show His love to others.** Lead children in prayer.

Discussion Questions

1. **When have you felt ignored? How did another person help you?**

2. **Who are some people kids your age often ignore or don't pay any attention to?** (Younger children. Kids they don't like.)

3. **What are some things you could do to care for someone who doesn't seem to have any friends?**

Additional Information for Older Children

Elizabeth Fry made sure the women prisoners were given Bibles and other things they needed. Many of her ideas for helping women who were in prison became laws in England and other countries. Elizabeth became very famous for her good works. In addition to helping women in prisons, Elizabeth taught children to read in Sunday School, helped start libraries and even started a school to train nurses in caring for people.

Salt Surprise

Keep on telling about God your whole life, looking for ways in every situation to share God's love with others.

Teacher Materials

Bible with bookmark at 1 Peter 3:15, plastic wrap, bowl, tape, salt, measuring spoon, metal pan with lid.

Prepare the Object Talk

Tightly stretch a piece of plastic wrap over the bowl, taping it securely. Practice Step 1 below to make sure the plastic wrap is on tight enough.

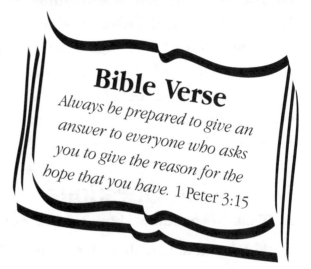

Bible Verse

Always be prepared to give an answer to everyone who asks you to give the reason for the hope that you have. 1 Peter 3:15

Introduce the Object Talk

It's important for God's followers to keep telling others about Him, giving reasons why we believe in and love God. See if you can figure out the reason, or explanation, for why something in this experiment moves without our touching it.

Present the Object Talk

1. Sprinkle one teaspoon of salt evenly onto the plastic. Then invite a volunteer to stand several feet (meters) from the bowl and bang the lid onto the pan at the level of the top of the bowl. The salt will move on the plastic.

2. As time permits, invite additional volunteers to take a turn banging the pan. Ask volunteers to tell reasons why they think the salt moves. Acknowledge each child's idea.

3. We've talked about some ideas about why the salt moves. Listen to the reason, or explanation, according to scientists: We can't see sounds, but they are vibrations in the air, so sounds make the air move. These vibrations in the air make the plastic move, or vibrate, so that the salt moves.

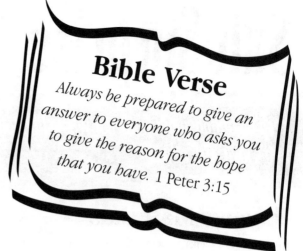

Bible Verse

Always be prepared to give an answer to everyone who asks you to give the reason for the hope that you have. 1 Peter 3:15

Conclude

Hearing a reason for why something is true helps us understand it better. Listen to 1 Peter 3:15 to find what God wants us to be ready to give a reason for. Read verse aloud. **The hope we have is our belief in God and His love and forgiveness for us. This verse reminds us to tell others about what we believe.** Lead children in prayer, asking His help in telling others about His love.

Discussion Questions

1. **What do you know about God that others should know? About Jesus?**

2. **Who has told you about Jesus and helped you learn about reasons to love and obey Him?**

3. **What are things kids your age can do to learn about Jesus?** (Read the Bible. Listen to stories from the Bible. Ask parents or teachers to help you understand what verses from the Bible mean.)

Sunday School

Show God's love by caring about the problems of others.

Teacher's Materials

Bible with bookmark at Philippians 2:4, newspaper.

Introduce the Object Talk

When we care about the problems other people have, we show God's love. Let's find out how a man who lived long ago cared about others and how he showed God's love to them.

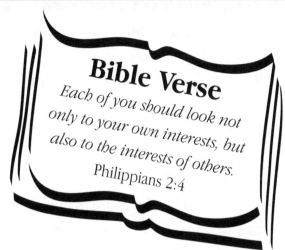

Bible Verse

Each of you should look not only to your own interests, but also to the interests of others.
Philippians 2:4

Present the Object Talk

1. Invite a volunteer to look through the newspaper to find names of people who write for the paper. **What do you think would be fun about working for a newspaper? What might be hard? Let's find out about a newspaper editor from a long time ago.**

2. Robert Raikes was born in England in 1736. Robert was the editor of a newspaper called the Gloucester (GLAHS-tuhr) Journal.

But Robert was more than just a newspaper editor. He cared about the problems of the people who lived around him. Robert wrote stories in the newspaper about problems in prisons. He wanted other people to know about the problems, so they would help to make changes. Robert realized that the prisons were full of people who had grown up without learning about God's love.

Many poor children at that time didn't go to school or church. Instead they had to work from early morning to late at night in dark and dirty factories, even on Saturdays! The only day on which they didn't have to work was Sunday. Robert and a friend started a school for those children—a Sunday School. The children learned to read the Bible and heard stories about God's love. Robert wrote about the Sunday School in his newspaper. Soon churches all over the country were starting Sunday Schools to show God's love to poor children.

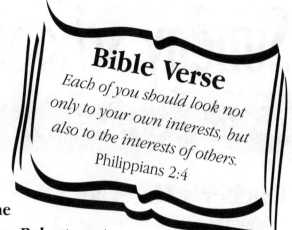

Bible Verse

Each of you should look not only to your own interests, but also to the interests of others.
Philippians 2:4

Conclude

Read Philippians 2:4 aloud. **This verse uses the word "interests" to describe problems, or things that a person worries about. How did Robert Raikes show that he cared about the worries and needs of others?** (He started a Sunday School to help children who had to work during the week.) Lead children in prayer, asking God to help them find ways to show care for other people. **God showed He cares about our needs when He sent His Son, Jesus, so that we can become members of God's family.** Talk with interested children about becoming members of God's family (refer to "Leading a Child to Christ" article on p. 8).

Discussion Questions

1. How can you show your friends that you care about their worries and needs?

2. Why do you think God wants us to care about problems other people have? What might happen if we didn't care about other people's problems?

3. When has someone cared about a worry or need you had?

Additional Information for Older Children

Robert Raikes wrote books for children to learn from and gave money to support these early Sunday Schools. The success of the Sunday Schools was noticed by people all over England. Robert even met King George III. After Robert Raikes died, the Sunday Schools continued to grow and in 1833 the government started to pay money to support them. Eventually, Sunday Schools spread to the United States, Ireland, Scotland and all over the rest of the world!

Circle Talk

God's love is for everyone, not just people like us.

Teacher Materials

Bible with bookmark at Romans 15:7, large sheet of paper, marker.

Prepare the Object Talk

Draw two large intersecting circles (called a Venn diagram) on a large sheet of paper (see sketch).

Bible Verse

Accept one another, then, just as Christ accepted you, in order to bring praise to God.

Romans 15:7

Introduce the Object Talk

It's important to remember that God's love is for everyone. Let's find out what some of the people whom God loves are like.

Present the Object Talk

Write the names of two volunteers at the top of each circle. Then interview them to find several differences and similarities between them, writing the similarities in the overlapping area of the circles and writing the differences in the remaining areas of the circles. **What do you like to do at school? What is your favorite TV show? Favorite color? Favorite food? What color are your eyes?** As you fill out the diagram, talk about the ways children are the same and different. **God made people alike in some ways and different in others.** Continue activity with other volunteers and new circles.

Small Group Option

Group children into pairs. Give each pair a Venn diagram and invite them to draw pictures or write words to show their differences and similarities.

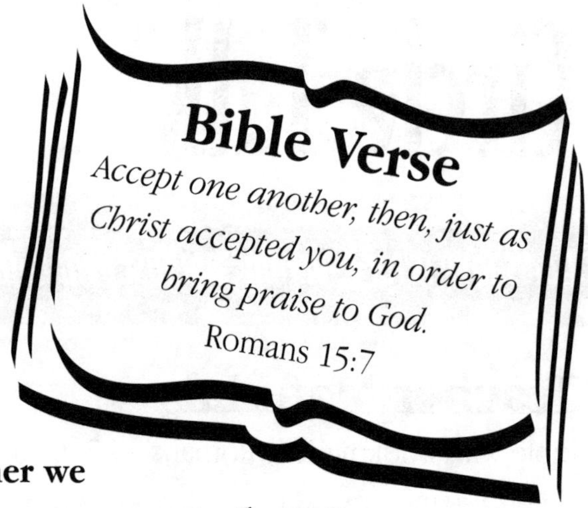

Bible Verse

Accept one another, then, just as Christ accepted you, in order to bring praise to God.

Romans 15:7

Conclude

Listen to Romans 15:7 to find out what God wants us to do for each other whether we are alike or different. Read verse aloud. **When we accept others, it means that we want to show God's love by telling them the good news about Jesus and treating them in kind and fair ways. God's love is for everyone.** Write "Loved by God" in overlapping area of circles. Pray, thanking God for His love and asking His help in showing love to others.

Discussion Questions

1. **How are you alike or different from the people in your family? A friend in your neighborhood or class at school?**

2. **How do you think you might be alike or different from a kid your age who lives in a country far away from here?**

3. **How might you help someone who is different from you learn about God's love? How might you accept that person and treat him or her fairly?** (Invite him or her to go to church or the park. Speak up when others are picking on him or her.)

Gifts of Love

The greatest love is God's love for us!

Teacher Materials

Bible with bookmarks at John 15:13 and 1 Corinthians 13:4, 8½ x11-inch (21.5x27.5-cm) sheet of paper, scissors, marker, variety of Valentine's Day gifts (heart-shaped candy box, valentine cards, flowers, etc.) in a large bag.

Bible Verse
Love is patient, love is kind.
1 Corinthians 13:4

Prepare the Activity

Make pop-up card. Fold and cut paper (see sketch a). Keeping card closed, fold as shown in sketch b. Open the card, draw and cut heart and draw a cross (see sketch c). Fold top portion of heart down inside the card at an angle. Decorate the front of the card to resemble a valentine.

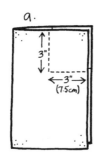
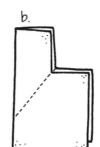
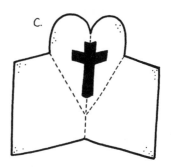

Introduce the Object Talk

The greatest love in all the world is God's love for us! Valentine's Day is a day to thank God for His love and show love to others. Let's look at some of the ways people tell others they are loved.

Present the Object Talk

1. What kinds of things do people give each other on Valentine's Day? As children suggest gifts, display examples from the Valentine's Day gifts you brought.

2. On Valentine's Day we give cards and gifts to tell people that we love them. But the best, the greatest, gift of love ever given was not given on Valentine's

Day. Open pop-up card you prepared. **What gift does this card remind you of?** (God's gift of salvation through His Son, Jesus.) **When was it given?** Volunteers respond. God's gift of His Son, Jesus, is the greatest gift of love ever given. Read, or ask an older child to read, John 15:13 aloud.

Bible Verse
Love is patient, love is kind.
1 Corinthians 13:4

Conclude

Listen to this verse which tells what we can do to show God's love to others. Read 1 Corinthians 13:4. **What are the ways to show love this verse tells us about?** (Be patient. Be kind.) **What are some ways you can show patience and kindness this week?** (Wait for someone else to share. Help someone who is hurt.) Pray, thanking God for His great love and His greatest gift, Jesus.

Discussion Questions

1. **Why is God's love the greatest love of all?** (He always loves us, no matter what. He is always patient and kind toward us. We may forget to love people all the time, but God always loves us.)

2. **How does God show His love for us?** (Sent Jesus to teach people about God and to die on the cross for our sins. Cared for people since the world began. Hears and answers our prayers. Gives us families and friends to love us.)

3. **What words would you use to describe God's love to someone else?** (Huge. The greatest. Faithful. Patient. Kind.)

4. **What are some ways we can show God's love to others?**

Additional Information for Older Children

There are several stories about who Saint Valentine was. According to tradition, around 270 a man named Valentine was put in prison because he worshiped God. While in prison, he continued to show love for God by helping others. Because of his faith, Valentine was killed. After his death, leaders in the church began a feast, or holiday, to help members of God's family remember His love.

Honorable Mention

Teacher Materials

Bible with bookmarks at Matthew 19:14-15 and 1 John 3:1, objects used to recognize deserving people (trophy, blue ribbon, certificate, award, etc.).

Prepare the Activity

Place objects around room. (Optional: Arrange to have a pastor or other church leader say a prayer of blessing for the children.)

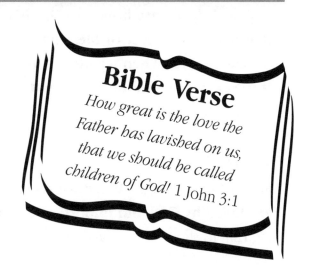

Bible Verse
How great is the love the Father has lavished on us, that we should be called children of God! 1 John 3:1

Introduce the Object Talk

Each of you is important to God! Let's talk about some of the ways we show we think people are important.

Present the Object Talk

1. What are some awards or honors you've received? contests you've won? Volunteers respond. **When people win contests or are given awards, we find ways to let them know what they did was important.** Ask volunteers to search for and identify the objects you placed around the room.

2. Many times today people are honored because they have done something special. But Jesus didn't honor children because they had done something special. Jesus loves all children. Jesus made sure the disciples knew children were important to Him when He showed how glad He was to see them. Read Matthew 19:14-15. **Jesus recognized**

how important children are. Today many countries, schools and other organizations set aside special days on which to honor children and show how important they are.

3. Some churches have a Sunday on which children are honored. On this day, a special prayer or blessing is said for each child. When we bless someone, it means we ask God to do good things for the person. (Optional: Pastor or other church leader says a blessing for the children.)

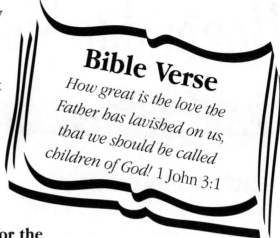

Bible Verse

How great is the love the Father has lavished on us, that we should be called children of God! 1 John 3:1

Conclude

Read 1 John 3:1 aloud. **When we are members of God's family, we know that we are loved by God and important to Him.** Pray, thanking God for His love and asking Him to show His care and protection to each child in the group.

Discussion Questions

1. **How are important people usually treated?** (Given a red carpet. Given a special seat. Get driven around in a special car. Have people to help them do everything.)

2. **How do we know that we are important to God?** (The Bible tells us. We are called His children.)

3. **What things does God do to show you that you are important to Him?** (Listens to and answers my prayers. Sent Jesus to take the punishment for my sins so that I can live forever with God. Gives me people who love and care for me.)

Additional Information for Older Children

Many countries, including Japan, Australia and Turkey, have national holidays in honor of children. In Turkey on Children's Day, children switch places with government leaders. The president, prime minister, the cabinet minister, and city and state leaders turn over their jobs to children who even sign laws into effect!

Link Up!

God's love for us is so great we can share it with others.

Teacher Materials

Bible with bookmark at 1 John 4:19, pencils, 1x6-inch (2.5x15-cm) strips of paper (several for each child), tape.

Introduce the Object Talk

Our love and caring for others begins with God's love for us. Let's help each other make a paper chain that shows some of the people we can show God's love to.

Bible Verse

We love because he first loved us. 1 John 4:19

Present the Object Talk

1. Print the name of one child on your own paper strip and say the name aloud. Tape the ends of the strip together, forming a link.

2. Ask for volunteers to suggest another child's name (or the name of a friend or family member) that begins with the last letter of the name you wrote. One volunteer writes one of the suggested names on a paper strip, inserts it through your link and tapes the ends together, forming a second link (see sketch).

3. Continue process, making paper chain as long as possible. Children may also make a paper chain with words of 1 John 4:19, repeating the verse until each child has added a word.

The Really Big Book of Kid Sermons and Object Talks

Conclude

When our names are linked together in this chain, it reminds us that we can show God's love to each other. Read 1 John 4:19 aloud. **What does 1 John 4:19 say about God? How does knowing about God's love help us?** Thank God for His love and ask His help in showing care to others.

Bible Verse

We love because he first loved us. 1 John 4:19

Discussion Questions

1. **What are some ways God has shown His love to us?**

2. **How has someone shown God's love to you?**

3. **How can you show God's love to others?**

4. **When might it be difficult to show God's love to someone?**

Measure Up!

Jesus loved us so much He was willing to suffer and die to take the punishment for our sins.

Teacher Materials

Bible with bookmark at John 15:13, a variety of items used for measuring—ruler, measuring stick, thermometer, rain gauge, measuring cup, tape measure, scale.

Bible Verse

Greater love has no one than this, that he lay down his life for his friends. John 15:13

Introduce the Object Talk

When we want to find out how big something is, we measure it. But there's one thing that is so great it can't be measured. As we measure some things today, be thinking about what this great thing might be.

Present the Object Talk

One at a time, show each measuring item. Allow children time to experiment with each item. If possible, children measure themselves and/or other items in room. Discuss items used for measuring: **What does this item measure? What's something small this item might measure? What might be the biggest thing this item could measure?**

Conclude

It's fun to measure all kinds of different items. Listen to what the Bible says is so great. Read John 15:13 aloud. **Who is this verse talking about?** (Jesus.) **What does this verse say Jesus did? Why did Jesus give up His life?** (To show His love for us.) **Jesus loves us so much He was willing to die, taking the punishment for our sins. His love for us can't be measured.** Lead children in prayer, thanking Jesus for His great love.

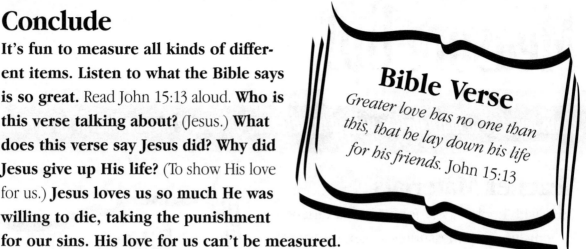

Bible Verse

Greater love has no one than this, that he lay down his life for his friends. John 15:13

Discussion Questions

1. **What are some other words you would use to describe Jesus' love? Why can't Jesus' love be measured?** (It's too big!)

2. **How does Jesus show His love for us today?** (Forgives our sins. Promises always to be with us and help us. Hears and answers our prayers.)

3. **When Jesus lived on earth, what else did He do to show His great love?** (Taught people about God. Healed sick people. Cared for many people.)

Memory Lane

God's actions show His love for us.

Teacher Materials

Bible with bookmark at Psalm 105, baby book or photo album of baby pictures; optional— paper, pencils, markers.

Introduce the Object Talk

God shows His love for us through His actions. Often, we make memory books or photo albums showing the actions of other people. Let's look at an example of a memory book and find out how we can remember God's loving actions.

Bible Verse

Sing to him, sing praise to him; tell of all his wonderful acts.

Psalm 105:2

Present the Object Talk

1. **How many of you know the name of the city where you were born? How old you were when you first walked? The day your first tooth came in?** Volunteers respond. Display a baby book or photo album. **This is a special book that some parents put together to help them remember the actions of their children when they were babies.** Describe some of the contents of the baby book or photo album you brought.

2. **In Old Testament times, God's people wanted to remember the loving actions of God. So when the people gathered together to celebrate special occasions, one of the priests would read special songs to remind the people of all the amazing things God had done for them.** Read, or ask an older child to read, Psalm 105:1-5. **Psalm 105 describes some of the**

wonderful things God did for Abraham, Jacob, Joseph, Moses and all the Israelites! These reminders of God's loving care gave the Israelites good reason to celebrate! (Optional: Children write or draw their own reminders of things God has done for them and their families.)

Bible Verse

Sing to him, sing praise to him; tell of all his wonderful acts.

Psalm 105:2

Conclude

Read Psalm 105:2 aloud. **What are some of the things God has done for you or your family?** Volunteers respond. **As we remember all the good things God has done for us, we have reason to celebrate, too!** Pray, thanking God for His love and all the great things He has done for us, remembering things mentioned by volunteers.

Discussion Questions

1. **When is a time a kid your age might experience God's loving care?** (When He answers prayer. When He provides food.)

2. **What are some good ways to learn more about God's loving acts?** (Read the Bible. Ask older people who love God about His great acts.)

3. **What has God done for you or people you know to show His love?** (Given families to care for us. Given us a house to be warm in. Given us people to tell about Him.)

4. **What can you do to tell others about God's loving acts?**

Additional Information for Older Children

Many psalms were written by David to praise God. Often we can find out what was happening in David's life at the time he wrote a particular psalm. Find Psalm 105:1-15 and 1 Chronicles 16:8-22 in your Bibles. Compare the verses in these passages. Children read verses and describe similarities and differences. Then ask children to read 1 Chronicles 16:1 to find the event for which David wrote these words.

Missionaries of Charity

Our kind actions demonstrate God's love.

Teacher's Materials

Bible with bookmark at Colossians 3:12, one or more objects with slogans (T-shirt, bumper sticker, poster, ads, etc.); optional—photo of Mother Teresa.

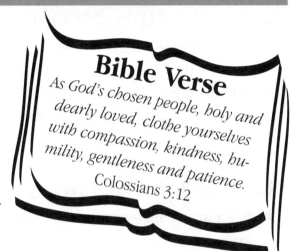

Bible Verse

As God's chosen people, holy and dearly loved, clothe yourselves with compassion, kindness, humility, gentleness and patience.
Colossians 3:12

Introduce the Object Talk

Our kind actions demonstrate God's love. Let's learn about a woman whose kind actions helped people around the world experience God's love.

Present the Object Talk

1. Show object(s) and ask volunteers to read the slogans aloud. **When people want others to know important things they believe, they often write slogans.**

2. In 1910 a special girl was born in Macedonia, a country in Eastern Europe. During her teenage years, this girl joined a group of young people who raised money for the poor and learned about missionaries in

foreign lands. The motto of this group was "What have I done for Christ? What am I doing for Christ? What will I do for Christ?" This motto showed how important these teenagers thought it was to love and obey Jesus.

When this young lady was 18, she decided to serve Christ by becoming a missionary in India. For the rest of her life, she lived among the poorest people in India. She taught street children and comforted the sick and dying. She became known as Mother Teresa. Other women joined her, forming a group called the Missionaries of Charity. "Charity" is another word for "love." Today this group has more than 500 centers around the world where the hungry, the sick and the dying are cared for. (Optional: Show photo of Mother Teresa.)

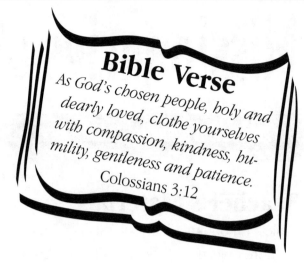

Bible Verse

As God's chosen people, holy and dearly loved, clothe yourselves with compassion, kindness, humility, gentleness and patience. Colossians 3:12

Conclude

Read Colossians 3:12 aloud. **How did Mother Teresa obey this verse?** Volunteers tell. Lead children in prayer, asking for God's help serving those who are in need so that others can learn more about God's love.

Discussion Questions

1. **What are some ways people have shown kindness to you or someone you know?**

2. **What are some kind actions you can do at home? At school? In your neighborhood?** (Let a brother or sister choose which video to watch. Help parents empty the dishwasher. Invite a new kid to play a game at school. Carry groceries for a neighbor.)

3. **Why do your kind actions help other people learn about God's love?** (They can see some of the ways God cares for them.)

4. **What is one kind action you can do this week? For whom?**

Additional Information for Older Children

The Missionaries of Charity spend their time cleaning people's bloody wounds, feeding dying people and rocking abandoned babies. When one missionary was asked if she got tired of doing this difficult work, she said that she could never get tired because she loves and cares for each person as if he or she were Jesus Himself (see Matthew 25:40).

Never-Ending Love

God keeps His promises to show His faithfulness.

Teacher Materials

Bible with Psalm 117:2 marked with a bookmark, two 12x2-inch (30x5-cm) strips of paper, scissors, tape.

Bible Verse

For great is his love toward us, and the faithfulness of the Lord endures forever.
Psalm 117:2

Introduce the Object Talk

God's love and His faithfulness last forever. Something that lasts forever has no end. Let's make something that doesn't have an end or a beginning—and gets bigger and bigger.

Present the Object Talk

1. Hold up two strips of paper. **Where's the beginning of these strips? The end?**

2. Tape strips together at one end to make one long strip. Flip one end of the strip over (see sketch a) and tape it to the other end, so paper loop has a twist. Make sure joined ends are completely covered with tape.

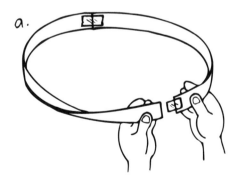

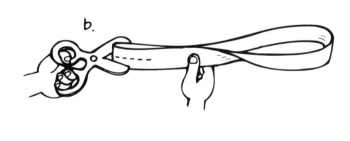

3. Fold strip and cut down the middle of the loop (see sketch b). (Loop will expand to double size.) Cut down the middle of the loops at least one more time.

Small Group Option

Prepare two strips for each child to tape together. Child will then cut the loop at your direction.

Bible Verse

For great is his love toward us, and the faithfulness of the Lord endures forever.
Psalm 117:2

Conclude

Now our paper strips have become a big loop which has no beginning or end. What does Psalm 117:2 say lasts forever? Read Psalm 117:2 aloud. **"Faithfulness" means always keeping your promises and doing what you say you will do. God is faithful and His promises last forever.** Thank God for keeping His promises.

Discussion Questions

1. What are some things other than God's love and faithfulness that don't seem to have a beginning or end? (Sky. Ocean.)

2. What are some of God's promises to us? (Always hear our prayers. Always help us. Never leave us.)

3. When might someone your age need to remember one of these promises?

Overflowing Love

God's gift of the Holy Spirit made it possible for the family of believers to grow as they showed God's love and care.

Teacher Materials

Bible with bookmark at Romans 5:5, small or medium-sized glass jar, large baking pan with sides, measuring utensils, baking soda, vinegar, food coloring.

Bible Verse
God has poured out his love into our hearts by the Holy Spirit, whom he has given us.
Romans 5:5

Introduce the Object Talk

The Holy Spirit is God at work in our lives or in the world. God's gift of the Holy Spirit makes it possible for His followers to show love and care for others. When we accept God's love, it overflows to others. Watch to see what overflows in this experiment.

Present the Object Talk

1. Set the jar in the middle of the baking pan. Pour one tablespoon of baking soda into the jar. Measure one cup of vinegar and add several drops of food coloring to the cup. Pour vinegar into the jar. The liquid will bubble up and overflow the jar.

2. When the vinegar and baking soda were mixed together, they formed a gas called carbon dioxide. The gas pushed the liquid out the top of the jar so that the liquid overflowed.

Conclude

The Bible talks about how God's love can overflow. Read Romans 5:5 aloud. **God loves us so much He wants each of us to show His love to others. God showed His love to us by sending the Holy Spirit. The Holy Spirit helps us show love to others so that the family of people who believe in God can grow.** Lead children in prayer, thanking God for sending the Holy Spirit and asking His help in showing His love to others.

Bible Verse

God has poured out his love into our hearts by the Holy Spirit, whom he has given us. Romans 5:5

Discussion Questions

1. **What are some other things you have seen that overflow?** (A river or lake that overflows its banks. A soda can that has been shaken before opening.)

2. **God made all these things that overflow. What are some of the other ways God has shown His love to us?**

3. **What are some ways we can show God's love to others?**

4. **How has someone shown God's love to you?**

Special Love

The same God who made the world and us, shows His love to all who are His children.

Teacher Materials

Bible with bookmark at 1 John 3:1.

Materials for Children

Several leaves from a variety of trees (small rocks, potatoes or other nature items may be substituted); optional—a leaf (or other nature item) for each child.

Bible Verse

How great is the love the Father has lavished on us, that we should be called children of God! 1 John 3:1

Introduce the Object Talk

When God made the world, He did many things to show His love for us. One thing God did was make each thing He created special. Try to figure out what is special about the leaf I give you.

Present the Object Talk

1. Select six to eight volunteers and give each volunteer a leaf. Allow volunteers a short time to examine leaves. **What do you notice about the size of your leaf? Its color? How does your leaf feel?** Volunteers briefly compare leaves. **Look carefully at your leaf, so you can find your leaf again when they're all mixed up.**

2. Collect leaves (include extra leaves) and group them together on table or floor. Volunteers try to find their leaves. **How hard was it to find your leaf? What helped you find your leaf?** Volunteers answer. **The more you knew about your leaf, the easier it was to find it.**

Small Group Option

All children are given leaves and participate.

Conclude

Because God made each of us, He knows us and loves us. No matter how many people there are in the world, God knows and loves each person. We are so special to Him that He wants us to love Him and be in His family.

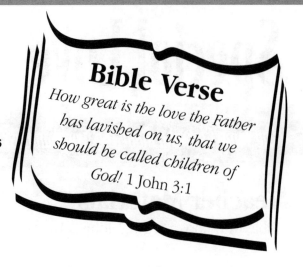

Bible Verse

How great is the love the Father has lavished on us, that we should be called children of God! 1 John 3:1

Read (or ask a volunteer to read) 1 John 3:1 aloud. **The word "lavish" means to give more than is needed. This verse reminds us of God's love. The reason God made the world and us is to show love.** Pray, thanking God for His love and for the special way in which He made the world and us.

Discussion Questions

1. **What are some other things in creation that look similar but are really different from each other?** (Snowflakes. Stars.)

2. **What are some ways God made each person unique?** (Our fingerprints. Our voices. Our smiles.)

3. **What are some ways God has shown love to you and your family?**

Ties of Love

God shows His love through the actions of people He gives to care for us.

Teacher Materials

Bible with bookmarks at Ephesians 6:1-3 and
1 John 4:11, variety of neckties; optional—one
or more medals.

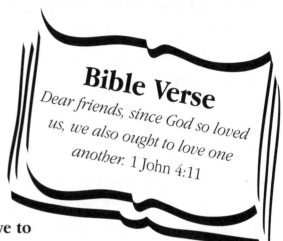

Bible Verse

Dear friends, since God so loved us, we also ought to love one another. 1 John 4:11

Introduce the Object Talk

**Through the actions of the people God
gives to care for us, we can see His love.
Let's find out about something we can give to
honor people who care for us.**

Present the Object Talk

1. (Optional: Show one or more medals.) **What kinds of things do people receive medals for?** (Winning a game or contest. Courageous action in rescuing someone.) **Some medals are called badges of honor.** Display neckties you brought. **A necktie is also a badge of honor. In 1660, King Louis XIV of France saw brightly colored silk handkerchiefs around the necks of some war heroes from a country called Croatia. He decided to make silk neckwear a sign of royalty. Over time, men everywhere started wearing ties.**

**2. Who do you know who wears
neckties? When are some times
you might give a necktie as a
gift? Many people give their
fathers and other important
men in their lives neckties on
Father's Day. The next time you
give someone a necktie, remember
that you are giving a badge
of honor for all the ways that
this person cares for you!**

(Optional: Distribute neckties to children and allow them to experiment with tying them around their own necks.)

3. Read Ephesians 6:1-3 aloud. **What does this verse say is the right thing to do?** (Obey parents. Honor parents.) **God gave us fathers and other people to love us and take care of us. Who is someone who loves and cares for you? What might you give that person to honor him or her?** Volunteers respond.

Bible Verse

Dear friends, since God so loved us, we also ought to love one another. 1 John 4:11

Conclude

God loves us so much that He gives us fathers and other people to take care of us. Read 1 John 4:11. **What are some ways you can show love to others? By showing love to others, we are showing our love for God! Loving and caring for others is one of the best ways we can show God's love.** Pray, thanking God for all the people He gives to care for us and asking for His help in showing love to others.

Discussion Questions

1. **How does knowing that God gives us people who care for us make you feel? Why do you think God wants us to have people who care for us?**

2. **What are some ways that fathers care for their children? Who are some people who care for you in this way?**

3. **How can you thank people who care for you? Why do you think these people want to care for you?**

Additional Information for Older Children

When we say the word "father," we are usually talking about our parents. In the Bible, instead of referring only to parents, the word "father" is used as a title of respect for rulers, elders and priests. Children find and read Scriptures about men who were called father as a way of showing respect for them: Joseph—Genesis 45:8, Elijah—2 Kings 2:11-12, Elisha—2 Kings 13:14.

The Really Big Book of Kid Sermons and Object Talks

What Do You Need?

No matter what we need, God helps and cares for us.

Teacher Materials

Bible with bookmark at Philippians 4:19, picture or photo of a baby (or a baby doll), apple, sharp object.

Introduce the Object Talk

No matter how young or old we are and no matter what we need, God says He will give us what we need. Sometimes it seems like we don't get the things we need. Let's talk about why we might feel that way and discover if it's really true.

Bible Verse

My God will meet all your needs according to his glorious riches in Christ Jesus. Philippians 4:19

Present the Object Talk

1. Show picture or photo of baby, or pass around doll, letting volunteers pantomime ways of caring for a baby. **What are some of the ways people care for babies? How do babies get the things they need?** Someone who cares for a baby will make sure to give the baby things like food, water, milk, hugs and toys to play with.

2. Listen to this verse about the things we need. Read Philippians 4:19 aloud. What does this verse say God does? (God gives us the good things we need.)

3. The Bible tells us to ask God for the things we need. But sometimes we ask God for something and we don't get it. Because God loves us so much, He might say no to our request because He knows that what we've asked for isn't good for us. Show sharp object, keeping out of children's reach. **If a baby wants to play with a (knife), how do people protect the baby?**

4. Other times when we ask God for something, His answer is to wait. Show apple. **Why is an apple good for you to eat? Why is an apple not good for a baby to eat?** (Baby might choke on apple pieces.) **Just as babies have to wait until they are older to eat apples, God knows we have to wait for some things.**

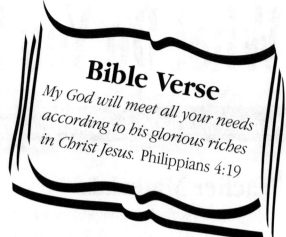

Bible Verse

My God will meet all your needs according to his glorious riches in Christ Jesus. Philippians 4:19

Conclude

When we pray and ask God to give us the things we need, we know that His answers are always best. Lead children in prayer, thanking God for meeting our needs.

Discussion Questions

1. **What are some of the things God provides for us?** (People to care for us. Food to eat. Friends.)

2. **How do people show that they are depending on God to give them what they need?** (Ask God for needs. Don't complain about things they want but don't have.)

3. **What's something you are thankful God has given to you?**

A Chance to Learn

Don't miss an opportunity to show goodness by doing what is right.

Teacher's Materials

Bible with bookmark at Galatians 6:10, item typically given to a teacher as a gift (bell; apple; sign saying "Thank you, teacher!"; etc.).

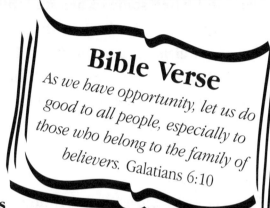

Bible Verse

As we have opportunity, let us do good to all people, especially to those who belong to the family of believers. Galatians 6:10

Introduce the Object Talk

We should use every chance we have to show goodness by doing what is right. Let's find out about someone who showed goodness and helped others because she did what was right.

Present the Object Talk

1. Hold up teacher gift. **Have you ever given something like this to one of your teachers or seen anything like this on one of your teachers' desks? What other kinds of gifts might make a teacher feel special?** Volunteers respond. **A long time ago, a teacher named Prudence Crandall got the opposite of a thank-you gift from the people who lived around her school.**

Teachers change the world one child at a time!

2. In the early 1800s, when people were still fighting about slavery, Prudence Crandall started a school for teenage girls in Connecticut. All the girls attending the school were white. At that time, some people did not want to be friends with African-Americans. So when Prudence welcomed an African-American girl to attend the school, the people in her town got angry. They took their daughters out of the school. But Prudence loved all of God's people and wanted to give African-American students a chance to learn. She invited more African-American girls to the school to take the place of the students who had left.

Now the townspeople became very upset! When a group of angry townspeople attacked her school, Prudence closed the school because she was afraid the girls would get hurt. It seemed like anger and hatred had won. But when some of her students grew up, they helped other African-American girls get an education. The good choices Prudence Crandall made caused many people to be able to learn. That was even better than receiving a thank-you gift!

Bible Verse

As we have opportunity, let us do good to all people, especially to those who belong to the family of believers. Galatians 6:10

Conclude

Read Galatians 6:10 aloud. **What does this verse tell us to do for all people? How did Prudence Crandall do good for others?** (She tried to help young girls by teaching them, even though other people didn't want her to.) Close in prayer, thanking God for the opportunity to do good and asking for His help in choosing to do what is right.

Discussion Questions

1. **When might a kid your age be able to show goodness by choosing to do what is right?** (Choosing to say something nice to a kid who is being teased. Let your brother or sister have the first turn, instead of fighting about whose turn it is.)

2. **When has someone shown goodness to you by doing what was right? How did that make you feel?** Tell your own answer as well as asking volunteers to respond.

3. **What are some ways to learn the right things to do?** (Read the Bible. Listen to parents or teachers. Watch older people who love Jesus.)

Additional Information for Older Children

Prudence Crandall was arrested and put on trial because of her efforts to help young African-American girls. Even though Prudence was found guilty and had to spend time in jail, her trial ended up helping others. More than 100 years later, some of the things said at her trial were used in the Supreme Court of the United States to make new laws that help African-Americans get good educations.

Choose That Gift!

Love God with your actions and your attitudes.

Teacher Materials

Bible with bookmark at Matthew 22:37, one large box, one small box, penny, dollar bill, heavy nonbreakable item (book, brick, etc.), wrapping paper, scissors, tape, ribbon.

Prepare the Object Talk

Place the penny and nonbreakable item in the large box and wrap it. Place the dollar in the small box and wrap it.

Bible Verse

Love the Lord your God with all your heart and with all your soul and with all your mind.
Matthew 22:37

Introduce the Object Talk

Loving God is something we can show not only with our actions but also in our attitudes—the way we think about things. Sometimes a person might say and do one thing but think something totally different. See if you can figure out what's really on the inside of these gifts.

Present the Object Talk

1. Place wrapped boxes on table or floor, so children can see them.

2. Invite several volunteers to take turns examining and shaking boxes.

3. Ask children to raise hands showing which of the two boxes they would like to receive. Ask several volunteers to tell why they chose the boxes and what they think is inside.

4. Have two volunteers open boxes and show the contents.

Conclude

What made some people think the biggest box was best? What made some people think the smallest box was best? Sometimes the way people or things look on the outside isn't the same as how they are on the inside. Listen to what Matthew 22:37 says about what should be on the inside—or in the attitudes—of God's followers. Read verse aloud. **When we love God with our attitudes, we want to please Him in everything we do. Loving and obeying God is what's most important to us.** Pray, expressing your love for God and thanking Him for His love for all people.

Bible Verse

Love the Lord your God with all your heart and with all your soul and with all your mind. Matthew 22:37

Discussion Questions

1. When have you been given a gift that was better than it looked on the outside? Eaten a food that tasted better than it looked?

2. How do people show love for their friends and family members?

3. What are some ways in which people show their love for God?

4. How has God shown He loves you? How can you show your love for Him?

Direction Signals

Loving and obeying God your whole life are the wisest things to do.

Teacher Materials

Bible with bookmarks at Psalm 62 and Mark 12:30, music cassette/CD or video and player.

Introduce the Object Talk

Loving God and obeying His directions our whole lives are the wisest things to do. Let's look at some ways people are directed to do things.

Bible Verse

Love the Lord your God with all your heart and with all your soul and with all your mind and with all your strength. Mark 12:30

Present the Object Talk

1. Ask children to identify various hand directions or signals. For instance, place index finger in front of puckered lips. **What am I directing you to do when I do this?** (Be quiet.) Continue with hand directions that mean "come here," "go away," "stop," "time out" and so on. (Variation: Ask volunteers to suggest and demonstrate hand directions.)

2. Another time when hand directions are used is when a director is leading a band or a choir. Ask a volunteer to read the phrases written under Psalm 62: "For the director of music. For Jeduthun. A psalm of David." **Who wrote the psalm?** (David.) **Who is Jeduthun?** (The director of music.) **This psalm was written for the director of music, Jeduthun, to use when he directed the songs of praise to God during worship services.**

3. Lead children in singing a song from the music cassette/CD or video. Divide children into two groups. Ask a volunteer to alternately point to each group. Only group being pointed at sings. Volunteer may also use hand signals to direct each group in singing loudly or softly.

Conclude

Read Mark 12:30 aloud. **What are the four ways we are directed to love God?** Volunteers respond. **The more we love God, the more we want to obey Him. And that's the wisest thing we can do!** Pray, asking God for His help to love Him and obey His directions every day.

Bible Verse

Love the Lord your God with all your heart and with all your soul and with all your mind and with all your strength. Mark 12:30

Discussion Questions

1. **Why are loving and obeying God our whole lives the wisest things we can do?** (God tells us the best ways to live. We avoid making mistakes when we do things the way God tells us to.)

2. **Who are some Bible people who showed by their actions that they loved and obeyed God? What are some of those actions?**

3. **What can you do to show that you love and obey God?** (Praise Him with songs. Pray to God, telling God why you love Him. Obey God's commands in the Bible. Tell the truth. Care for others.)

Additional Information for Older Children

The Hebrew word *selah* (SEE-lah) occurs twice in Psalm 62 as well as in many other psalms. No one really knows what *selah* means! Some people believe it is a musical direction that tells when the musicians should play loudly in between the phrases of the song. Other people think *selah* indicates when a pause in the singing should take place. Read Psalm 4 where the word *selah* appears and decide which definition you think is correct. Guide children to find and read verses, and then discuss the usage of the word *selah*.

Emergency Kit

God helps us do what's right, even when it's hard.

Teacher Materials

Large bag with these objects inside: Bible with bookmark at Psalm 119:66, eraser and a framed photo of a friend and/or family member.

Introduce the Object Talk

A first-aid or emergency kit usually has bandages and medicine in it. This bag is like an emergency kit for people who love God. Let's find out what's in the bag.

Bible Verse
Teach me knowledge and good judgment, for I believe in your commands. Psalm 119:66

Present the Object Talk

1. Show bag to children and shake it slightly, so children hear the objects inside. Invite one or more volunteers to feel the outside of the bag and try to guess what the objects might be.

2. As you take each item out of the bag one at a time, explain how the object reminds us of what it means to do what's right.

This eraser reminds us of making mistakes. Obeying God doesn't mean we'll never make mistakes. God erases our wrong actions by forgiving our sins when we ask Him to.

This picture of a friend reminds us that God gives us moms and dads, grandmas and grandpas, sisters and brothers and friends who will pray for us and help us know what God wants us to do.

The Really Big Book of Kid Sermons and Object Talks

Conclude

The best part of obeying God is that God gives us the Bible to help us obey Him. Read Psalm 119:66 aloud. **To have good judgment means to be wise and know the right things to do and say. We know that we can depend on God to help us be wise and make good choices.** Ask God's help in doing what's right.

Bible Verse

Teach me knowledge and good judgment, for I believe in your commands. Psalm 119:66

Discussion Questions

1. What promises in God's Word do you remember? Instructions? Tell an example of a promise or instruction that has helped you obey God. Older children may find and read a promise or two: Joshua 1:9; Psalm 23:1; Proverbs 3:5-6.

2. Who is someone God has given you to help you learn what God wants you to do?

Eyes of Faith

Our right actions can help others do what is good.

Teacher's Materials
Bible with bookmark at 1 Timothy 4:12, one or more old eyeglasses or sunglasses with petroleum jelly smeared on the lenses.

Bible Verse
Don't let anyone look down on you because you are young, but set an example for the believers in speech, in life, in love, in faith and in purity. 1 Timothy 4:12

Introduce the Object Talk
The good things we do and the right choices we make can help other people do good things, too. Let's find out how someone who couldn't see very well was an example to many people.

Present the Object Talk

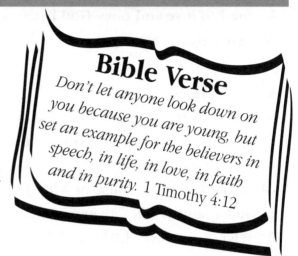

1. Volunteers try on the glasses you prepared. **What are some things it would be hard to do if this is how you could see?** Children tell ideas. **A woman named Henrietta Mears had very poor eyesight, but that didn't stop her from doing great things.**

2. When Henrietta Mears was a child, her doctor said that she would probably become blind. So as she grew up, Henrietta decided to study hard, read a lot and memorize large portions of the Bible in case she later lost her eyesight. Henrietta's eyes were a problem for her through-out her life, but the doctor's prediction never did come true. She was never completely blind.

When Henrietta grew up, she became a high school teacher in a small town. She was determined to help her students learn to do good things. When Henrietta discovered that her school didn't have a football team, she hired a coach and helped organize the team. Henrietta went to every game to cheer for her students. Soon the football players started coming to Henrietta's Sunday School class where she taught them about the Bible. By the end of one year, many young people had decided to believe in Jesus and had learned to love and obey God because of Henrietta's teaching.

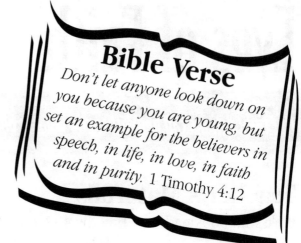

Bible Verse

Don't let anyone look down on you because you are young, but set an example for the believers in speech, in life, in love, in faith and in purity. 1 Timothy 4:12

Conclude

Read 1 Timothy 4:12 aloud. **How was Henrietta Mears an example to others?** Children tell ideas. **Let's ask God to help us do what is right so that other people can learn about Him.** Lead children in prayer. **Jesus is the best example any of us can follow. Because of what Jesus did for us, we can become members of God's family.** Talk with interested children about becoming members of God's family (refer to "Leading a Child to Christ" article on p. 8).

Discussion Questions

1. **Whose good example have you followed? Who might follow your good example?** (Younger brother. Friend. Someone at school.) How?

2. **What kinds of good actions might happen in a living room? In a kitchen? In a bedroom?** (Helping a child with his or her homework. Clearing the dishes from the table. Reading a story to a younger brother or sister at bedtime. Sharing the computer.)

3. **How might our right actions help another family member do good?** (Reading a story to a younger brother might help him fall asleep. Clearing a table might help a parent have time to call a lonely friend.)

Additional Information for Older Children

Henrietta Mears was an example to many well-known Christian leaders, including Billy Graham. Henrietta started a publishing company that produces Sunday School curriculum. She also started a Christian camp that many children and adults attend every year. Her poor eyesight did not stop her from doing good!

Get Ready!

God gets us ready to do good things for Him.

Teacher Materials

Bible with bookmark at Philippians 2:13, one or more of the following diagrams or maps: blueprints, highway map, city street map, topographical or trail map, ocean depth chart, map of school, map of museum or mall.

Bible Verse

It is God who works in you to will and to act according to his good purpose. Philippians 2:13

Introduce the Object Talk

We've all done things to get ready for an important event like a birthday party or a Christmas celebration. God wants us to get ready to do the good things He wants us to do, too. Look at these maps and diagrams and think about how they help you prepare for something.

Present the Object Talk

One at a time, show each kind of map or diagram you have brought. **What would this (map) help you get ready for? What kind of information do you learn from this (diagram)? Why is the information on here important? What might happen if you didn't have this map or diagram?** (Might get lost. Wouldn't know how long trip would take. Couldn't plan how to get to the place we're going.)

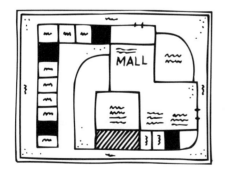

Conclude

Before we take a trip or build a building, it's important to get ready so that we can do a good job. **Who helps us get ready to do the good things God wants us to do?** Read Philippians 2:13 aloud. **This verse tells us that we don't have to try to obey God by ourselves. He promises to help us love and obey Him.** Pray, thanking God that He is with us to help us do good.

Bible Verse

It is God who works in you to will and to act according to his good purpose. Philippians 2:13

Discussion Questions

1. **What are some other things kids your age need to get ready for?** (Spelling test. Piano recital. Basketball game.) **How do you get ready for them?** (Practice. Ask God's help.)

2. **What are some of the ways we can get ready to do the good things God wants us to do?** (Learn about God. Read the Bible. Talk to God.)

3. **What's something good you think God might want you to do?** (Be honest. Treat others fairly.)

Growing in Obedience

When we know God's Word, it shows in our lives.

Teacher Materials

Bible with bookmark at Psalm 119:11, samples of different grains (barley, rice, rye, corn, rolled oats, wheat, wheat germ, cracked wheat flour, muesli cereal, puffed oat or rice cereal, etc.).

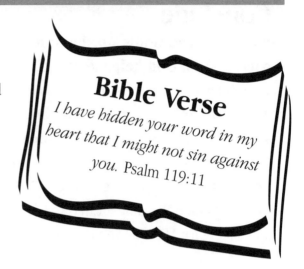

Bible Verse

I have hidden your word in my heart that I might not sin against you. Psalm 119:11

Introduce the Object Talk

When we know God's Word, it shows in our lives by the good decisions we make and the right actions we take. One of the ways people in Bible times celebrated the Feast of Weeks was by bringing offerings of grains they had grown and harvested. Let's discover how these growing things remind us of obeying God's Word.

Present the Object Talk

1. Show samples of different grains, passing samples around to children and allowing them to taste if desired. (Check for allergies.) **Where do all these kinds of food come from?** (They are grown. You can make bread or cereal from them.) **These are grains. Unlike fruits or vegetables that also grow from the ground, grains are the seeds of plants, mostly different types of grass.**

2. **At the Feast of Weeks, also called Shavuot (shah-voo-OHT), the Hebrew word for "weeks," God's people celebrated and thanked God for the good things that grow from the earth. When we plant a seed and care for it by giving it light and water, the seed grows and produces grain. When we read and think about God's Word, it grows and produces good things in our**

lives. What are some of the good things that can grow out of our lives by studying God's Word? (Courage to be honest. Kind ways to treat others. Patience. Knowledge to make good choices.)

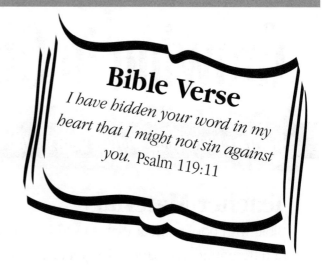

Bible Verse
I have hidden your word in my heart that I might not sin against you. Psalm 119:11

Conclude

When we read God's Word and follow what it says, God helps us live the very best way. Read Psalm 119:11 aloud. **According to this verse, what should we do to keep from sinning? What do you think it means to hide God's Word in our hearts?** (Read God's Word and remember it.) **One important thing God's Word tells us about is how to become members of God's family.** Talk with the children about becoming Christians (see "Leading a Child to Christ" on p. 8). Pray, thanking God for His Word and asking for His help in obeying it.

Discussion Questions

1. When might kids your age read and think about God's Word? (When hearing a Bible story at church. When reading a Bible story with parents.)

2. Who has helped you learn from God's Word? (Parents. Grandparents. Teachers.)

3. What do we learn from reading God's Word? (How to love and obey God. How to show His love to others. How to become members of God's family.)

Additional Information for Older Children

The Feast of Weeks took place at the end of the barley harvest. Because the first sheaf of the barley harvest was to be dedicated, or given, to the Lord, the first day of the Feast of Weeks is called Firstfruits. Read Leviticus 23:9 aloud. **Until the dedication was made, no bread, grain or anything from the harvest could be eaten! The people wanted to give God the first and best part of their harvest.**

Magnetic Leaders

Look for good leaders who will help you do what's right in God's eyes.

Teacher Materials

Bible with bookmark at Deuteronomy 6:18, sheet of paper or card stock, magnet (toy magnet or refrigerator magnet), several iron or steel items (paper clips, nails, pins, washers, etc.).

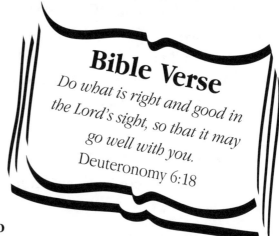

Bible Verse

Do what is right and good in the Lord's sight, so that it may go well with you.
Deuteronomy 6:18

Introduce the Object Talk

The Bible talks about leaders, people who help others think and act in certain ways.
God wants us to look for leaders who will help us do what's right in God's eyes. Look at the way in which these objects follow their leader.

Present the Object Talk

Hold paper or card stock horizontally. Invite a volunteer to experiment with the magnet and the items you have collected by placing an item on top of the paper and then moving the magnet under the paper to lead the item around on the paper. Repeat activity with other volunteers and items.

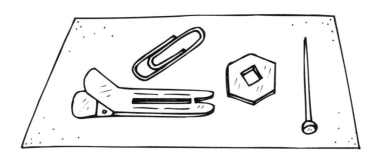

Conclude

These metallic items followed their leader—the magnet. We can choose the kind of people or leaders we want to follow. God gives us people who can lead us to obey Him. Read Deuteronomy 6:18 aloud. **What does this verse say we should do?** Volunteer answers. **We all need leaders who will help us do what's right in God's eyes and obey Him.** Pray, thanking God for people who help us obey Him.

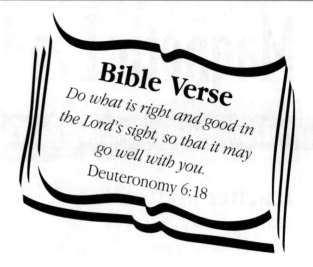

Bible Verse

Do what is right and good in the Lord's sight, so that it may go well with you.
Deuteronomy 6:18

Discussion Questions

1. **What kind of people do we often think of as leaders?** (Teachers. Parents. Coaches.)

2. **What kind of people make the best leaders?** (People who will help us do what's right in God's eyes.)

3. **Who has helped you obey God?**

4. **Who is someone you can help obey God? What is a way you can help that person obey God?** (Pray with him or her. Show him or her a good example by obeying God.)

Making Friends

Patiently continue to do what is right in all situations.

Teacher's Materials

Bible with bookmark at 1 Corinthians 15:58, bucket, rope, small prize for each child.

Prepare the Activity

Tie rope onto bucket's handle. Place prizes in bucket.

Bible Verse

Stand firm. Let nothing move you. Always give yourselves fully to the work of the Lord.
1 Corinthians 15:58

Introduce the Object Talk

Doing what's right, even in difficult situations, is a way to show patience. Let's find out how a man showed patience in a hard situation.

Present the Object Talk

1. What kind of gift would you give a friend? Volunteers respond. **I'm going to give you a gift in an unusual way today.** Hold bucket by the rope and invite each child to take a prize from the bucket. **Usually when people exchange gifts, it shows that they are friends. Let's find out how a man named Jim Elliot gave gifts in a bucket to try to make friends with some dangerous people.**

2. Jim Elliot and four other missionaries lived in the country of Ecuador in South America. The missionaries wanted to tell a group of people called the Aucas (OW-kuhs) **about Jesus. But there was a BIG problem. The Aucas were not friendly people. In fact, they usually killed anyone who came near their villages!**

But the missionaries didn't give up. First, they patiently learned how to say words in the Aucan language. Then for several months, they flew over the Aucas' villages, lowering buckets filled with gifts for the Aucas. As they lowered the buckets, they called out greetings to the people. Even in this hard situation, Jim Elliot patiently kept trying to make friends with the Aucas. Eventually, the missionaries were able to meet the Aucas face-to-face.

Bible Verse

Stand firm. Let nothing move you. Always give yourselves fully to the work of the Lord.

1 Corinthians 15:58

Conclude

Read 1 Corinthians 15:58. **"Stand firm"** means you should keep doing what is right and trust in God. What is one way Jim Elliot and his friends stood firm and did the work of the Lord? (They continued to try to make friends with the Aucas, even though it was hard.) Pray, asking God to help children patiently do what is right.

Discussion Questions

1. **What are some situations in which it is hard to have patience and do what is right?** (Your brother or sister keeps bothering you. Someone is yelling at you. You are tired and don't want to do what is right.)

2. **What is one right action you can take (when your younger brother keeps taking your markers)?** Repeat question, substituting other situations in which patience might be needed.

3. **What is "the work of the Lord"?** (Loving others. Obeying God's commands.)

4. **Name one time (at school) when it is hard to do what is right. How can you patiently keep doing right in that situation?** Repeat question, substituting other times, places or situations for the words "at school."

Additional Information for Older Children

Shortly after Jim Elliot and his friends met the Aucas, they were killed by the Aucas. Some people thought that all of Jim's efforts to make friends had been wasted. But several years later, Jim's wife and another woman became friends with the Aucas and lived in their village. Because the missionaries patiently kept doing what was right, many Aucas became Christians.

Rainbow Fun

People who love God obey Him.

Teacher Materials

Bible with bookmark at John 14:15; six glasses; measuring cup; light corn syrup; glycerin (found in most pharmacies); water; cooking oil; rubbing alcohol; red, yellow, green and blue food coloring; four spoons.

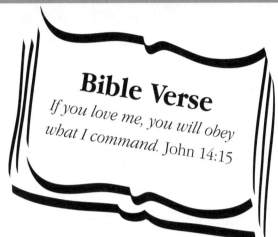

Bible Verse

If you love me, you will obey what I command. John 14:15

Introduce the Object Talk

God's instructions help us know the best way to live. Watch what happens when I follow these instructions.

Present the Object Talk

Read directions aloud as you complete each step. Or have an older child read aloud as you work.

1. Set out the glasses and pour a half cup of each liquid into separate glasses in the following order: light corn syrup, glycerin, water, cooking oil, rubbing alcohol.

2. Using separate spoons, stir several drops of food coloring into the liquids: red into light corn syrup, yellow into glycerin, green into water, none into cooking oil, blue into alcohol.

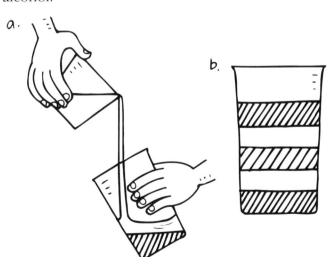

3. Pour about 1 inch (2.5 cm) of each liquid into the remaining glass as follows: *(a)* pour red into the center of the glass without letting liquid hit the side; *(b)* tilt the glass and pour yellow into point where red meets the side of the glass (see sketch a); *(c)* pour green liquid down the side of the tilted glass; then clear; then blue.

Each liquid should float on the top of the previous liquid. Hold the glass upright to see rainbow (see sketch b).

Bible Verse
If you love me, you will obey what I command. John 14:15

Conclude

Following these directions helped me make a rainbow. Following God's directions, or commands, is even better! They help us know the best way to live. Read John 14:15 aloud. **Because I love God, I want to obey Him.** Ask God's help in obeying.

Discussion Questions

1. **What would have happened if I hadn't followed the directions?**

2. **Being honest is a direction, or command, God wants us to obey. What are some of the results of being honest?** (Parents and friends trust you and like to be with you. Teachers know they can depend on you.)

3. **What are some ways you can show love for God and obey His commands?** (Be honest. Care about the needs of others.)

Running the Race

We show goodness by choosing to obey God, even when it is hard.

Teacher's Materials

Bible with bookmark at Acts 5:29, sports medal or trophy.

Introduce the Object Talk

We show goodness by choosing to obey God. Let's find out about one man who chose to obey God, even when it was hard.

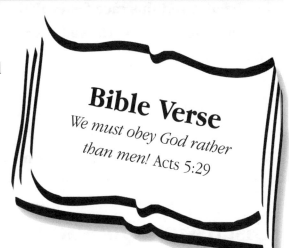

Bible Verse
We must obey God rather than men! Acts 5:29

Present the Object Talk

1. Show sports medal or trophy. **How do you think I got this award?** Volunteers tell ideas. Briefly explain to children where the item came from. **Many athletes dream of the chance to win Olympic medals.**

2. Eric Liddell (lih-DEHL) **was an athlete in England who could run very fast! In 1924, he hoped to win a gold medal at the Olympics. But when the race schedules were announced, Eric discovered that he was supposed to run in a race on a Sunday. Years before, Eric had said that he would not work or play sports on Sundays. He made this choice to show his love and obedience to God. Eric wanted to spend time worshiping God on Sundays, not running races. So Eric said he would not run in the Sunday race.**

GOLD MEDAL

1ST Place

When people in England heard about Eric's decision, they were furious! They thought that Eric didn't care about his country. But Eric started training for a different race that did not take place on Sunday. No one thought he could win this race, however, because it was longer. On the day of the race, much to everyone's surprise, Eric not only won the race and the gold medal, but he also ran this race faster than anyone else in the world had ever run it!

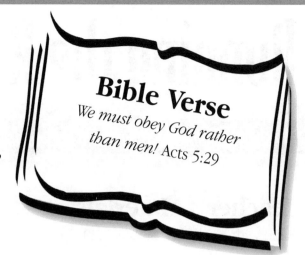

Bible Verse
We must obey God rather than men! Acts 5:29

Conclude

Read Acts 5:29 aloud. **How did Eric Liddell show that he wanted to obey God? Why might it have been hard for him to show goodness in this way?** Children respond. Pray, asking God to help children choose to obey Him, even when it is hard.

Discussion Questions

1. **How do we know what God wants us to do?** (He tells us in His Word, the Bible. By listening to our parents.) **What are some things God's Word tells us to do?** Volunteers respond. Invite older children to read one or more of the following verses aloud: Exodus 20:12, Galatians 5:14, 1 Thessalonians 5:16-18, James 1:19, 1 John 3:11.

2. **Why is it most important to obey God?** (His laws are the best, even when they are hard. He loves us. He is God, the maker of everything. His laws tell us how to follow God's plans.)

3. **When are some times it is hard to obey God's commands?** (When you feel tired or angry. When you don't know God's commands. When everyone else is disobeying God's commands.) **Why do you think it's important to obey God, even in those hard times?**

4. **Name one way you can show goodness by obeying God's commands this week.**

Additional Information for Older Children

Throughout his life, Eric Liddell made choices that showed goodness. Just one year after winning the Olympic gold medal, Eric went to the country of China as a missionary. For 20 years, Eric Liddell helped people in China learn about Jesus. The story of Eric Liddell's life and his good choices was told in the movie *Chariots of Fire*.

Seek and Find!

Ignoring God's instructions always leads to trouble.

Teacher Materials

Bible with Psalm 119:2 marked with a bookmark, blindfold.

Introduce the Object Talk

We follow God's instructions because He knows the best way for us to live. But sometimes things make it hard to follow instructions. Watch to see what happens when we make it hard to follow instructions.

Bible Verse
Blessed are they who keep his statutes and seek him with all their heart. Psalm 119:2

Present the Object Talk

Invite a volunteer to wear a blindfold. Then instruct the volunteer to complete a task such as one of the following: walk to the table across the room and pick up the Bible,

find the chalk and write your name on the chalkboard or play a music tape in the cassette player. Repeat with other volunteers and additional tasks. Occasionally ask volunteers, **What would make it easier to find what you're looking for? If you really wanted to do what I asked you to do, what would make it easier?** (Take off the blindfold.)

Conclude

Wearing a blindfold makes it difficult to find what you're looking for. Ignoring or disobeying God's instructions is like wearing a blindfold, and it gets us into lots of trouble. Listen to Psalm 119:2 to find what happens to people who learn about and follow God's instructions. Read verse aloud. **"Statutes" is another word for God's instructions. When we seek or try to follow God's instructions, we can find the best way to live.** Thank God for His instructions and ask His help in following them.

Bible Verse

Blessed are they who keep his statutes and seek him with all their heart. Psalm 119:2

Discussion Questions

1. **What are ways kids your age might be tempted to disobey God? What might be the results? What kind of trouble might happen?**

2. **Why is it so important to God that we obey His commands?** (He loves us so much, He wants us to have the good things that result from obeying Him.)

3. **When can you obey God?**

Talk Radio

Being careful in what you say shows self-control.

Teacher's Materials

Bible with bookmark at James 1:19, one or more copies of Chronicles of Narnia books (available in most church and public libraries).

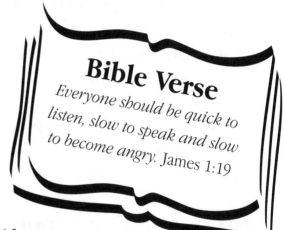

Bible Verse

Everyone should be quick to listen, slow to speak and slow to become angry. James 1:19

Introduce the Object Talk

One way to show self-control is to be careful about what you say. Let's find out how one man was careful about what he said.

Present the Object Talk

1. Show book(s) you brought. **The Chronicles of Narnia is a series of books written by a man named C. S. Lewis. What do you know about these books?** Volunteers tell about stories they know. **C. S. Lewis wrote these books to help children learn about loving and obeying God. But Mr. Lewis also did many other things in his life.**

2. Clive Staples Lewis was born in Ireland in 1898. He joined the army to fight for England during World War I and was a brave army officer. But during World War II, C. S. Lewis helped people in another way in England.

The Lion, the Witch and the Wardrobe by C.S. Lewis

During the war, while the Nazis were bombing cities in England, many people listened to C. S. Lewis talk on the radio about what it meant to be a Christian. C. S. Lewis carefully chose what to say so that all kinds of people could understand God's love for them, even when bad things, like a war, happened. The talks helped people see that loving and obeying God was the most important thing to do. So many people were helped by the radio talks that later some of the talks were written down in a book called *Mere Christianity*. Even today people learn about being part of God's family from this book.

Bible Verse

Everyone should be quick to listen, slow to speak and slow to become angry. James 1:19

Conclude

Read James 1:19 aloud. **Being "slow to speak" means being careful about what you say. How did C. S. Lewis show that he was careful in the things he said?** (When talking on the radio, he was careful about what he said so that all kinds of people could learn about God.) **When we listen to others and are careful about what we say, we show self-control. Let's ask God to help us listen to each other and use self-control in what we say.** Lead children in prayer.

Discussion Questions

1. **When might it be hard to show self-control when you talk to others?** (When angry or upset. When someone says something unkind.)

2. **When are some times it might be difficult for kids your age to listen?** (When they're tired. When they're hungry. When someone is taking a long time to speak.)

3. **What can you do that will help you listen better and control what you say?** (Follow James 1:19 and be "quick to listen" and "slow to speak." Pray and ask God for His help. Count to 10 before speaking if upset. Walk away before saying something that shouldn't be said.)

4. **What should we do when we make mistakes and say things we shouldn't?** (Ask for God's forgiveness and apologize to the people we were talking to.)

Additional Information for Older Children

Many people wrote letters to C. S. Lewis, and he spent a lot of time answering the letters, many of them from children who read the Chronicles of Narnia. Some of the letters he wrote back to these children were published in a book called *Letters to Children*. Invite children to tell what they would write in letters to C. S. Lewis. (Optional: Read aloud some of the letters from *Letters to Children* by C. S. Lewis.)

Timed Tasks

Be ready to trust and follow God's good commands.

Teacher Materials

Bible with bookmark at Psalm 119:60, stopwatch or watch with second hand.

Introduce the Object Talk

When someone tells us what to do, sometimes we obey right away and sometimes we put off obeying. God wants us to be ready and quick to obey Him. Let's see how quickly you can do what I say.

Bible Verse
I will hasten and not delay to obey your commands.
Psalm 119:60

Present the Object Talk

1. Hold up your watch. **What are some of the things we use watches for? How do watches help us?** Volunteers respond (tell what time it is, get to places on time, bake a cake, play the right number of minutes in a game, etc.).

2. Sometimes people use watches to find out how fast they can do things. Invite volunteers to take turns completing one or more of the following tasks while you time them: say the letters of the alphabet, do 10 jumping jacks, say his or her name five times, shake the hands of six people in the room, touch all four corners of the room, etc. Add new tasks or repeat tasks as needed. Older children may take turns giving commands to rest of group. (Optional: Children repeat Psalm 119:60 before doing tasks.)

Conclude

We had fun trying to do these things in a hurry. **What does Psalm 119:60 say we should hurry to do?** Read verse aloud. **Whose commands are we to obey? When we hurry, or hasten, to obey God's commands, it means that we don't try to put off doing what God wants. Because God's commands help us know the best way to live, we are ready and glad to obey them.** Pray, thanking God for His commands and asking His help in following them.

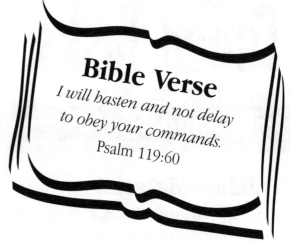

Bible Verse
I will hasten and not delay to obey your commands.
Psalm 119:60

Discussion Questions

1. **What are some other things you can do quickly?**

2. **What kinds of things do you like to take your time to do?**

3. **Why do you think God wants us to hurry to obey His commands?** (To not waste time. So we don't forget to obey.)

4. **God tells us to treat others honestly and fairly. How can you be ready to quickly obey this command during the week?** (Always tell the truth. Be fair when sharing toys or snacks.)

Use Your Senses

Don't make excuses for not obeying God.

Teacher Materials

Bible with bookmark at Job 12:13, blindfold, several small objects (quarter, eraser, walnut, plastic letter, etc.) in a bag; optional—one of each object for each group of six to eight children, bell.

Bible Verse

To God belong wisdom and power; counsel and understanding are his. Job 12:13

Introduce the Object Talk

The Bible tells us a lot about what God is like and why He is greater than anyone else. We're going to discover one way God shows that He is wiser and greater than anyone.

Present the Object Talk

Select several volunteers—one volunteer for each object. Blindfold the first volunteer, hand him or her an object and ask volunteer to identify the object. Repeat with each object, using a different volunteer.

Variation: Bring a variety of scents for volunteers to smell while blindfolded (orange peel, cotton ball sprinkled with vanilla flavoring, onion slice, etc.).

Small Group Option

1. Groups of six to eight children sit in circles, with their hands placed behind their backs.

2. Secretly give one child in each circle an (eraser).

3. Allow time for child to feel the object with his or her hands, trying to identify the object but keeping its identity a secret. At your signal, child passes the object behind his or her back to the next child in the circle, keeping the object hidden in his or her hands. (Optional: Ring bell as signal.) Continue process until all children have had an opportunity to feel the object. Then identify the object aloud. Repeat with a variety of objects.

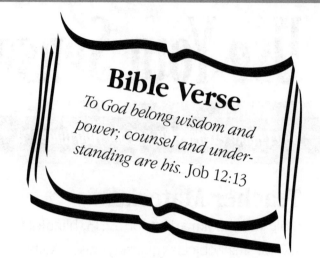

Bible Verse

To God belong wisdom and power; counsel and understanding are his. Job 12:13

Conclude

How did we figure out what each object was? Volunteers answer. **The awesome way in which God made us shows how great and wise He is. How does Job 12:13 describe God?** Read verse aloud. **The words "counsel" and "understanding" mean that God's knowledge is greater than anyone else's. Discovering how great God is helps us see why it's so important to obey Him and never think that our ideas are better than His.** Thank God for His wisdom and power.

Discussion Questions

1. **What are some other ways our sense of touch helps us?** (Tells us when something's too hot to eat. Lets us know when we need to wear a coat.)

2. **What other senses did God give us? How do they help us?** (Sense of smell helps us smell fire.) **How would our lives be different if we didn't have these senses?**

3. **What are some other ways we see God's greatness and wisdom?** (The way trees and flowers are made.)

4. **How can you obey this wise and great God?** (Be kind to others. Help friends. Be honest.)

Who Am I?

Jesus teaches us to live in ways that show we belong to Him and follow Him.

Teacher Materials

Bible with bookmark at Ephesians 4:1, a variety of objects that represent occupations or hobbies (computer disk, gardening glove, book, wrench, basketball, paintbrush, guitar); optional— blindfold.

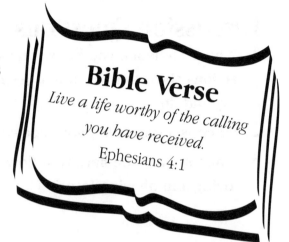

Bible Verse

Live a life worthy of the calling you have received.

Ephesians 4:1

Introduce the Object Talk

Our friends and families can learn from our words and actions whether or not we have chosen to belong to Jesus and follow Him. The things we do and say every day help people learn about us. See if you can learn what people are like by looking at objects they might use.

Present the Object Talk

1. Show one of the objects you collected. (Optional: Blindfold a volunteer who feels the object and then identifies it.) Children tell what they learn about a person who uses the object. For example, if the object is a gardening glove, children might say "likes to be outdoors," "grows lots of plants" and "works hard."

2. We can tell what a person is like by the things they do and say. Jesus talks about the words and actions of people whose job it is to follow Him— people who are called Christians. What might Christians do to show that they belong to Jesus? (Be honest. Help others. Forgive others. Depend on God to give them what is needed. Say kind words to enemies. Don't put bad things into their bodies.) **Christians do these good things to show their love for God.**

Conclude

Reading the Bible helps us learn ways of showing we belong to Jesus. And we learn that God promises to help us obey Him. Read Ephesians 4:1 aloud. Pray, asking God's help in following Him.

Discussion Questions

1. **Who is someone you know whose actions show they belong to Jesus? What does that person say and do?**

2. **When is a time a kid your age can show they follow Jesus? How?**

3. **When might it be hard to follow Jesus? What can we do when we need help loving and obeying Jesus?**

Bible Verse

Live a life worthy of the calling you have received.
Ephesians 4:1

Worldwide Travel

Show God's goodness by making sure your words and actions match.

Teacher's Materials

Bible with bookmark at 1 John 3:18, world map.

Introduce the Object Talk

We can show God's goodness by making sure that our words and actions match. Let's find out about a man who became known for loving and obeying God with both his words and actions.

Bible Verse

Let us not love with words or tongue but with actions and in truth. 1 John 3:18

Present the Object Talk

1. Show world map. Invite a volunteer to point out the country in which you live. **What other countries have you traveled to or heard of?** Volunteers name countries. Invite volunteers to locate countries on map. Give help as needed. **Today**

we are going to talk about a man named Billy Graham. He has traveled to over 185 countries!

2. In 1934, Billy Graham went to a church meeting and heard a preacher talk about Jesus. Because of what he learned about Jesus at that meeting, Billy decided to love and serve God for his whole life. So after Billy went to college, he started telling people about Jesus' love and how to become a member of God's family.

Billy not only told people about Jesus' love, but his actions also showed Jesus' love. Billy traveled to cities all over the world to preach about Jesus. He talked to people who were kings and to people who were members of tribes in Africa. He preached in huge football stadiums and in small villages. Every

place that Billy preached, many people decided to become members of God's family. Everyone that met Billy saw that both his actions and words showed Jesus' love.

Bible Verse
Let us not love with words or tongue but with actions and in truth. 1 John 3:18

Conclude

Read 1 John 3:18 aloud. **Billy Graham's words and actions showed that he obeyed this verse. Who are some other people you know who love God and others with their actions as well as with their words?** Volunteers briefly tell about people they know. **Let's ask God to help us show goodness by making sure our words and actions match.** Lead children in prayer. **Billy Graham used his words to help other people become members of God's family.** Talk with interested children about becoming members of God's family (refer to "Leading a Child to Christ" article on p. 8).

Discussion Questions

1. **Why is it important for what you do to match what you say you believe?** (Our actions show what we really believe. Our good actions can help others do what is good.)

2. **When are some times it might be hard for a kid your age to act in ways that show goodness? How could you help a friend in a situation like this?**

3. **Making our words match our actions is one way to show goodness. How does God help us have the fruit of goodness?** (Gives the Bible to help us understand right ways to act. Reminds us of ways to speak and act to show goodness. Answers our prayers for help.)

Additional Information for Older Children

Billy Graham's son, Franklin Graham, also traveled and preached about God. Franklin Graham also became the leader of Samaritan's Purse, a group of people who help people all over the world. For many years at Christmastime, Samaritan's Purse has collected shoe boxes of gifts that are given to poor children in many countries. (Optional: Find additional information at www.samaritanspurse.org.)

Zigzag Pictures

No matter where you are or what happens in your life, you can experience God's goodness and live as God wants you to.

Teacher Materials

Bible with bookmark at 1 Corinthians 2:9, two identically sized magazine pictures, sheet of paper that is the same height and twice as wide as one picture, ruler, scissors, glue.

Bible Verse

No eye has seen, no ear has heard, no mind has conceived what God has prepared for those who love him. 1 Corinthians 2:9

Prepare the Object Talk

Accordion-fold the paper and both pictures, making each pleat about 1 inch (2.5 cm) wide. Open up the pictures and cut along the folded lines. (Discard any end pieces less than 1 inch [2.5 cm] wide.) Glue alternating strips of the pictures in order to the sheet of paper. Fold up the paper.

Introduce the Object Talk

We can't see ahead to what will happen to us; but we know that no matter where we are or what happens to us, God is with us, giving us the good things we need. All through the Bible, God's people discovered how good it is to follow God. Look at this paper to discover two pictures.

Present the Object Talk

1. Show the paper to children, holding it at an angle so that only one picture can be seen. Ask volunteers to describe what they see. Then show paper from another angle to show the other picture.

2. Allow time for children to experiment with holding the paper to see both zigzag pictures.

Conclude

When we looked at the paper, we discovered two pictures. The Bible tells us about something we haven't seen yet, but we'll discover as we grow older. Read 1 Corinthians 2:9 aloud. **This verse helps us remember that we can experience God's love and goodness now and in the future.** Lead children in prayer, thanking Him for His love and for the good things He gives us.

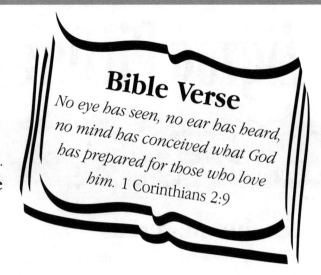

Bible Verse

No eye has seen, no ear has heard, no mind has conceived what God has prepared for those who love him. 1 Corinthians 2:9

Discussion Questions

1. **What are some of the good things God gives the people who love and obey Him?** (Courage. Wisdom to make good choices. Answers to prayer.)

2. **How has God helped you and your family in the past? What good things has He provided for you?**

3. **How has God helped our church?**

4. **What can you do to show your love for God?**

A Dangerous Journey

We can ask God for wisdom to settle arguments and live in peace with others.

Teacher's Materials

Bible with bookmark at Romans 14:19, sheriff's badge; optional—construction paper, marker, scissors, straight pin.

Prepare the Activity

(Optional: Make badge from construction paper [see sketch].)

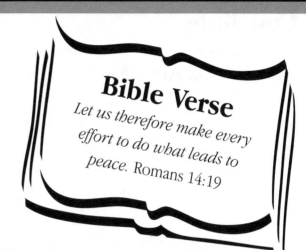

Bible Verse

Let us therefore make every effort to do what leads to peace. Romans 14:19

Introduce the Object Talk

God will help us live in peace with others when we ask Him for help and wisdom to settle arguments. Let's find out about a man who had to be very brave to live in peace.

Present the Object Talk

1. Invite a volunteer to wear sheriff's badge. (Optional: Volunteer wears paper badge.) **What is the job of someone who wears a badge like this?** (Sheriff. Police officer.) **How does a sheriff or police officer keep the peace?**

2. In the 1800s a young man named Samuel Morris had a chance to help others live in peace. Samuel was sailing on a ship from the African country of Liberia to America, because he wanted to go to school to learn more about God.

The sailors on the ship, however, didn't like Samuel because he was African. One angry sailor even threatened to kill him! One day, that sailor thought others were making fun of him, so he swung his sword to attack them. Samuel jumped in the way, putting his own life in danger, and shouted, "Don't kill!" The angry sailor surprised everyone by putting down his sword and walking away. Everyone was amazed! After that, whenever there was a fight, Samuel helped to stop it and kept the peace by praying for the men. Samuel Morris showed that he was willing to do whatever he could to help people live peacefully together.

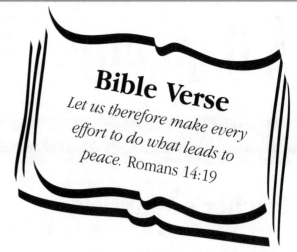

Bible Verse

Let us therefore make every effort to do what leads to peace. Romans 14:19

Conclude

Read Romans 14:19 aloud. **What does it mean to "make every effort"?** (To try as hard as you can. To do something to the best of your ability.) **How did Samuel Morris show that he made every effort for peace?** (Even though he could have been hurt or killed, he stopped the sailor with the sword from hurting anyone.) Invite volunteers to pray, asking God to help them do actions that will help friends and family members live in peace.

Discussion Questions

1. **When have you been a peacemaker or settled an argument while playing with friends? With your family?** Tell children an age-appropriate example about God giving you wisdom to be a peacemaker before asking children to share their stories.

2. **When is one of the hardest times for you to remember to be a peacemaker?**

3. **How can you make every effort to do what leads to peace at home? At school?** (Let a brother or sister be first or borrow something when he or she asks. Ask God for wisdom about how to treat a classmate who is being mean. Don't argue. Don't tease.)

Additional Information for Older Children

Samuel Morris was born a prince in Africa. When he was a teenager, he was taken prisoner when his people lost a battle. Samuel was tortured when his father could not pay the ransom. After sailing to America, Samuel attended Taylor University in America for only one year before he died from injuries he had received when he was tortured. But during that year, Samuel helped many people learn to trust and obey God. Many people at Taylor University decided to become missionaries because of Samuel's actions.

Fair Pay for All

Putting others first can help us be peacemakers.

Teacher's Materials

Bible with bookmark at Romans 12:18, Help Wanted section of newspaper.

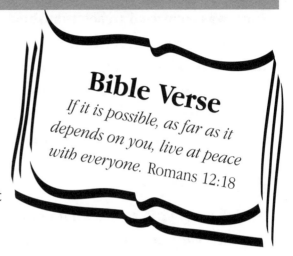

Bible Verse

If it is possible, as far as it depends on you, live at peace with everyone. Romans 12:18

Introduce the Object Talk

Every day we have opportunities to help others live in peace. Peacemakers do what they can to put the needs and interests of others first. Let's find out what one man did to be a peacemaker.

Present the Object Talk

1. Show Help Wanted section of newspaper. **What do people use this part of the newspaper for? Why might finding a job be hard?** Children tell ideas. **There are all kinds of reasons people might have a hard time finding jobs. Some people have had trouble finding good jobs just because of the color of their skin.**

2. John Perkins was an African-American who had a hard time finding a job for fair pay. He once worked for a farmer all day and received only 15 cents as payment! Because of problems like these, many African-American people believed they needed to fight to be treated fairly.

3. When John Perkins grew up, he became a Christian. He wanted to help African-Americans be treated fairly without fighting. So John started telling people in Mississippi about Jesus. Sometimes he was yelled at and even beaten, but he still worked hard to help African-Americans get fair pay.

One time a friend of John's told him about a man and woman who were so poor that they didn't have any food or a place to live. John said he would help the man and woman. When they came for help, however, John was surprised to see that they were not African-American! John wondered if he should help them or not. But he soon realized that because God loves everyone the same, white people deserved help from him, too. John's hard work helped people of all races get good jobs and fair pay.

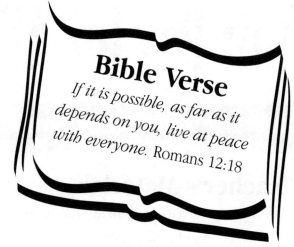

Bible Verse

If it is possible, as far as it depends on you, live at peace with everyone. Romans 12:18

Conclude

Read Romans 12:18 aloud. **What does the verse mean when it says we should live at peace with others "as far as it depends on [us]"?** (It means we should not start fights or arguments. It means we should try to end arguments or fights, instead of continuing them.) **In what ways was John Perkins a peacemaker?** (He helped others to get good jobs and fair pay without fighting.) Lead children in prayer, asking God to help them do what they can this week to live at peace with others.

Discussion Questions

1. **When might a kid your age need help to live in peace with others?** (When someone says something mean. When someone cheats in a game.)

2. **Who are some peacemakers you know?** (Police officers. People who break up fights. People who walk away from arguments.)

3. **What can you do to make peace if someone wants to quarrel?** (Stop a quarrel instead of continuing it. Ask an adult for help. Pray, asking God for courage to be a peacemaker.)

Additional Information for Older Children

John Perkins started the Harambee (HAR-ahm-bay) **Christian Family Center in Pasadena, California. The word "Harambee" is Swahili and means "let's pull together." The people who work at this center help teenagers go to college, so they can come back to help others.**

Home Security

When we trust in God's care, His peace helps us not to worry.

Teacher's Materials

Bible with bookmark at Psalm 29:11, one or more items people use for home security (warning sign, lock, keys, light, etc.).

Introduce the Object Talk

When we trust in God's care, the peace He gives us will help us not to worry. Let's find out how some people trusted in God and how God helped them in a very scary situation.

Bible Verse

The Lord gives strength to his people; the Lord blesses his people with peace. Psalm 29:11

Present the Object Talk

1. Show items you brought. **What do people use these items for? What are some other things people depend on to protect them?** Children respond. **Two missionaries, John Paton and his wife, knew one night that they needed protection.**

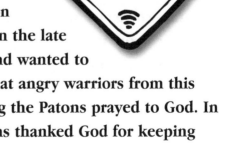

2. John Paton and his wife were missionaries on Tanna, an island near the country of Australia in the late 1800s. One tribe didn't like the missionaries and wanted to kill them. Late one night the Patons realized that angry warriors from this tribe had surrounded their home. All night long the Patons prayed to God. In the morning the warriors were gone! The Patons thanked God for keeping them safe.

About a year later, the tribal chief who had planned the attack became a Christian. The chief asked John who the men were the chief had seen guarding the missionary home the night of the attack. John told the chief that he and his wife were the only people there. Both men then realized that the warriors had seen angels God sent to protect the missionaries.

Conclude

Read Psalm 29:11 aloud. **What does this verse say that God does? What does it mean to say we have God's peace?** (We can feel safe because we know God always cares for us.) **How did the Patons show that they believed this about God?** Children respond. Lead children in prayer.

Bible Verse

The Lord gives strength to his people; the Lord blesses his people with peace. Psalm 29:11

Discussion Questions

1. **What are some scary situations kids your age often face? What do you know about God that might help someone in a situation like this to have peace?**

2. **What are some ways God has cared for you or for someone you know?** Describe one or more ways God has cared for you before asking children to respond.

3. **How can you remember to trust God's care when you are worried or afraid?** (Pray. Read a Bible verse. Talk to someone who loves God.)

Additional Information for Older Children

When John Paton became a missionary, one of the first things he had to do was learn the language of the people on the island of Tanna. Their language, Tannese, had never been written down! But John thought of a way to write down the words. He was even able to print the Bible for the people of Tanna. John later wrote the story of his life in a book titled *John G. Paton, Missionary to the Cannibals.*

Our Daily Bread

We can have peace because God knows what we need and promises to care for us.

Teacher's Materials

Bible with bookmark at John 14:27, loaf of bread and carton of milk.

Introduce the Object Talk

God knows just what we need and He promises to take care of us! Because we can depend on God, we can have peace. Let's find out how one man showed that he had peace and trusted God.

Bible Verse

Peace I leave with you; my peace I give you. I do not give to you as the world gives. Do not let your hearts be troubled and do not be afraid. John 14:27

Present the Object Talk

1. What is your favorite breakfast food? Children respond. Show bread and milk. **People often eat bread and milk as part of their breakfast. Let's find out about some children who didn't know if they would have any food to eat for breakfast.**

2. In the early 1800s, George Müller was a preacher in England. George was also the leader of an orphanage for poor children. One morning the tables in the orphanage dining room were set, but there was no food and no money to buy food. George didn't know where he would get food for breakfast. George and the children prayed, "Dear Father, we thank You for what You are going to give us to eat."

As soon as they finished praying, the town baker knocked at the door. He had loaves of fresh bread! The baker had gotten up early to make bread because he felt that God wanted him to give this gift to the children at the orphanage. A moment later, there

was another knock at the door. The milkman's cart had broken down outside of the orphanage, and he needed to empty the cart before he could repair it. The milk would be wasted, so he offered to give the milk to the children. Time after time, God answered George's prayers just like this! George and the orphans had peace because they trusted God's care.

Bible Verse

Peace I leave with you; my peace I give you. I do not give to you as the world gives. Do not let your hearts be troubled and do not be afraid. John 14:27

Conclude

Read John 14:27 aloud. **How did God care for George Müller and the orphans?** Children respond. **What are some other ways God cares for people?** Lead children in prayer, thanking God for taking care of us, so we can have peace and depend on Him.

Discussion Questions

1. **What are some things a kid your age might worry about?** (A test in school. A sick parent or grandparent. Being liked by others.)

2. **What is something a kid can do if he or she is feeling worried about something?** (Remember God's promise to care for us. Tell God what he or she is worried about. Read in God's Word about how He takes care of His family.)

3. **What does Jesus tell us about worrying?** (There is no need to worry, because God knows what we need and will provide for us.)

4. **How can we get the peace that Jesus said He left with us?** (Ask Jesus to forgive our sins and tell Him that we want to be members of God's family. Keep trusting God, even when we're worried.) Talk to interested children about salvation (see "Leading a Child to Christ" article on p. 8 in this book).

Additional Information for Older Children

Before George Müller opened his orphanage, only rich children were allowed to stay in England's orphanages. George said that he opened his orphanage for two reasons: he wanted to care for poor orphans and he wanted to show that God would supply the needs of anyone who prayed and trusted in Him. Over ten thousand boys and girls were cared for because George prayed and trusted God.

Peace in the Congo

Because God has forgiven us through Christ, encourage people to forgive each other and make peace.

Teacher's Materials

Bible with bookmark at 1 Peter 3:8, world map.

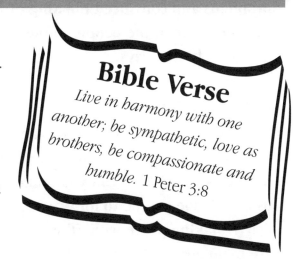

Bible Verse
Live in harmony with one another; be sympathetic, love as brothers, be compassionate and humble. 1 Peter 3:8

Introduce the Object Talk

We can encourage people to forgive each other and make peace, because God has forgiven us. Let's find out about one man who worked hard to help people and make peace.

Present the Object Talk

1. Show children the map. **Where is the country in which we live?** Volunteer locates country on map. Show children or ask an older child to find the country of the Democratic Republic of the Congo (formerly Zaire). **William Sheppard was an African-American missionary to the Congo in 1890. He went to this country because many of the tribes of people who lived there did not know about Jesus.**

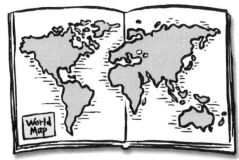

2. William learned the different languages the people in the Congo spoke and helped the people build churches, schools and homes for children. William even became friends with a tribe of people who had always killed any outsiders who came to their area. William's work with these people made him so famous that he was invited three times to the White House, home of the president of the United States.

William could have felt like he had done enough to help the people in the Congo, but he knew that there was a lot more important work left to do. At that time, the king of Belgium was in control of the Congo. His soldiers forced many people in the Congo to work under terrible conditions. William began to write about the problems he saw. Soon people all around the world learned about these problems and convinced the king of Belgium to treat the people in the Congo in better ways.

Bible Verse

Live in harmony with one another; be sympathetic, love as brothers, be compassionate and humble. 1 Peter 3:8

Conclude

Read 1 Peter 3:8 aloud. **Which instructions in this verse tell ways to make peace?** ("Live in harmony with one another." "Be sympathetic.") **How did William Sheppard obey this verse? How can you make peace with others? Let's ask God to help us encourage people to forgive each other and make peace.** Lead children in prayer. **Making peace with others is a good way to show that we love God and are members of His family.** Talk with interested children about becoming members of God's family (refer to "Leading a Child to Christ" article on p. 8).

Discussion Questions

1. **People can "live in harmony" with each other when they choose to respect each other. What can you do to show more respect and kindness to your friends? Your family?**

2. **How do you think living in harmony, or respecting each other, can make peace?**

3. **Forgiving others is one way to "live in harmony" with others. What can a kid your age do when it seems difficult to forgive others?** (Ask for God's help. Read about God's forgiveness in the Bible. Forgive, even when it's hard.)

Additional Information for Older Children

William Sheppard's wife, Lucy Gantt Sheppard, traveled with her husband to the Congo. She worked hard to help the people in the Congo have a good education. Lucy wrote books in the language of the people who lived in the Congo. She wrote the very first reading book written in their language.

Prison Peace

Working to make peace helps us build friendships.

Teacher's Materials

Bible with bookmark at Colossians 3:15, bell or other item used as signal for quiet (whistle, etc.).

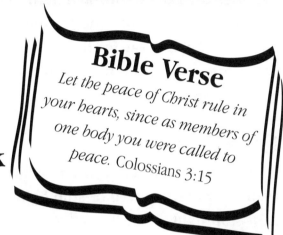

Bible Verse

Let the peace of Christ rule in your hearts, since as members of one body you were called to peace. Colossians 3:15

Introduce the Object Talk

When we do our best to make peace, it helps us make friends. Let's find out how one woman worked to make peace and what happened as a result.

Present the Object Talk

1. Get children's attention by ringing bell or using other item you brought. **If you were trying to signal a crowd of fighting people to be quiet, what would you do?** Volunteers tell. **In 1932, a woman named Gladys Aylward was asked to quiet down a crowd of fighting prisoners.**

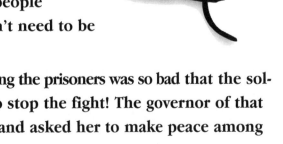

2. Gladys Aylward had moved from England to China so that she could tell people about Jesus. "People who trust Jesus don't need to be afraid," Gladys said.

One day at a nearby prison, a fight among the prisoners was so bad that the soldiers were afraid to go into the prison to stop the fight! The governor of that area remembered what Gladys had said and asked her to make peace among the prisoners.

Gladys walked into the prison courtyard and shouted for quiet. When the men quieted down, Gladys asked them to tell her why they were fighting.

The Really Big Book of Kid Sermons and Object Talks

"This prison is crowded and the prisoners have nothing to do," the men said. "We fight over food because we don't have enough to eat." As Gladys talked and listened to the men, they agreed to make peace and stop fighting. Then Gladys worked hard to help keep peace among the prisoners. She even found a way for the prisoners to earn money, so they could buy enough food.

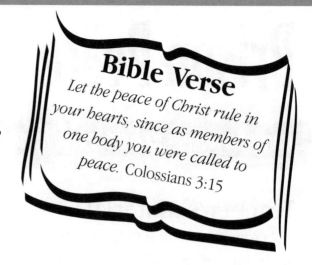

Bible Verse

Let the peace of Christ rule in your hearts, since as members of one body you were called to peace. Colossians 3:15

Conclude

Read Colossians 3:15 aloud. **When we have Christ's peace in our hearts, it means we do our best to avoid or stop fights and arguments. How did Gladys Aylward help stop fights?** (She listened to the men in the prison and helped them settle their arguments.) **Let's ask God to help us make peace with others.** Lead children in prayer.

Discussion Questions

1. **When are some times kids your age have to work to make peace at school? At home?** (When friends are arguing. When brothers or sisters are angry.)

2. **When have you seen someone else work to make peace? What happened?** Tell your own example of a situation in which working to make peace resulted in friendship.

3. **When are some times people might need help to make peace?** (When they are too mad to talk to each other. When they don't understand each other.)

4. **How can we get God's help when we're working to make peace?** (Pray to God. Read His Word. Ask older people who love God for help.)

Additional Information for Older Children

Before Gladys Aylward went to China, no one thought she would be a good missionary. But Gladys refused to give up her plan to be a missionary. She worked hard and saved money until she was able to buy a ticket to China. In China, God helped Gladys learn to speak the difficult Chinese language and to become a great missionary.

Branches of Praise

God gives us everything we need.

Teacher Materials

Bible with bookmark at Philippians 4:19, several tree branches; optional—one or more objects used at sporting events (pom-pom, pennant, foam hand, etc.).

Bible Verse

My God will meet all your needs according to his glorious riches in Christ Jesus.
Philippians 4:19

Introduce the Object Talk

It's important to remember all that God has done for us. In the Old Testament God's people celebrated the Feast of Tabernacles to help them remember how God took care of them when they left Egypt. Let's find out some of the things they used in this celebration and how the celebration got its name.

Present the Object Talk

1. Show branches. **At the Feast of Tabernacles, called Sukkot** (suh-KOHT) **in Hebrew, God told His people to gather different types of tree branches and fruit.** (Optional: Read Leviticus 23:40 aloud.) **The branches and fruit were used in several ways. One way was to decorate small booths the people built. Traditionally, the people lived in these booths for the seven days of the celebration. Living in the booths reminded them of the time after they escaped from Egypt when they had no houses to live in. The word "sukkot" means booths or tabernacles, and that's why this celebration was called the Feast of Tabernacles.** (Optional: Read Leviticus 23:42 aloud.) **Even today Jewish people build and decorate booths as part of this holiday.**

2. Besides being used to decorate the booths, the branches were used to show praise to God. What are some objects people use to cheer for or praise a sports team? Volunteers tell. (Optional: Display objects used at sporting events.) Invite volunteers to wave branches (or hands) in the following traditional pattern for Sukkot: to the front, sides, back, up and down. **The branches were waved in all directions to show that God is ruler over all the earth.**

Bible Verse

My God will meet all your needs according to his glorious riches in Christ Jesus.
Philippians 4:19

Conclude

We can praise God, too, not just at the Feast of Tabernacles, but all year long. Read Philippians 4:19 aloud. **What does this verse tell us about God?** Volunteers answer. **This verse tells us a good reason to celebrate!** Pray, thanking God for giving us all that we need.

Discussion Questions

1. **What are some times in the Bible when God gave people what they needed?** (Manna and water to the Israelites in the desert. A dry sea for the Israelites to get away from Pharaoh. Instructions for Noah to build an ark, so he could be safe during the flood.)

2. **With the things God has given us, how can He use us to help provide for other people's needs?** (Share what you have with people who need it. Help serve food to people at a homeless shelter. Give offering at church, so the church can use the money to help people with their needs.)

3. **In what ways can you thank God for giving you everything you need?** (Pray. Tell others about His gifts. Sing songs of praise to God.)

Additional Information for Older Children

Traditionally, branches from three trees—myrtle, willow and palm—were collected at the Feast of Tabernacles. (Optional: Show one or more of the named branches.) **The branches were braided together and then waved in the air as a way of praising God. A fruit—called a citron—was also held and waved. A citron looks like a lemon.** (Optional: Show lemon.) **In Hebrew, the branches were called a *lulav* (LOO-lahv) and the fruit was called the *etrog* (EH-trog).**

Cheerful Praise

Use your abilities to give praise to God.

Teacher Materials

Bible with bookmark at Psalm 136, objects used to cheer sports teams (pom-poms, pennants, large foam fingers, etc.).

Bible Verse
Give thanks to the Lord, for he is good. His love endures forever. Psalm 136:1

Introduce the Object Talk

We can give praise to God when we use the abilities and talents He gave us. Let's look at a way people praised God in Old Testament times.

Present the Object Talk

1. When a sports team scores a goal, what does the crowd do? (Cheers.) Display objects used to cheer sports teams. (Optional: **What are some of your favorite cheers?** Lead children in a few cheers—"Give me an A!" "We've got spirit; yes, we do!" "2, 4, 6, 8! Who do we appreciate?")

2. Because God is so good to us and because He loves us so much, we want to cheer for joy! One meaning of the word "cheer" is to praise someone or something. The book of Psalms is a book of praise songs. The writers of the psalms used their abilities and talents to praise God.

3. Psalm 136 is a psalm written in an interesting way. After each sentence said by the Old Testament song leader, the choir or worshipers would say "His love endures forever." What does it mean when the psalm says

"**His love endures forever**"? (It will never end. God will always love us.) Lead a reading of Psalm 136 in the manner described (i.e., read, or ask an older child to read, the verses and lead children in saying the refrain "His love endures forever").

Bible Verse

Give thanks to the Lord, for he is good. His love endures forever. Psalm 136:1

Conclude

Because God loves us so much, He gives us abilities that we can use to celebrate and praise Him. Pray, thanking God for the abilities He gives us.

Discussion Questions

1. **How have you seen people at church use their abilities to praise God?** (Make banners. Sing songs. Play music.)

2. **What are some things kids your age can do to praise God? What abilities do you have that you could use to praise and worship God?**

3. **Why do you think praising God is important?**

Additional Information for Older Children

When things are scary or difficult, it may seem hard to praise God. But in the Old Testament, we can read about King Jehoshaphat and how he praised God even when three different armies were coming against his country! To show that they believed God's promise to fight the battle for them, the king and his people chose singers to lead the army instead of soldiers! The singers didn't carry swords—they carried cymbals and harps and other instruments! Read what happened in 2 Chronicles 20:20-22.

Day of Rest

God gives us a day to rest from work and to worship Him.

Teacher Materials

Bible with bookmarks at Exodus 20:8 and Leviticus 23:3, two white candles in candlesticks, matches or lighter.

Introduce the Object Talk

Because He loves us, God gives us a day to rest and worship Him. Let's look at the way people in Bible times celebrated the day of rest, the Sabbath.

Bible Verse

Remember the Sabbath day by keeping it holy. Exodus 20:8

Present the Object Talk

1. The Sabbath, the seventh day of the week, was the very first holiday God told His people to celebrate. Read, or ask an older child to read, Leviticus 23:3. **In fact, God was the first to celebrate the Sabbath. What did God do on the seventh day after creating the world?** (He stopped His work and rested.) **The Hebrew word for the Sabbath is *Shabbot* ** (shah-BAHT)**, which means "to rest."**

2. **Traditionally, God's people worship God together and with their families by celebrating the Sabbath from Friday at sunset to Saturday at sunset.** Display candles in candlesticks and light the candles. **At every Sabbath celebration two candles are lit; and prayers, called blessings, are said. The blessings ask God to show His love and care to the people in the family. During the day-long Sabbath, God's people are to rest from all work and take time to celebrate God's love for them—especially shown by His creation of the world, His rescue of them from slavery in Egypt and all that He does for His people.**

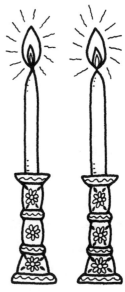

Conclude

Read Exodus 20:8 aloud. **The Sabbath is called holy because it is a special day, a day that is set apart or different from all others. On the Sabbath, we honor and worship God and get the rest we need! Today, Christians all over the world celebrate this day of rest on Sunday, the first day of the week, as a way to joyfully remember that Jesus was raised from the dead on the first day of the week.** Pray, thanking God for His gift of the Sabbath to use to rest and worship Him. Blow out candles.

Bible Verse
Remember the Sabbath day by keeping it holy. Exodus 20:8

Discussion Questions

1. **What are some reasons to rest from work and to worship God?** (God knows that everyone needs to rest. To follow God's example of resting. To obey His command to remember the Sabbath.)

2. **What did God create when He made the world? How can we enjoy those things as part of our Sabbath celebration?** (Take a picnic to a forest or park and enjoy the trees and plants God made. Go to a garden and look at the growing things. Go to the zoo and look at all the different types of animals God made. Look at nature books.)

3. **What are some other ways we rest and take time to worship God?** (Stay home from work and school. Go to church. Sing songs to praise God. Visit a sick or lonely person. Show our love for God by obeying Him.)

4. **What's an example of a way your family rests and worships God?** (Read God's Word together. Pray together. Meet with other members of God's family.)

Additional Information for Older Children

Traditionally, two loaves of a braided bread called *challah* (HAH-lah) are eaten at the special Sabbath meal. These two loaves are reminders of the double amount of manna that God provided for the Israelites on the day before the Sabbath while they were traveling in the desert. God gave the extra manna so that the Israelites wouldn't have to work to gather manna on the Sabbath. Children read Exodus 16:22-23. (Optional: Serve *challah* to children.)

Foreign Phrases

Because Jesus is God's Son, we can worship Him as King now and forever.

Teacher Materials

Bible with bookmark at Zechariah 14:9, large sheet of paper, marker, world map or globe.

Prepare the Activity

On large sheet of paper, print the following language names and phrases—English: Jesus is Lord; Spanish: *Jesús es Señor* (HAY-soos ehs seh-NYOHR); French: *Jesus est le Seigneur* (JHAY-soo eh leh seh-NYOOR); Tagalog (Philippines): *Si Hesus ay Panginoon* (SEH hay-SOOS ay PAH-nee-nah-ahn); German: *Jesus ist Herr* (YAY-soos eest HEHR); Italian: *Il Jesus é il Signore* (EEL HAY-soos eh eel seeg-NOH-ree). Practice saying the phrases.

Bible Verse

The Lord will be king over the whole earth. On that day there will be one Lord, and his name the only name. Zechariah 14:9

Introduce the Object Talk

People all over the world can praise and worship Jesus. One way to worship Jesus is by celebrating a special day called Christ the King Sunday. On this day, Christians all over the world worship Jesus as King of heaven and earth for all time. Let's find out what some of these Christians might say to worship Jesus.

Present the Object Talk

1. The Bible tells us that one day, everybody on the earth will say that Jesus is Lord. Lord is a special name for Jesus that shows He is Ruler or King of all things and of all people. (Optional: Read Philippians 2:9-11 aloud.) **At our church, we speak (English) when we say ("Jesus is Lord").** Show map or globe and point out the area where your church is located.

2. **People in each country of the world say these words in their own languages.** Show paper you prepared with "Jesus is Lord" written in several languages. **This is how people say "Jesus is Lord" in (Spanish).** Repeat for each language, including languages spoken by the children in your group. On map or globe, find locations where each language is spoken as you help children pronounce the phrases.

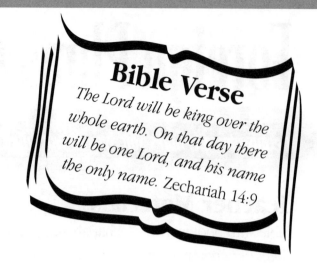

Bible Verse

The Lord will be king over the whole earth. On that day there will be one Lord, and his name the only name. Zechariah 14:9

Conclude

Read Zechariah 14:9. **This verse talks about the day when Jesus returns to earth. Then everyone will understand that Jesus really is the King. How would you explain to a friend what this verse means?** Volunteers tell ideas. Close in prayer, inviting children to call out "Jesus is Lord" in any of the languages written on large sheet of paper.

Discussion Questions

1. **What does it mean to say that Jesus is our King?** (We want to love and obey Him. He is our ruler.)

2. **When can we worship Jesus as King?** (When we pray. When we sing songs of praise. When we talk about Jesus to others.)

3. **Why is it important to worship Jesus?** (To show our love to Him. To help others worship Him, too.)

4. **What can we do to show that we believe Jesus is King and worship Him?** (Obey what the Bible, His Word, tells us to do. Sing songs of praise to Him. Give Him offerings of love, time and money.)

Additional Information for Older Children

Kings or leaders of countries sometimes gain power because they lead their armies into war. Jesus' war was not against people or countries but against sin, death and God's enemy, Satan. By dying on the cross and rising from the dead, Jesus won the war against all the sin in the world. The Bible tells us that one day all people will recognize that Jesus is the King of kings.

Full of Beans

God doesn't give up on us.

Teacher Materials

Bible with Psalm 136:1 marked with a bookmark, one bowl or bucket filled with several cups of beans (or dry cereal), one empty bowl or bucket, one teaspoon; optional—additional teaspoons.

Bible Verse
Give thanks to the Lord, for he is good. His love endures forever. Psalm 136:1

Introduce the Object Talk

God never gives up loving or helping us. As we work together on a big job, see if you feel like giving up.

Present the Object Talk

1. Place the filled bowl or bucket on one side of the room. Place the empty bowl or bucket on the other side of the room. Select six to eight volunteers. Volunteers line up by the filled container. Hand each volunteer a teaspoon.

2. How long do you think it will take to move all these beans to the empty container—one spoonful at a time? Children take turns carrying beans to the empty container. If time is short, give each volunteer a spoon and let them all work at the same time. Several times during the activity ask children how this job makes them feel and make comments such as the following: **Moving all these beans is a big job! A job like this might make you feel like quitting. If we don't give up on this job, it will get done!** Allow the activity to continue until all beans are moved or until children lose interest.

Small Group Option

All children line up and take turns carrying beans to the empty container.

Conclude

One of the things I'm glad to know about God is that He doesn't give up loving us. How does Psalm 136:1 describe God? Read verse aloud. **God is good, and because He is so good He will never give up loving or helping us.** Thank God for His love and help.

Bible Verse

Give thanks to the Lord, for he is good. His love endures forever. Psalm 136:1

Discussion Questions

1. What are some jobs you've felt like quitting?

2. Why do you think God doesn't quit loving us so much? (His love is so great!)

3. How has God shown love and help to you and your family?

4. When we've disobeyed God, how do we know God still loves us? (We can tell God we're sorry for our sin. He cares for us and promises to forgive us.)

Light of the Menorah

Come together to worship God for His power and protection.

Teacher Materials

Bible with bookmark at Psalm 18:2, a variety of candles (birthday cake candles, decorative candles, votive candles, etc.), menorah (or nine candles and candlesticks), matches.

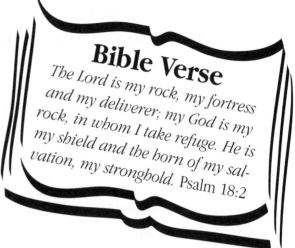

Bible Verse

The Lord is my rock, my fortress and my deliverer; my God is my rock, in whom I take refuge. He is my shield and the horn of my salvation, my stronghold. Psalm 18:2

Introduce the Object Talk

God's power and protection are great reasons to come together and worship Him. In New Testament times God's people worshiped Him at a holiday called the Feast of Dedication. Today we call this holiday Hanukkah (HAH-nih-kah)**. Let's find out how this holiday started and what was done to celebrate it.**

Present the Object Talk

1. Show different candles one at a time. (Optional: Light candles.) **How is this type of candle used?** Volunteers answer.

2. Show menorah (or nine candles and candlesticks). **This is called a Hanukkah menorah. Many years ago, God's people used a menorah in the Temple in Jerusalem. The Temple was where God's people came to worship Him. But in between the time of the Old Testament and the coming of Jesus in the New Testament, a Greek ruler who hated God did many wrong things in the Temple. The menorah was not lit for many years.**

After a group of Israelites defeated the army of this general, the religious leaders of the Israelites wanted to dedicate the Temple so that they could worship God in the

Temple again. To dedicate something means to set it apart for a special purpose. The menorah was lit as part of the dedication of the Temple.

3. **To remember God's power, Hanukkah, which is the Hebrew word for dedication, is celebrated for eight days. The Hanukkah menorah is a symbol of that celebration. Each day one candle is lit.** Light the candles, using the middle candle to light them from left to right. **When Jesus lived on earth, this holiday was celebrated by the Jews as a reminder of God's power in helping His people defeat their enemies.** (Optional: Read John 10:22-23 aloud.)

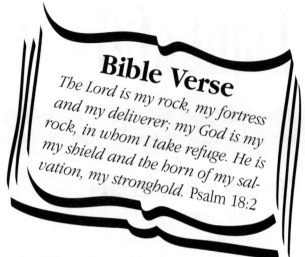

Bible Verse
The Lord is my rock, my fortress and my deliverer; my God is my rock, in whom I take refuge. He is my shield and the horn of my salvation, my stronghold. Psalm 18:2

Conclude

Read Psalm 18:2. **What does this verse say about God's power?** Pray, thanking God for His power to help and His protection from harm.

Discussion Questions

1. **What stories about God's power have you read in the Bible?** (The parting of the Red Sea. Elijah being fed by ravens. Jesus healing the blind man.)

2. **Why is it good to know about God's power?** (We can be sure of His help when we need it. We know we can depend on Him.)

3. **When have you been helped by God's power? How has God cared for you?**

4. **How do you need God's help and care today?**

Additional Information for Older Children

Hanukkah is sometimes called the Festival of Lights. This name not only reminds people of the lighted candles on the menorah but also of a story that was told about the relighting of the menorah. In Bible times, the branches of the menorah held oil, not candles. The story is told that there was found only enough oil for the menorah to burn for one day. However, the menorah continued to burn for eight days until more oil was made. God's people said that it was God's power that kept the menorah burning.

Magnificent Music

We can worship God for His love and His promise to send the Savior.

Teacher Materials

Bible with bookmark at Luke 1:46-56, rhythm sticks or other rhythm instrument; optional—recording of "The Magnificat" and player.

Introduce the Object Talk

God's love and His promise to send a Savior are good reasons to worship Him! Singing is one important way people worship God. Let's find out about one of the oldest songs ever sung about Jesus' birth.

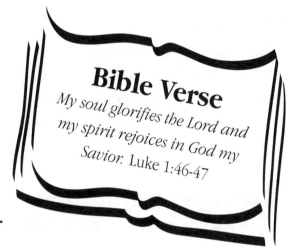

Bible Verse

My soul glorifies the Lord and my spirit rejoices in God my Savior. Luke 1:46-47

Present the Object Talk

1. What are some songs that people sing at Christmas? ("Silent Night," "Jingle Bells," "Away in a Manger," etc.) Use rhythm sticks or other rhythm instrument to play the rhythms to several Christmas songs. Ask children to guess the names of the songs. (Optional: Lead children in singing one or more of the songs.)

2. All of these songs are sung at Christmastime, but the very first Christmas song was sung by Mary after the angel told her she was going to be Jesus' mother. The words of Mary's song are now part of a song called "The Magnificat" (mahg-NEE-fee-kaht)**, which is a Latin word. "The Magnificat" is sung in many churches, not just at Christmastime, but all year long. It is said to have been set to music more often than any other hymn!** Read, or ask several children to take turns reading, Luke 1:46-47. (Optional: Also read verses 48-50 and/or play a portion of "The Magnificat.")

3. **What did Mary praise God for in this song?** (For being her Savior. For doing great things for her. For His mercy.) **How is this song the same or different from the other Christmas songs we named?** Volunteers respond.

Bible Verse

My soul glorifies the Lord and my spirit rejoices in God my Savior. Luke 1:46-47

Conclude

The word "magnificat" means "to magnify." When we magnify God, we are praising Him and telling others how wonderful He is. Pray, praising God for His wonderful gift of His Son, Jesus. Talk with interested children about becoming members of God's family (see "Leading a Child to Christ" on p. 8).

Discussion Questions

1. **What are some reasons to worship and thank God at Christmastime?** (He showed His love by sending Jesus as our Savior. He promised a Savior for many years.)

2. **What are some ways to worship God at Christmastime?** (Thank God in prayer and song for sending Jesus. Show God's love to others by giving gifts. Put up decorations that are reminders of Jesus' birth.)

3. **What is one way you would like to worship God this week?**

4. **How does giving and receiving gifts help us celebrate Jesus' birth?** (Jesus is God's gift to us.)

Additional Information for Older Children

Mary's song of praise is similar to a song sung by Hannah in the Old Testament. Mary sang her song to praise God for the great things He had done for His people and for loving her and allowing her to be the mother of Jesus, the Savior of the world. In a similar way, Hannah was praising God for giving her a son, Samuel, who would be dedicated to God's work. Children read some or all of Hannah's song in 1 Samuel 2:1-10.

Message Fun

To help others learn about God, tell about the great and wonderful things He has done.

Teacher Materials

Bible with bookmark at Psalm 105:1, paper, markers.

Prepare the Object Talk

On each sheet of paper, write one of the following personalized license-plate messages: "CRE8OR" ("Creator"), "GDLVSU" ("God loves you"), "GDS4EVR" ("God is forever"), "GD4GIVS" ("God forgives") and "GDSGR8" ("God is great").

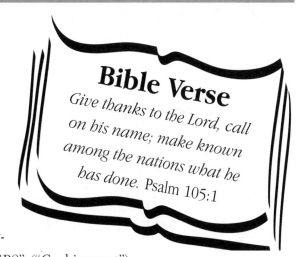

Bible Verse

Give thanks to the Lord, call on his name; make known among the nations what he has done. Psalm 105:1

Introduce the Object Talk

Because we're glad to know about God and His love for us, we want others to know about Him, too. See what you can discover from these special messages.

Present the Object Talk

1. When have you seen a personalized license plate? Volunteers answer. **People get personalized license plates because the plates tell messages the people want others to know.**

2. Listen to this Bible verse to find out what messages we can tell. Read Psalm 105:1 aloud. **When we tell about the great and wonderful things God has done, we help others learn about Him.**

3. One at a time, show the license-plate messages you prepared. Allow volunteers time to discover what the message on each plate says. (Optional: Give paper and markers to children for them to create additional messages about the great and wonderful things God has done, limiting messages to seven characters. Display papers in a well-traveled area of your church.)

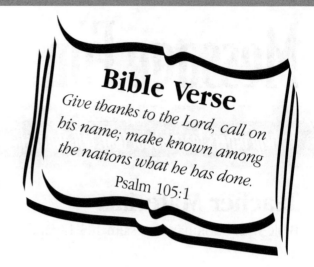

Bible Verse

Give thanks to the Lord, call on his name; make known among the nations what he has done.

Psalm 105:1

Conclude

Lead children in prayer, inviting volunteers to name great and wonderful things God has done.

Discussion Questions

1. **What are some great and wonderful things God has done?**

2. **Who has told you about how great God is? When?**

3. **How did people learn about God in Bible times? How do people learn about God today?** (Listen to others who tell about God. Read His Word.)

Passover Plates

Remember what God has done for you and praise Him!

Teacher Materials

Bible with bookmarks at Exodus 12:14 and Psalm 77:12-13; plate; several of these foods—parsley, salt water, horseradish, *matzo* crackers, *haroset* (chopped apples and nuts mixed with honey), lamb or other clean bone, hard-boiled egg; optional—*seder* plate.

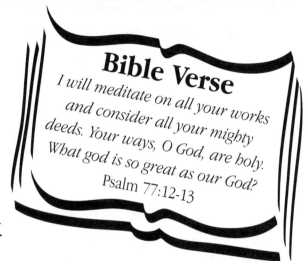

Bible Verse

I will meditate on all your works and consider all your mighty deeds. Your ways, O God, are holy. What god is so great as our God?

Psalm 77:12-13

Introduce the Object Talk

It's important to praise God and remember all that He has done for us. After God rescued His people from slavery in Egypt, He told them to eat a special meal to help them remember and celebrate His help and protection. Let's find out what foods are eaten at this special meal.

Present the Object Talk

1. What is the name of the celebration at which God's rescue of His people from slavery is remembered? (Passover.) **Another name for the Passover meal is** *seder* (SAY-dehr). *Seder* **means "order." As the foods are eaten in order, questions are asked and answered to tell the story of the escape from Egypt.**

2. Show and discuss each food item you brought. (Optional: Place food items on seder plate. Invite volunteers to taste items.) **The Hebrew word for green plants is** *karpas* (CAHR-pahs). **This green parsley reminds us that everything that grows is a gift from God.** Dip parsley in salt water. **The salt water reminds us of the tears of the Hebrew slaves in Egypt.** Place horseradish on a piece of *matzo*. **The horseradish tastes bitter and reminds us of the terrible years of slavery in Egypt.** *Haroset*, **made with apples, nuts and honey, reminds us of the mortar between the bricks**

that the Hebrew slaves used to build in Egypt. The bone reminds us of the lamb that was sacrificed at the first Passover. The hard-boiled egg is another reminder of the sacrifices made by God's people in Bible times. The *matzo* crackers (*matzo* is bread made quickly without yeast) remind us how fast the Hebrews left Egypt.

Bible Verse
I will meditate on all your works and consider all your mighty deeds. Your ways, O God, are holy. What god is so great as our God?
Psalm 77:12-13

3. Why did God want His people to celebrate the Passover? Read, or ask an older child to read, Exodus 12:14 aloud. **The Passover celebration reminds us all of God's power.**

Conclude

Read Psalm 77:12-13 aloud. **What does Psalm 77:12-13 tell us about God?** (God is holy. He is the greatest.) Pray, asking for God's help to remember all the great things He has done and thanking Him for His love and power.

Discussion Questions

1. **What are some of the great things God has done that you have read about in the Bible?** (Helped the Israelites escape from Pharaoh's army. Helped the Hebrew people get to the Promised Land. Healed people. Sent Jesus to die for our sins.)

2. **What are some of the great things God has done for you and your family?** Tell your own answer as well as inviting volunteers to respond.

3. **When can you praise God for the ways He helps you?**

Additional Information for Older Children

During the *seder* meal, a large cup is placed in the center of the table for the Old Testament prophet Elijah. In Old Testament times, people believed that Elijah would appear to announce the coming of the Messiah. Placing a cup on the table showed that the people were ready for the Messiah. Now we know that the Messiah, Jesus, has already come!

Praise Parade

God's family celebrates and praises God together!

Teacher Materials

Bible with bookmarks at Psalm 24 and Psalm 149:1, large sheet of paper, marker, masking tape; optional—objects used at parades (serpentine rolls, confetti, balloons, batons, whistles, drums, etc.).

Bible Verse
Praise the Lord. Sing to the Lord a new song, his praise in the assembly of the saints.
Psalm 149:1

Prepare the Activity

On the large sheet of paper, draw one line for each letter of the name of several objects used at parades (see suggested list above). (Optional: Use objects associated with specific parades in your community.) Tape paper to wall.

Introduce the Object Talk

When God's family gets together, we celebrate and praise God! Let's look at one way big crowds of people get together and celebrate special occasions.

Present the Object Talk

1. Display paper you prepared. Invite volunteers to suggest letters of the alphabet. As volunteers suggest letters, print letters on the correct lines. If a letter is not used in any of the words you are using, write the letter at the bottom of the paper. As letters fill in the words, children guess what the words are. **All of these words are the names of things used at a special event. Guess what the event is!** Volunteers respond until the event, a parade, is revealed.

2. **Another word like "parade" is "procession."** **A procession is a group of people moving forward together, usually as part of a very special ceremony. Processions are an important part of funerals, graduations and weddings. Often, music accompanies processions. Psalm 24 is a song that was written for the procession David led when he brought the Ark of the Covenant to Jerusalem. (The Ark was a special box that reminded the people of God's presence.)** Read, or ask an older child to read, Psalm 24:7-10 aloud. (Optional: As verses are read, children walk in a procession around the room.)

Bible Verse

Praise the Lord. Sing to the Lord a new song, his praise in the assembly of the saints.
Psalm 149:1

Conclude

When David brought the Ark to Jerusalem, the Israelites celebrated and praised God. As members of God's family, we can celebrate and praise God, too! Read Psalm 149:1 aloud. **An assembly is a large group of people. When are some times large groups of people come together to praise God?** Pray, thanking God that the members of His family can celebrate and praise Him together.

Discussion Questions

1. **What has God given you to show His love for you?** Volunteers respond. **How has God given you courage? When has God forgiven you?**

2. **Why is it important to celebrate these gifts God gives us?** (To recognize God's constant goodness to His people. To remember the good gifts God gives us every day.)

3. **What are some ways to praise God with other members of His family?**

4. **What is one way you can praise God with your family this week?** (Sing a praise song together before eating dinner. Each person in the family thanks God for something when you pray together. Together, make a poster telling God reasons you love Him.)

Additional Information for Older Children

Many psalms were written for special occasions. Psalm 132 may have been written for two occasions: the Temple dedication (children compare Psalm 132:8-10 to 2 Chronicles 6:41-42) **and when the king was crowned** (children read Psalm 132:18).

Sing a Song

Worship God with joy because of the great things He has done.

Teacher's Materials

Bible with bookmark at Psalm 100:2, cassette/CD recording of "Hark! the Herald Angels Sing" and player or photocopies of words and music, large sheet of paper, marker.

Bible Verse
Worship the Lord with gladness; come before him with joyful songs. Psalm 100:2

Introduce the Object Talk

God has done so many great things! We can joyfully worship God when we think about the great things God has done. Let's find out about one man who worshiped God and helped others worship God, too.

Present the Object Talk

1. Invite children to sing "Hark! the Herald Angels Sing" or listen to song on cassette/CD. **When do we usually sing this song? What does this song say about Jesus?** Children respond. **A man named Charles Wesley wrote this song and many other songs about Jesus.**

2. Charles Wesley grew up in a very big family in England in the 1700s. He went to church and did many good things all his life, but he didn't really understand what it meant to be a Christian or how much God loved him.

When Charles was a grown-up, he lived with some Christians in London. While he was there, Charles saw how kind and gentle they were, and he heard them talk about how they lived as part of God's family. Those Christians helped Charles understand God's love for him.

Charles was so glad to know of God's love that he began to write songs about God's love and forgiveness. For many years Charles and his brother, John, preached and sang about God's love and forgiveness to people all over England. Charles eventually wrote 6,000 hymns! Many people learned to love and worship God because of Charles's music and preaching.

Bible Verse

Worship the Lord with gladness; come before him with joyful songs. Psalm 100:2

Conclude

Read Psalm 100:2 aloud. **How did Charles Wesley show his joy for the great things God has done?** (He wrote and sang songs about God.) **What are some things God has done for which you are thankful?** List children's responses on a large sheet of paper. Lead children in prayer, thanking God for items children listed.

Discussion Questions

1. **How do people often show that they are joyful or happy?** (Smile. Sing.)

2. **How can we show joy when we worship God?** (Sing songs that tell of God's greatness. Tell others about the ways in which God helps us. Thank God in prayer for the good things He gives us.)

3. **What is one way we have worshiped God today?**

Additional Information for Older Children

"Hark! the Herald Angels Sing" is often sung to celebrate Jesus' birth. Another of the hymns Charles Wesley wrote is often sung to celebrate Jesus' **resurrection.** Ask volunteers to take turns reading one or more stanzas of "Christ the Lord Is Risen Today." **What words from this song help us tell about our joy that Jesus is alive?**

The End Is Just the Beginning

God's gifts to us make it possible for us to worship Him in everything we do and obey Him in all situations so that others may come to know and love Him.

Teacher Materials

Bible with bookmark at Psalm 67:1-2, objects from graduations (pictures, mortarboard, diploma, etc.).

Bible Verse

May God be gracious to us and bless us and make his face shine upon us, that your ways may be known on earth, your salvation among all nations. Psalm 67:1-2

Introduce the Object Talk

Others may come to know and love God when we worship and obey Him in all situations. Let's talk about a time in our lives that may seem like the end but that is also a beginning.

Present the Object Talk

1. **Have you ever been to a graduation? What are some of the things you saw there?** Show objects you brought. Ask volunteers to identify objects and explain how they are used at a graduation. **What do you think is the reason for a graduation celebration?** Volunteers respond. **Some people think of a graduation only as the end of something—the end of going to a particular school. But a graduation is also a time to begin something new—the beginning of a new school, for example, or a job.**

2. **At the end of most worship services, a pastor or church leader will usually say a prayer called a benediction. A benediction is something good that is spoken to people to help people remember that God is with them even after the worship service is over. Reading or singing a benediction not only means that the worship service is ended, but it also means that now we can begin the new week loving and obeying God with the gifts He has given us.** Read or ask an older child to

read the benediction in Psalm 67:1-2.
(Optional: Lead children in singing the
song or saying the words that your church
uses as a benediction at worship services.)

Bible Verse

May God be gracious to us and bless us and make his face shine upon us, that your ways may be known on earth, your salvation among all nations. Psalm 67:1-2

Conclude

**Prayers or songs of benediction
remind us that even though the
worship service is ending, we can
begin the new week worshiping God
every day as we love and obey Him.
God's gifts to us make it possible for us to love Him and help others become
part of His family, too.** Talk with children about becoming members of God's family,
following the guidelines in the "Leading a Child to Christ" article (see p. 8). Pray, asking for God's help to love and obey Him in all situations.

Discussion Questions

1. What are some of the gifts God has given members of His family? (His love
and care. Prayer. Other people who believe in and love Jesus.)

**2. In what ways can kids your age show that they want to love and obey
God?**

3. How can we help others become members of God's family? (Care for them.
Pray for them.)

Additional Information for Older Children

**The word "benediction" comes from the Latin *bene* ("good") and *dicuts*
("speaking"). This tells us that the benediction is a blessing pronounced
over everyone present, asking God to bless the hearers with help and
strength as the new week begins. A benediction may also be a blessing
to God, praising Him for His goodness.**

Thumb Wrap!

Believing in God and His power makes us want to worship Him.

Teacher Materials

Bible with bookmark at Psalm 95:6-7, masking tape, a variety of objects (pencil, paper, book, a cup of water, marker, paper clip).

Introduce the Object Talk

Getting to know what God is like helps us believe in Him and worship Him. Try this experiment with me to learn about a special way God made us that shows His great power.

Bible Verse

Come, let us bow down in worship, let us kneel before the Lord our Maker; for he is our God. Psalm 95:6-7

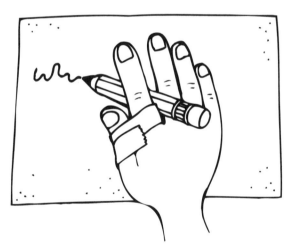

Present the Object Talk

1. With masking tape, wrap together the thumb and first finger of a volunteer's writing hand. Then ask the volunteer to try to write his or her name on a piece of paper.

2. Repeat with other volunteers and these tasks: turn pages of a book, drink cup of water, pick up a paper clip, open a door, button or unbutton a coat or sweater, etc.

3. Discuss the activity by asking, **What made your task so hard to do? What would happen if you didn't have a thumb? What would happen if you only had thumbs on your hands?** Volunteers tell ideas.

Conclude

God made our fingers and thumbs to work just right. Listen to these verses that talk about God as the One who made us. Read Psalm 95:6-7 aloud. **One way to worship God is by thanking Him for making us.** Lead children in prayer, thanking God for making us in such special ways.

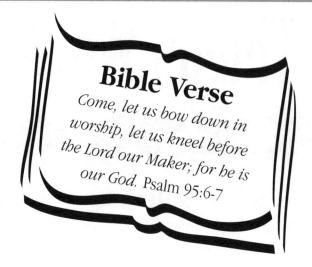

Bible Verse

Come, let us bow down in worship, let us kneel before the Lord our Maker; for he is our God. Psalm 95:6-7

Discussion Questions

1. **What are some other special ways that God has made us?** (We can taste different flavors. Our arms and legs have joints, so they can bend.)

2. **What's something about the way you're made for which you want to thank God?** Tell children something you're glad God has made you able to do.

3. **What are some of the ways people in our church thank and worship God?** (Sing songs of praise. Pray. Tell others about God's greatness.)

Wave Bottles

Jesus is so great that we can't help but praise Him.

Teacher Materials

Bible with bookmark at Psalm 145:3, 12-ounce clear plastic bottle, water, blue food coloring, mineral oil, tape; optional— picture of ocean or starry sky.

Bible Verse

Great is the Lord and most worthy of praise; his greatness no one can fathom.
Psalm 145:3

Prepare the Object Talk

Fill bottle half full with water. Add several drops of blue food coloring. Fill remainder of bottle with mineral oil. Fasten cap tightly and wrap with tape. (If you have a large group, prepare more than one bottle.)

Introduce the Object Talk

The more we get to know about Jesus, the more we want to praise Him. Let's look at something that reminds us of how great Jesus is.

Present the Object Talk

1. Show bottle. Ask a volunteer to hold the bottle horizontally and gently tilt the bottle from end to end, creating a wavelike motion. Allow time for children to experiment with the bottle.

2. The waves in this bottle remind me of the ocean. What words would you use to describe an ocean? How hard do you think it might be to see to the very bottom of the ocean or a deep lake? Why? Volunteers tell ideas. (Optional: Show picture of ocean instead of using wave bottle, or show starry sky picture and talk with children about the impossibility of counting all the stars in the sky.)

Conclude

The ocean is so big and so deep we can't understand exactly what it is like. Listen to what the Bible says about the Lord. Read Psalm 145:3 aloud. **The word "fathom" means to understand. This verse tells us that the Lord is so great we can never understand exactly how great He is! Because Jesus is so great, we want to praise Him.** Lead children in prayer, thanking Jesus for His greatness.

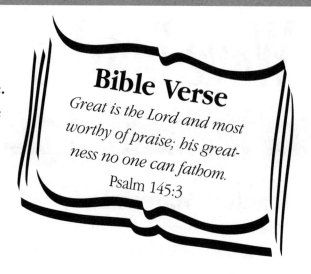

Bible Verse

Great is the Lord and most worthy of praise; his greatness no one can fathom.
Psalm 145:3

Discussion Questions

1. What are some other things that remind us of how great Jesus is? (The miracles He did on earth. His resurrection.)

2. What are some of the ways people praise Jesus for His greatness? (Sing songs about Him. Pray. Tell others about His greatness.)

3. What would you like to praise Jesus for?

Welcoming Ways

Jesus is so great that we can't help but praise Him.

Teacher Materials

Bible with bookmark at Psalm 147:1; optional—objects used to welcome and praise others (medal, red carpet, confetti, pennants, pom-poms, etc.).

Bible Verse

Praise the Lord. How good it is to sing praises to our God, how pleasant and fitting to praise him! Psalm 147:1

Introduce the Object Talk

We can't help but praise and honor Jesus because He is so great! Let's look at some of the ways great people are honored.

Present the Object Talk

1. One at a time, pantomime, or ask volunteers to pantomime, ways to praise or honor people. (Lay out a red carpet, drop flower petals down an aisle, cheer for a sports team, salute, bow, curtsy, throw confetti, etc.) As each action is pantomimed, children guess the action. **Who might be honored that way?** (Optional: Show objects used to honor others and ask children to describe how objects could be used to praise others.)

2. Why do we do special things to praise people? (To show they are important to us. To show that we admire or love them.) **On the first Palm Sunday, people praised and honored Jesus when He arrived in Jerusalem. They clapped and cheered, waved palm branches in the air and laid palm branches and their coats on the road for Jesus to ride on. Every year we remember and celebrate Palm Sunday because it was the beginning of the time when Jesus died for our sins and then rose again to give us new life.**

Conclude

During the week that followed Jesus' kingly parade into Jerusalem, Jesus died on the cross to make a way for all of us to become members of God's family. He deserves all the honor we can give Him! Read Psalm 147:1 aloud. **What are some of the things God has done in your life for which you would like to praise and honor Him?** Praise God in prayer, mentioning children's responses.

Bible Verse

Praise the Lord. How good it is to sing praises to our God, how pleasant and fitting to praise him! Psalm 147:1

Discussion Questions

1. **What are some of the reasons we want to praise Jesus?** (He is God's Son. He was willing to die on the cross to pay the punishment for all people's sins. He rose from the dead. He loves us all. He taught us the best way to live.)

2. **What are some ways we can praise Jesus?** (Sing songs to Him. When we pray, tell Him why we love Him or what we are thankful for. Tell others how wonderful He is.)

3. **What is your favorite way to praise Jesus?** Volunteers respond.

Additional Information for Older Children

We may not think of a donkey as a royal animal; but in Bible times, the donkey was considered a sign of humility, peace and royalty! Read 1 Kings 1:38-40 to learn about a kingly parade similar to the one we celebrate on Palm Sunday.

In Zechariah 9:9, you can read the Old Testament prophet Zechariah's prediction of a King coming to save God's people—riding on a donkey! Now we know the King he wrote about was Jesus! Volunteer reads verse aloud.

Ask God!

Teacher Materials

Bible with bookmark at 1 Thessalonians 5:17-18, flashlight with batteries, plant, votive candle, match, large wide-mouthed jar, snack for each child.

Bible Verse

Pray continually; give thanks in all circumstances.
1 Thessalonians 5:17-18

Introduce the Object Talk

If we want to get to know God and obey Him, we need to talk to Him every day. Let's look at these objects and talk about what they need in order to work.

Present the Object Talk

1. Show flashlight and ask children to tell what it needs to work (batteries). **What are some other items which need batteries in order to work?** (CD player, handheld video games, toys, etc.)

2. Show plant and ask children to tell what it needs to grow (water, sunlight). **What are some other things which need water and sunlight to grow?** (Trees, flowers, etc.)

3. Light candle. **What does this candle need to burn?** (Oxygen.) Cover candle with jar and watch to see the candle flame go out. Repeat experiment, inviting children to count how long it takes for the flame to go out.

4. What do you need to do every day to live and grow? (Eat food. Drink water. Breathe air.) Serve snack to each child.

Bible Verse
Pray continually; give thanks in all circumstances.
1 Thessalonians 5:17-18

Conclude

We've talked about what all these items need. What does 1 Thessalonians 5:17-18 say we need to do? Read verses aloud. **Sometimes we only think about praying to God when we have a problem or need something. But when does 1 Thessalonians 5:17-18 say we should pray? Talking to God every day about what we are doing and the choices we are making helps us love and obey Him.** Lead children in prayer, thanking Him that we can talk to Him.

Discussion Questions

1. When can you talk to God?

2. What are some things a kid your age could tell God about school?

3. Who might help you remember to pray?

4. What's something you'd like to thank God for right now?

Light Lesson

Prayer helps us get to know Jesus, God's Son.

Teacher Materials

Bible with bookmarks at Matthew 17:2 and Psalm 69:13, sheet of white paper, marker, flashlight or lamp with bare bulb.

Prepare the Activity

Fold paper in half. Draw a sun on folded paper.

Bible Verse

I pray to you, O Lord, in the time of your favor; in your great love, O God, answer me with your sure salvation. Psalm 69:13

Introduce the Object Talk

We can get to know Jesus, God's Son, when we pray. One time when three of Jesus' disciples were praying with Him, they learned that Jesus was God's Son. Let's find out what happened.

Present the Object Talk

1. Holding paper so that drawing faces you, shine light from flashlight or lamp directly on the blank side of the paper. **When I shine this light directly on the sheet of paper, what do you see?** (Nothing but the paper.) Without moving paper, move light source behind paper. **When I shine the light from behind the paper, what do you see?** (The sun drawn on the paper.)

2. The Bible tells us about a time when light made Jesus' disciples see Him in a different way. His face shone as bright as the sun and made them know He was God's Son. Jesus' appearance changed so much that the Bible says He was transfigured. The word "transfigure" means to change. Read, or ask an older child to read, Matthew 17:2. **Many churches remember Jesus' transfiguration on a special Sunday**

each year. Celebrating this event reminds God's followers that Jesus is God's Son, the Savior sent by God.

Conclude

We can get to know Jesus by reading about Him in the Bible. We also get to know Jesus through prayer. In the same way you become better friends with others by talking with them, **you get to know Jesus better whenever you pray.** Read Psalm 69:13 aloud. **The writer of this verse is praying to God because he knows God loves him and will answer his prayers.** Pray, thanking God for Jesus, His Son, and asking God's help in getting to know who Jesus is. Talk with children about becoming Christians. Follow the guidelines in the "Leading a Child to Christ" article on page 8.

Bible Verse
I pray to you, O Lord, in the time of your favor; in your great love, O God, answer me with your sure salvation. Psalm 69:13

Discussion Questions

1. **What are some things you know about Jesus?** (He is God's Son. He loves us. He is always with us.) **How have you gotten to know who Jesus is?** (From teachers and parents. From reading God's Word.)

2. **Why do you think praying helps us get to know Jesus?** (When we pray, it reminds us of Jesus' love and care for us.)

3. **What kinds of things can you talk to Jesus about?**

4. **When are some times you pray every day? When are some other times you can pray?**

Additional Information for Older Children

About a week prior to Jesus' transfiguration on the mountain, Jesus asked His disciples who people thought He was. Jesus also asked who THEY thought He was. Read what Peter said in Matthew 16:13-16.

The Bells Are Ringing

When we talk to God, we can worship Him for who He is and what He has done.

Teacher Materials

Bible with bookmarks at Psalm 100 and Daniel 2:20, bell(s); optional—pictures of bells.

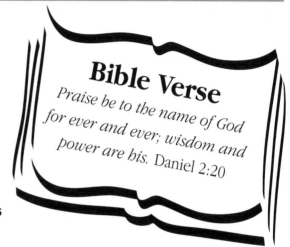

Bible Verse

Praise be to the name of God for ever and ever; wisdom and power are his. Daniel 2:20

Introduce the Object Talk

For all that God is and all that He has done, we can worship God by talking to Him. Let's look at a way to know that it is time to come together and worship God.

Present the Object Talk

1. Display bell(s) you brought. (Optional: Show pictures of bells.) Allow volunteers to ring the bell(s). **Bells often tell people when it's time to do something. What kinds of bells can you think of that tell you it's time for something?** (School bells. Dinner bells. Customer-service bells. Emergency Broadcast System warning bells. Church bells.) **Many churches have bell towers and bells that are rung to let people know it is time for a worship service.**

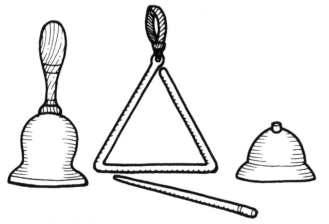

2. **When God's followers come together, they sometimes read verses from the Bible that tell everyone it's time to worship God. The verses that are read are called a call to worship. Psalm 100 is a call to worship.** Ask older volunteers to read the psalm, one verse at a time. **The words of this psalm help people think about how and why we should worship God.** At the beginning and end of the psalm, as well as at the end of each verse, invite volunteers to ring the bell(s) as another reminder to worship God.

Conclude

When Daniel lived in Bible times, he worshiped God, too. Read Daniel 2:20 aloud. **What two words does this verse use to describe God?** ("Wisdom" and "power.") **What are some of the ways God's wisdom and power help people today?** (Answer our prayers. Give us courage. Help us do right.) Pray, thanking God and praising Him for His wisdom and power.

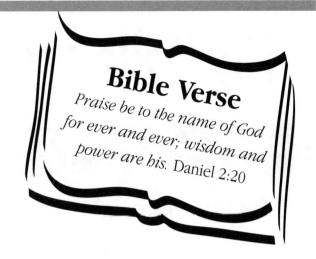

Bible Verse

Praise be to the name of God for ever and ever; wisdom and power are his. Daniel 2:20

Discussion Questions

1. **Who are some people who often receive praise in our world today?** (Athletes. Movie stars.) **Why is it important to worship and praise God?** (Because God is greater than anyone else, He deserves our worship and praise. We want to tell God we love Him and how glad we are about all the things He has done for us.)

2. **In Psalm 100, the words "gates" and "courts" are referring to places in the Temple where people worshiped God in Bible times. Where are some places that we could enter, giving thanks and praise to God?** (Church. Home. School.)

3. **What does Psalm 100 mean by describing God as faithful to all generations (a generation is a group of people born at the same time)?** (God has cared for people and loved people all through the history of the world.)

4. **What do you want to praise God for today?** Tell your own answer to this question before inviting volunteers to answer.

Additional Information for Older Children

Many psalms have the words "of David" written at the beginning of the psalm. This phrase could mean that David wrote the psalm or that the psalm was written by someone else and dedicated to David. Look at these psalms to find who Bible scholars think either wrote the psalm or used the psalm in worship. Children look at these psalms to find the probable authors: Psalm 19 (David, king of Israel), Psalm 42 (the sons of Korah, a group of musicians), Psalm 50 (Asaph, a choir leader in David's time), Psalm 90 (Moses, leader of God's people when they escaped from Egypt).

Watch and Wait

God always answers prayer–sometimes in ways we don't expect.

Teacher Materials

Bible with bookmark at Colossians 4:2, newspapers, several paper plates, glue, salt in a shaker, paintbrush, watercolor paint, container of water.

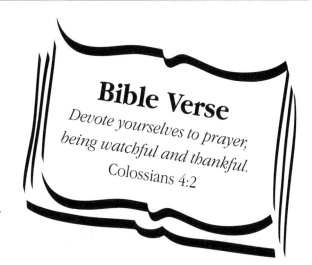

Bible Verse
Devote yourselves to prayer, being watchful and thankful.
Colossians 4:2

Prepare the Object Talk

Make a practice design, following the directions below.

Introduce the Object Talk

Sometimes when something takes a long time to happen, we get tired of waiting and watching for it to happen. When we pray to God, we need to wait and watch to see Him answer our prayers. Watch to see what happens in this experiment.

Present the Object Talk

1. Cover table or floor with newspapers. Squeeze glue onto a paper plate, creating a design of thick lines that intersect.

2. Immediately pour salt over the lines, making sure to cover the glue completely. Shake excess salt onto glue. Saturate the paintbrush with water so that it is very wet.

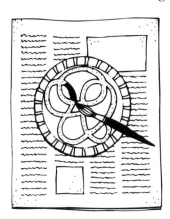

Then dab watercolor paint onto one of the lines, holding the brush at one place. The color will move along the lines as the salt absorbs the water in the paint. Encourage children to keep watching to see what happens to the paint.

3. After the color has stopped spreading, rinse the brush in water and apply another color of paint at a different place. The two paints will mix at the point where they meet. **What did you expect would happen? What did happen?**

Small Group Option

Provide materials for children to create their own designs.

Conclude

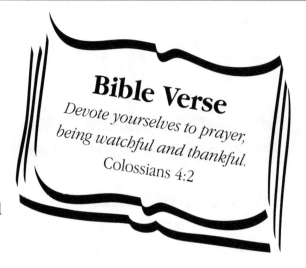

Bible Verse
Devote yourselves to prayer, being watchful and thankful.
Colossians 4:2

Just as we watched to see what would happen with the paint, it's up to us to keep watching to find out how God will answer our prayers. We know God will always keep His promise to answer our prayers. Read Colossians 4:2 aloud. **When we devote ourselves to prayer, we never give up praying and looking to see how God will answer our prayers. Sometimes God answers our prayers in ways we don't expect.** Lead children in prayer, thanking God for always hearing and answering our prayers.

Discussion Questions

1. **What are some things kids your age often talk to God about?** (When help is needed to do something. To thank Him for having something good or for something good happening.)

2. **Why might God answer a prayer by saying "no" or "later"?** (God knows what's best for us.)

3. **In what way has God answered a prayer for you or someone in your family?**

4. **What's something you want to talk to God about?**

Worldwide Prayer

Teacher Materials

Bible with bookmarks at Matthew 6:9 and Philippians 4:6, large sheet of paper, marker; optional—globe or world map, flags from countries listed below (pictures of flags may be found in encyclopedias or on the Internet).

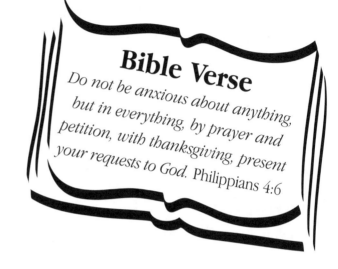

Bible Verse

Do not be anxious about anything, but in everything, by prayer and petition, with thanksgiving, present your requests to God. Philippians 4:6

Prepare the Activity

On large sheet of paper, print one or more of the following: Spanish—*Nuestro Padre en el cielo* (nyoo-EH-stroh PAH-dreh een ehl see-EH-loh); French—*Notre Père dans le ciel* (NOH-treh PEHR dahn leh SEE-ehl); German—*Unser Vater in Himmel* (OON-suhr VAH-tuhr ihn HIHM-uhl); Tagalog (Philippines)—*Ama Namin sumasa-langit ka* (Ah-mah NAH-meen soo-MAH-sah LAHN-geet kah); Norwegian—*Våre Far inne him-melen* (VAHR FAHR IHN-eh HIH-meh-lehn); Afrikaans (South Africa)—*Ons Vader in hemel* (AHNS VAH-duhr ihn HIHM-uhl); Kwazulu (South Africa)—*Ubaba Wethu Ebhakabhaka* (OO-bah-bah WEE-thoo EHB-hah-kahb-hah-kah). Practice saying the phrases.

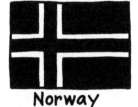

Norway

Introduce the Object Talk

When Jesus lived on earth, He taught us how to talk to God. One prayer that Jesus prayed, called the Lord's Prayer, is prayed by people all over the world. Let's find out about some of the first words in this prayer and practice saying them in different languages.

South Africa

Present the Object Talk

1. When Jesus taught the disciples to pray, what name did He use for God?
Read Matthew 6:9 aloud. **Jesus was speaking in the Aramaic language and the**

word He used for Father was *Abba* (AH-bah). *Abba* actually means "Daddy"! Jesus showed how much He was loved by His Father in heaven by calling Him Daddy.

2. **Jesus' example shows us that we can talk to God as our Daddy, too. People in each country of the world say the words of the Lord's Prayer in their own languages.** Show paper you prepared. **This is how people say "Our Father in heaven" in (Spanish).** Repeat for each language. Include volunteers in your group who speak other languages. (Optional: Show map or globe and identify locations of countries, or show flags or pictures of flags you have collected.)

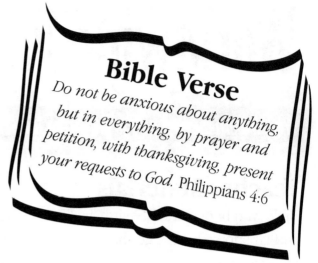

Bible Verse

Do not be anxious about anything, but in everything, by prayer and petition, with thanksgiving, present your requests to God. Philippians 4:6

Conclude

Read Philippians 4:6. **The word "anxious" means worried. What should we do instead of worry?** (Talk to God.) Ask children to thank God for His gift of prayer, inviting them to begin with "Our Father in heaven" in any of the languages written on large sheet of paper.

Discussion Questions

1. **What are some things Jesus prayed about? What did Jesus ask His Father in heaven to do?**

2. **What are some things kids your age worry about?**

3. **How do you think talking to God about your worries will help?** (God will listen to you. He will give you courage. God will remind you that He is with you. God always answers prayer in the very best way.)

4. **What are some things you can thank and praise God for? What are some things you need God to help you with?**

Additional Information for Older Children

When Jesus prayed at Gethsemane on the night He was betrayed by Judas, He again began His prayer with the Aramaic word *Abba*. Read this prayer in Mark 14:35-36.

Bigger Than All

God's love and power are bigger than the biggest fear.

Teacher Materials

Bible with Isaiah 12:2 marked with a book-mark, six to eight classroom or household objects ranging in size from very small to very large.

Bible Verse

Surely God is my salvation; I will trust and not be afraid. The Lord, the Lord, is my strength and my song; he has become my salvation.
Isaiah 12:2

Introduce the Object Talk

When we feel worried or afraid because of problems at school or in our neighborhoods, it helps to remember that God's love and power are bigger than our biggest fears. Let's name some things that are bigger than others.

Present the Object Talk

1. Invite volunteers to arrange objects in order of size. Hand volunteers one object each and have them line up in order.

2. Beginning with the smallest object, invite children to name a variety of objects which are bigger than the smallest object but smaller than the next object. For example, a pencil is bigger than a penny but smaller than a book. Continue until all objects have been discussed. **What are the biggest objects you can think of?** (Redwood tree. Skyscraper. Bridge.)

Conclude

We've been talking about a lot of things that are bigger than others. Listen to Isaiah 12:2 to find out what we can remember about God when we're afraid or worried. Read Isaiah 12:2 aloud. **We can remember that God's strength and His help for us are bigger than our fears or worries.** Thank God for His love and help when we're worried or afraid.

Bible Verse

Surely God is my salvation; I will trust and not be afraid. The Lord, the Lord, is my strength and my song; he has become my salvation.
Isaiah 12:2

Discussion Questions

1. What's a worry a kid your age might have? A fear?

2. Why might someone who's afraid forget about God's love and help?

3. How has God helped you when you've felt afraid?

4. What worry or fear do you want to talk to God about?

Breaking Bread Together

Teacher Materials

Bible with bookmarks at John 13:34-35 and 1 John 3:16, objects used by your church for communion (plates, cups, chalice, bread or wafers, juice, etc.).

Bible Verse

This is how we know what love is: Jesus Christ laid down his life for us. 1 John 3:16

Introduce the Object Talk

Because He loves us so much, Jesus was willing to die on the cross so that our sins could be forgiven. The night before He was killed, Jesus ate a special supper with His disciples. Let's look at the way our church family remembers that special supper and Jesus' death on the cross.

Present the Object Talk

1. Show objects one at a time. **What is this object? What are some ways to use it?** (Optional: Children taste food items.)

2. We use these objects when we celebrate the Lord's Supper. One of the names for this celebration is "communion," which means to share something with others. When we celebrate communion together, we share in celebrating and remembering the last supper Jesus ate with His disciples before He died on the cross to take the punishment for our sins. Explain and demonstrate use of objects. (Optional: Invite your pastor or other church leader to talk with children about how your church celebrates the Lord's Supper.)

3. One special day each year, many Christians celebrate Jesus' last supper with His disciples; this day is called Maundy Thursday. The word "maundy" comes from the Latin word *mandatus*

which means "command." Read, or ask an older child to read, John 13:34-35 aloud. **What is the new commandment Jesus gave His followers during the Last Supper?**

Conclude

Read 1 John 3:16 aloud. **What does this verse tell us that love really is?** (Jesus cares so much for us that He died for us.) Pray, thanking Jesus for dying on the cross for our sins. Talk with interested children about becoming members of God's family (see "Leading a Child to Christ" on p. 8).

Discussion Questions

1. **What are some ways Jesus loved and served people when He was here on earth?** (Healed them. Fed them. Taught them the best way to live. Washed the disciples' feet.)

2. **How does Jesus show love for us today?** (Answers our prayers. Promises to always bc with us.)

3. **What are some ways we can show Jesus' love to people today?** (Be patient with brothers or sisters. Help others at school. Play games fairly.)

Additional Information for Older Children

The day on which Jesus died is sometimes called Good Friday. No one knows for sure where the name Good Friday came from. Some people think that the word "good" came from the phrase "God's Friday." Other people, however, believe the name came about because even though Jesus' death was very sad, so much good happened as a result of His death. What are some of the good things that happened as a result of Jesus' death and resurrection? (Our sins can be forgiven. We can experience God's love.)

Great Greetings

Jesus' death and resurrection make it possible for us to have eternal life.

Teacher Materials

Bible with bookmark at 1 John 5:11, cassette/CD or music video and player.

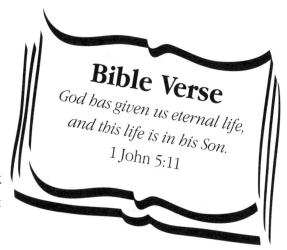

Bible Verse

God has given us eternal life, and this life is in his Son.
1 John 5:11

Introduce the Object Talk

Because Jesus died for our sins and rose again, we can have eternal life! Let's look at one way we remember Jesus' great gift every year at Easter.

Present the Object Talk

1. Wave hand at children. **What does it mean when I wave my hand at you?** (Waving is a way to say hello or greet someone.) Demonstrate, or ask children to demonstrate, other ways to greet people. (Say hello. Give a high five. Shake hands.)

2. During Easter, many Christians greet each other in a special way. One person says "Christ is risen," and the other says "He is risen indeed." For several minutes, play a song from the cassette/CD or music video as children walk around room and greet each other in the manner described above. (Note: If there are other Easter traditions followed in your church family, explain these traditions to children.)

Conclude

Jesus' resurrection makes it possible for us to become members of God's family! Read 1 John 5:11 aloud. **Eternal life means we can live with God in heaven, experiencing His love forever. According to this verse, where can we get eternal life?** (From God's Son, Jesus.) Pray, thanking Jesus for dying on the cross and rising from the dead so that we can have eternal life. Talk with interested children about becoming members of God's family (see "Leading a Child to Christ" on p. 8).

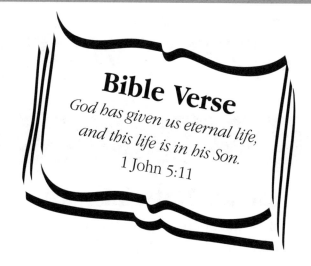

Bible Verse

God has given us eternal life, and this life is in his Son.
1 John 5:11

Discussion Questions

1. **Why was Jesus the only One who could take the punishment for our sins?** (Jesus is the only person who never sinned. He is the One God promised to send.)

2. **When we choose to become members of God's family, what does He give us?** (Forgiveness for our sins. Eternal life.)

3. **What are some ways we remember Jesus' death and celebrate His resurrection?** (Thank Jesus for His love. Sing special songs. Celebrate Easter with our church families at special worship services.)

4. **How does your family celebrate Jesus' resurrection at Eastertime?**

Additional Information for Older Children

Passion Week, also called Holy Week, begins with Palm Sunday and ends with Easter. Many churches are open for services daily or at least on Thursday and Friday as well as Sunday. This is the week during which Lent, which began 40 days earlier, ends. During Lent, many people choose to give up something they like or enjoy, in order to focus more on what Jesus gave up for them.

Joy in Salvation

God's gift of salvation brings great joy.

Teacher's Materials

Bible with bookmark at Habakkuk 3:18, shoe box with shoes inside.

Bible Verse
I will rejoice in the Lord, I will be joyful in God my Savior.
Habakkuk 3:18

Introduce the Object Talk

When we accept God's gift of salvation, it brings us great joy. Let's find out how one person learned about the joy that comes with God's gift of salvation.

Present the Object Talk

1. Show shoe box. **When have you gone to a store to buy new shoes? How did a salesperson help you?** Children respond. **Dwight Moody was a successful shoe salesman in Boston, but one day his shoe sales didn't go as planned.**

2. Dwight grew up in a very poor family. Dwight hated being poor and was determined to become rich. When he was 17 years old, he went to live with his Uncle Samuel in Boston. He worked in his uncle's shoe store. Soon Dwight was making a lot of money, because he was one of the best shoe salesmen around.

School teacher, Mr. Kimball, visited Dwight at the shoe store. Dwight thought that his teacher had come to buy shoes. But Mr. Kimball did more than that—right there in the store he invited Dwight to become a member of God's family! Dwight did. He said he felt a new kind of happiness and love and everything was different. Now Dwight knew that true joy came from

being a part of God's family! Dwight didn't want to keep his joy a secret. He went back home to visit his family to tell them about Jesus, too. And for the rest of his life, Dwight spent most of his time telling people about Jesus and the joy that comes from being a Christian.

Bible Verse
I will rejoice in the Lord, I will be joyful in God my Savior.
Habakkuk 3:18

Conclude

Read Habakkuk 3:18 aloud. **How did Dwight Moody show he was joyful to know Jesus?** (He wanted to tell his family and other people about Jesus.) **Let's thank God for His gift of salvation.** Lead children in prayer.

Discussion Questions

1. **What are some reasons we have to "be joyful in God"? What are some reasons we have for being thankful to God?**

2. **What are some of the ways people hear about God's gift of salvation and the joy it brings?** (Friends tell them. They go to church. They read the Bible.)

3. **The Bible tells us that God is joyful when we become a part of His family. Why?** (He loves us and wants us to be part of His family.)

4. **When we hear about God and accept God's gift of salvation by becoming members of God's family, we experience joy. Why?** (Our sins are forgiven by God. We can have eternal life. We know God loves us.) Talk with interested children about becoming members of God's family (refer to "Leading a Child to Christ" article on p. 8).

Additional Information for Older Children

Dwight Moody became known as a man who tried to honor and obey God in all his actions. Dwight traveled all over America and England to preach about Jesus. Many people learned about Jesus through his preaching. People today still learn about Jesus from organizations Dwight helped to start, such as the Moody Bible Institute and Moody Press in Chicago.

Paid in Full

Becoming a Christian is more than knowing facts about God. God invites each of us to choose to belong to God's family and accept Jesus' love.

Teacher Materials

Bible with bookmark at Romans 6:23, large sheet of paper, marker, calculator, blank check, pen.

Introduce the Object Talk

God wants us to be part of His family so much that He made it possible for us to receive His love and forgiveness for the wrong things we do. Let's find out how Jesus paid for our sins.

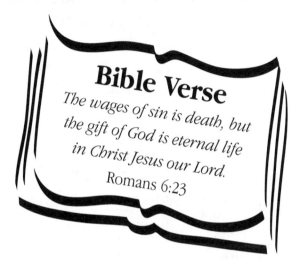

Bible Verse

The wages of sin is death, but the gift of God is eternal life in Christ Jesus our Lord.

Romans 6:23

Present the Object Talk

1. If we were to owe money for the wrong actions we've done, we would probably owe a lot of money. Ask children to name wrong actions. (Lying, stealing, cheating, fighting, etc.) As you list each wrong action on paper, have class decide on a dollar amount as penalty, or punishment, for each action (for example, $100 for lying), and write this amount next to the action. Ask a volunteer to add the amounts on the calculator and announce total to class. (Optional: Depending on the age of your group, you may add amounts on the calculator yourself.)

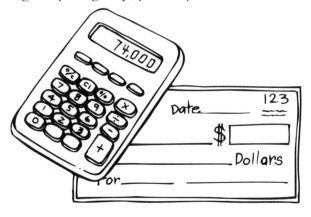

2. If someone loved you enough, he or she could pay what you owe for your wrong actions by writing a check for the full amount. Write out a check for the total amount, leaving the "to" and "from" portions blank.

Conclude

The good news we read in the Bible is that the amount or punishment owed for our sin has been completely paid by Jesus, God's Son. Read Romans 6:23 aloud. **When Jesus died on the cross, He made it possible for our sin to be paid in full so that we can be part of God's family. What a great gift He gave us!** Complete the check, making the check out to "God,"

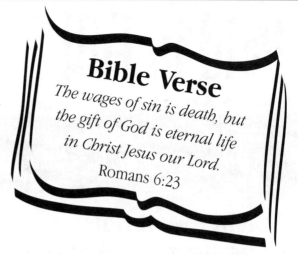

Bible Verse

The wages of sin is death, but the gift of God is eternal life in Christ Jesus our Lord.

Romans 6:23

signing it from "Jesus" and writing "For (your name)'s sin" in the check memo portion. Lead children in prayer, thanking God for His gift of salvation.

Discussion Questions

1. **How does doing wrong usually make a person feel?**

2. **How can asking God to forgive our sins help us?** (God promises to give us forgiveness and make us members of His family.)

3. **How do we know that God's love is big enough to forgive all the wrong things we and others do?** (The Bible tells us so. God always keeps His promises.)

4. **How have you learned about God's love for you?** (From reading God's Word. From people who show God's love to others.)

Signs of Change

God's gift of salvation can't be earned!

Teacher Materials

Bible with bookmark at Ephesians 2:8-9, a variety of signs or flyers (For Sale, Beware of Dog, No Trespassing, advertising flyers, etc.).

Introduce the Object Talk

Because God's love for us is so great, He wants us to accept His free gift of salvation. A long time ago, a man named Martin Luther wanted to make sure everyone heard the good news about salvation. Let's find out what he did.

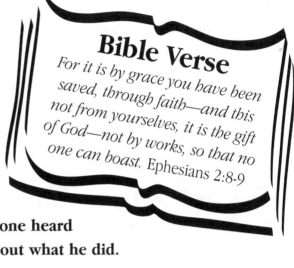

Bible Verse

For it is by grace you have been saved, through faith—and this not from yourselves, it is the gift of God—not by works, so that no one can boast. Ephesians 2:8-9

Present the Object Talk

1. One at a time, display and discuss the various signs you brought. **What does this sign tell you?** Volunteers answer. Explain signs as needed.

2. Signs help people by giving them information they need. What are some other ways to give people information? (Television. Radio. Bulletin boards. Internet and e-mail.)

3. On October 31, 1517, Martin Luther nailed to a church door in Germany a paper that was like a sign. This paper explained that God's Word teaches that people do not need to buy God's gift of salvation by paying money to a priest. When people realized that a believer is forgiven by faith alone and that a believer needs no other priest than Christ (see Hebrews 10:19-22), **many of them stopped trying to buy salvation and simply asked God for His great gift! Today many people**

remember Martin Luther's actions on a day called Reformation Day. "Reformation" means to improve something, or to make right something that has been wrong.

Conclude

Read Ephesians 2:8-9 aloud. **What do these verses say God gives us?** (Salvation.) **What does it mean to have faith?** (To trust and believe that God's Word is true and that Jesus died and rose again to pay for our sins.) Pray, thanking God for His free gift of salvation through Jesus. Talk with interested children about becoming members of God's family (see "Leading a Child to Christ" on p. 8).

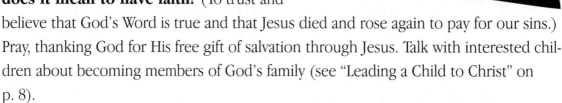

Bible Verse

For it is by grace you have been saved, through faith—and this not from yourselves, it is the gift of God—not by works, so that no one can boast. Ephesians 2:8-9

Discussion Questions

1. **Grace is love and kindness shown to someone who doesn't deserve it. What does Ephesians 2:8-9 say about grace?** (We are saved because of God's grace.)

2. **Why can't we boast or brag about being saved?** (We are only saved when we believe in Jesus' death for our sins, not because of any good actions we have done.)

3. **Why is salvation described as a gift from God?** (It is free. There is nothing we can do to earn it. He gives it to us because He loves us.)

Additional Information for Older Children

Martin Luther's writings spread quickly. Here's why: Although Martin Luther wrote his paper in Latin, which many people didn't understand, his writing was later translated into German, a language that most people in his country understood. Then, many people were able to read his writings.

About the same time, the printing press was invented by Johann Gutenberg in a nearby town. Thousands of copies of Luther's writings were printed. These copies were given out all over Europe. The good news of God's free gift of salvation traveled all over Europe and beyond!

A School for Girls

Use your abilities to show kindness to others.

Teacher's Materials

Bible with bookmark at Ephesians 6:7, long strips of cloth or an elastic bandage.

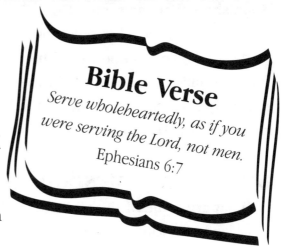

Bible Verse
Serve wholeheartedly, as if you were serving the Lord, not men.
Ephesians 6:7

Introduce the Object Talk

We can use our abilities to show kindness to other people. Let's find out how one woman's actions helped others learn to be kind.

Present the Object Talk

1. Invite a volunteer to wrap his or her arm or ankle in cloths or bandage. **When are some times people wrap their arms or ankles like this?** (When they've sprained or broken their arm or ankle.) **A long time ago in China, people wrapped the feet of girls for a very different reason. At that time in China, people thought that small feet were beautiful! Parents tightly wrapped their daughters' feet with the small toes bent under. The bones in the feet would break and then heal into tiny twisted feet that were very painful to walk on.**

2. In 1873, a woman named Lottie Moon went to China as a missionary. She wanted to help people learn about Jesus. Lottie started a school for girls. But Lottie soon found that her students had a hard time learning. The girls were in constant pain because their feet were bound so tightly!

Lottie felt so sorry for her students that she worked hard to convince one girl's family to let the girl unbind her feet. It wasn't easy for Lottie Moon to convince others to stop hurting girls by binding their feet. But in time, Lottie's actions convinced many people to treat girls kindly; and eventually, foot binding became illegal.

Conclude

Read Ephesians 6:7 aloud. **How did Lottie Moon show that she served God?** (She convinced people not to hurt girls by binding their feet.) **Lottie Moon used her ability to talk to people to help the girls in her school. Let's ask God to help us use our abilities to show kindness to others, too.** Lead children in prayer.

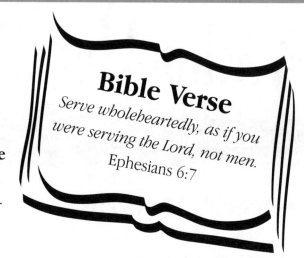

Bible Verse

Serve wholeheartedly, as if you were serving the Lord, not men.
Ephesians 6:7

Discussion Questions

1. **What are some of the abilities God has given you?** Guide children in discussing all kinds of abilities (reading well, playing soccer, being a good friend, singing, cooking, fixing things, painting, etc.).

2. **What are some ways you can use these abilities to show kindness to others?**

3. **When has someone showed kindness to you? What ability did he or she use?**

Additional Information for Older Children

During her life, Lottie Moon was very concerned that people not forget to help missionaries who teach about God in foreign countries. She wrote many letters to Christians in the United States, asking them to give money to missionaries. Lottie Moon died on Christmas Eve, 1912. To this day, in Lottie's honor, many churches still collect a Lottie Moon Christmas Offering that is used to help missionaries.

Care for Foster Children

Sharing what you have can show your love for God and bring kindness to many people.

Teacher's Materials

Bible with bookmark at Romans 12:13, food wrapper or bag from a fast-food restaurant.

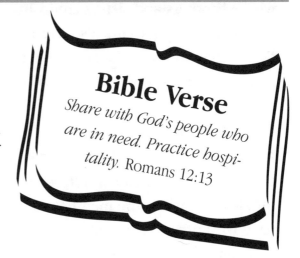

Bible Verse
Share with God's people who are in need. Practice hospitality. Romans 12:13

Introduce the Object Talk

We can bring kindness to many people when we share what we have. As we learn about one person who shared, think about how you can show God's love by sharing and bringing kindness to others.

Present the Object Talk

1. Show food wrapper or bag. **What do you know about the place where I got this (wrapper)?** Children respond. **S. Truett Cathy is one person who started a fast-food restaurant.**

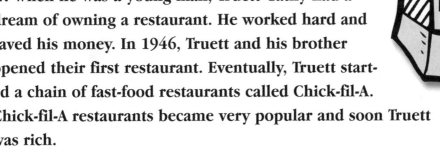

2. When he was a young man, Truett Cathy had a dream of owning a restaurant. He worked hard and saved his money. In 1946, Truett and his brother opened their first restaurant. Eventually, Truett started a chain of fast-food restaurants called Chick-fil-A. Chick-fil-A restaurants became very popular and soon Truett was rich.

Some rich people spend their money on big houses or new cars. But Truett loved God and believed the Bible verse that says that it is better "to give than to receive" (Acts 20:35). Truett chose to spend his money helping children in foster care—children who have to live away from their parents, because their parents can't take good care of them.

Bible Verse

Share with God's people who are in need. Practice hospitality. Romans 12:13

Many times children in foster care don't even get to keep living with their brothers and sisters. Truett felt sorry for these children, so he used his money to build foster homes where brothers and sisters could live together. Foster parents also live in the homes, so the children have a safe place to live and grow. Foster children in these homes are loved and cared for.

Conclude

Read Romans 12:13 aloud. **How did Truett Cathy obey this verse? How do you think his actions made a difference in other people's lives?** Children tell ideas. **It pleases God when the members of His family are kind and share what they have with others.** Lead children in prayer, asking for God's help to find opportunities to be kind and share with others. Talk with interested children about becoming members of God's family (refer to "Leading a Child to Christ" article on p. 8).

Discussion Questions

1. **What do you think are some good reasons for obeying Romans 12:13?** (To show God's love. To show that we thank God for His love.)

2. **What are some things needed by people you know?**

3. **What can you share with others?** (Clothes. Friendship. Knowledge of God's love.)

Additional Information for Older Children

In addition to sharing money to help foster children, Truett Cathy gave money to Chick-fil-A workers who wanted to go to college. Since 1973, the company has given more than $15 million to help their workers go to college.

Freeing the Slaves

Patiently continue to help others in the best ways you can.

Teacher's Materials

Bible with bookmark at Psalm 106:3, book of rules (game rule book, driver's manual, etc.).

Introduce the Object Talk

Even when it's hard, patiently continue to help others in the best ways possible. Let's find out about a man who was known for patiently helping others for many, many years.

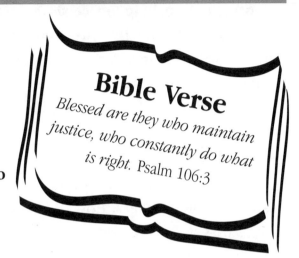

Bible Verse

Blessed are they who maintain justice, who constantly do what is right. Psalm 106:3

Present the Object Talk

1. Show book you brought. **What does this book tell about?** (Rules for [playing chess].) **Why do you think rules are important?** Children tell ideas. **William Wilberforce's job was making rules. He was a member of Parliament in England from 1780 to 1825. (That's like being a member of Congress in the United States.)**

2. **After William became a member of God's family, he realized that he could serve God and show his love for Him by doing his best to help others through his job in Parliament.**

In 1788, William made a long speech in Parliament. He asked the other people in Parliament to make a new law to end slavery. Many people didn't want to hear that slavery was wrong because they made a lot of money from selling slaves and from the work slaves did. Parliament voted down William's idea, but William didn't give up. Every year for 18 years, William tried to convince people to end slavery.

Finally, Parliament decided to pass a law that made it illegal to force people to be slaves. But there were still many people who were already slaves, and the new law didn't set them free, so William's job wasn't over! He patiently kept working to free slaves until the end of his life. Just four days before William died, Parliament passed a law saying that ALL slavery was illegal in England and in all the British colonies.

Bible Verse

Blessed are they who maintain justice, who constantly do what is right. Psalm 106:3

Conclude

Read Psalm 106:3 aloud. **This verse says that God is pleased when people do what is right to help others. How did William Wilberforce help others?** (He asked people to pass laws to end slavery.) Lead children in prayer, asking God to help them do their best to help others.

Discussion Questions

1. When might it be hard to help others? (When you're tired. When you have your own jobs to do.)

2. How can you remember to patiently do your best to help others? (Ask God's help. Remember God's patience.)

3. What are some things you can do to help others this week?

Additional Information for Older Children

After William Wilberforce became a member of God's family, he considered leaving Parliament to become a pastor or doing something else to serve God. His friends convinced him that he could serve God by staying in Parliament and passing laws that would help others. In addition to working to end slavery, William helped people get a good education and helped missionaries travel to other countries.

 The Really Big Book of Kid Sermons and Object Talks

Gifts to Grow By

God can do great things with our gifts to Him.

Teacher Materials

Bible with bookmark at 1 Timothy 6:18, popcorn kernels, measuring cup, popcorn maker, two bowls, napkins; optional—salt.

Bible Verse

Command them to do good, to be rich in good deeds, and to be generous and willing to share. 1 Timothy 6:18

Introduce the Object Talk

Our gifts to God can be used by Him in many ways. Even small gifts of love and time can make a big difference. Let's look at something that starts out small and grows to be big!

Present the Object Talk

1. Pour popcorn kernels into measuring cup until they measure half a cup (or the measurement appropriate for your popcorn maker). Ask a volunteer to look at the measuring cup and tell how much corn is in the cup.

2. What happens to these popcorn kernels when they are heated? (They pop. They get bigger.) Invite children to tell how much corn they think will be popped from the half cup of kernels.

3. Pop popcorn and measure it. (Optional: Ask Discussion Questions while waiting for kernels to pop.) Children compare their predictions with the actual number of cups of popped corn.

4. Serve popcorn to children. (Optional: Children sprinkle salt on popcorn.)

Conclude

Sometimes we think our gifts to God are small and won't make much of a difference. But even our small gifts can be used by God in great ways. Listen to 1 Timothy 6:18 to find out some ways we can give to God. Read verse aloud. **What does this verse say we can give to others? How are our right actions a gift to God?** (Our right actions show love for God and help others learn about Him.) Lead children in prayer, asking God to show us ways to give to Him and to others.

Bible Verse

Command them to do good, to be rich in good deeds, and to be generous and willing to share. 1 Timothy 6:18

Discussion Questions

1. **What are some other things that start out small and get bigger?** (Cookies, until they're baked. Babies, until they grow to be adults. Plant and tree seeds, until they're planted and watered.)

2. **In what ways might kids your age give to God?** (Give time to help others. Donate possessions we have that are needed by others.) Tell children about ways the people in your church give to others to show love for God.

3. **What is one way you can give to God?**

Good Soup

Listening to others and treating them fairly are ways to show God's goodness.

Teacher's Materials

Bible with bookmark at Zechariah 7:9, can of soup.

Introduce the Object Talk

God's goodness shows in our lives when we listen to others and treat them fairly. Let's find out how one man showed God's goodness in the way he treated others.

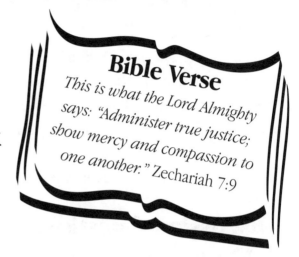

Bible Verse

This is what the Lord Almighty says: "Administer true justice; show mercy and compassion to one another." Zechariah 7:9

Present the Object Talk

1. Show can of soup. **When do you like to eat soup? What kinds of soup do you like best?** Volunteers tell. **One man was not happy when he saw some poor-tasting soup that was being served in his city.**

2. **Charles Tindley was born as a slave, just a few years before Abraham Lincoln set the slaves free. When he grew up, Charles became the pastor of a church in the city of Philadelphia. Charles worried about some poor people who** lived on the streets instead of in homes. He wanted to treat them in good ways, and he wanted to teach them about Jesus.

One day Charles went to a kitchen where poor people were given soup and bread to eat. But when Charles looked at the food, he saw that the soup was very watery and the bread was stale. Charles felt sorry for the people and wanted them to receive better food.

The next Sunday, Charles told his congregation that they were going to help the poor people in their city. The church members cooked good, healthy food and welcomed the poor people into their church. Charles often talked to the poor people and showed how much he cared about them. Many of these people considered Charles their own pastor because he cared enough to listen to them and treat them in good ways.

Conclude

Read Zechariah 7:9 aloud. **When we "administer true justice," it means we treat others fairly. What else does this verse say God wants us to do?** Children respond. **How did Charles Tindley show mercy and compassion to others?** (He helped poor people have good food to eat.) Lead children in prayer, asking God to help them listen to others and treat others fairly.

Bible Verse

This is what the Lord Almighty says: "Administer true justice; show mercy and compassion to one another." Zechariah 7:9

Discussion Questions

1. **When are some times it might be hard for you to listen to others? How does listening to someone help a person know the best ways to help?** (By listening, a person can learn what is really needed and what to pray for.)

2. **What does it mean to treat other people fairly?** (Respect each person. Care for all people in the same way you care for the people you like most.) **What can you do to treat your brother or sister more fairly? Kids at school?**

3. **How can listening to others and treating them fairly help them see God's goodness?** (It shows them that God thinks each person is important.)

4. **What are some other ways that your actions can show God's goodness?**

Additional Information for Older Children

When Charles Tindley was a boy, his father was very poor, so Charles worked for farmers doing chores. As he grew up, he had to work so much that he was unable to go to school. But Charles wanted to learn to read. He collected newspaper pages that other people had thrown away, and he slowly taught himself how to read. Then Charles was able to read the only book he had— the Bible.

Homes for the Homeless

Kindness is doing good without expecting anything in return.

Teacher's Materials

Bible with bookmark at 1 Thessalonians 3:12, hammer and/or other construction tools.

Introduce the Object Talk

When we do good without expecting anything in return, we are showing kindness. Let's look at a way some people work hard to show kindness even though they don't get paid any money for it.

Bible Verse

May the Lord make your love increase and overflow for each other and for everyone else, just as ours does for you.
1 Thessalonians 3:12

Present the Object Talk

1. Show hammer and/or other construction tools. **What do people use these tools for?** Volunteers tell ideas. **Carpenters who build furniture and houses usually get paid for their work. But some people who work as carpenters don't get paid at all! These people work for an organization called Habitat for Humanity. "Habitat" is a word that means the place where someone lives. "Humanity" is a word that means people. What do you think people who work for Habitat for Humanity might do?** (Build homes for people who don't have a good place to live.)

2. One man who works for Habitat for Humanity used to be the president of the United States. His name is Jimmy Carter. After a new president was elected, President Carter could have looked for a job to earn lots of money. But instead, because he loved God and wanted to show God's love to others, he decided to spend some of his time working for Habitat for Humanity.

Jimmy Carter and the other people who help Habitat for Humanity don't get any pay in return for building houses for poor people. They build houses because they want to show kindness to others in need.

Bible Verse

May the Lord make your love increase and overflow for each other and for everyone else, just as ours does for you.
1 Thessalonians 3:12

Conclude

Read 1 Thessalonians 3:12 aloud. **How does this verse describe how we should show love? Something overflows when there's so much of it that it won't stay in one place. It spreads out everywhere! How does Jimmy Carter's kindness show God's love?** (He helps others without expecting to get money or anything else in return.) Pray, asking God to help your children find ways to be kind to others.

Discussion Questions

1. **What are some ways to show kindness to others without expecting anything in return?** (Help a younger brother or sister. Donate items to a homeless shelter.)

2. **When has someone been kind to you? What did that person do? Why do you think that person chose to be kind?**

3. **When have you been kind to another person? What happened as a result of your kindness?**

Additional Information for Older Children

In 1981, the United States had a new president. Even though Jimmy Carter wasn't the president anymore, he and his wife, Rosalynn, still wanted to help people all over the world. They started the Carter Center, a nonprofit organization to help people be peaceful and treat others fairly. Through the years, the Carter Center has worked with many different countries to improve the way the people in those countries live. In 1999, Jimmy and Rosalynn Carter were presented with a very important award, the Presidential Medal of Freedom.

It's Free!

When we love God, we give generously.

Teacher Materials

Bible with bookmark at Matthew 10:8, marker, one index card per child and one bite-sized snack item, sticker or small prize for each child.

Bible Verse
Freely you have received, freely give. Matthew 10:8

Prepare the Object Talk

Print the word "FREE" on several cards. Shuffle "FREE" cards in with blank cards.

Introduce the Object Talk

Everyone likes to get something for free! The Bible tells us that even though His love is more valuable than anything in the world, Jesus freely gives it to us. Today we're going to get something for free and talk about how we can give freely to God and to others.

Present the Object Talk

1. Give each child a card, keeping cards facedown.

2. At your signal, children pass cards facedown around the group. When you signal "stop," each child looks at his or her card. Children holding cards marked "FREE" get (snacks) for themselves and pass out (snacks) to other children.

Small Group Option

1. Print only one "FREE" card. Shuffle "FREE" card in with blank cards. Seat children in a circle. At your signal, children pass cards facedown around the circle.

2. When you signal "stop," child holding "FREE" card gets a (snack) for him- or herself and gives a (snack) to one other child. Repeat the activity until all children have received a (snack).

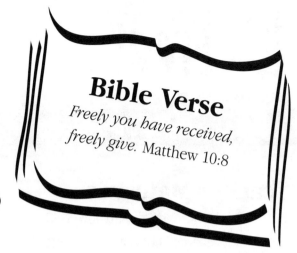

Bible Verse
Freely you have received, freely give. Matthew 10:8

Conclude

In this activity we received our (snacks) for free. Matthew 10:8 talks about the way in which Jesus gives us what we need. Read verse aloud. **Jesus said these words when He was telling His followers to help and care for others. Jesus has given His love to us for free! We don't have to do anything to earn it!** Lead children in prayer, thanking God for His free gift of love and asking His help in giving freely in return.

Discussion Questions

1. What are some other things God freely gives us? (Answers to prayer. Forgiveness of sins. Friends and family.)

2. What can we give to God that money can't buy? (Our love. Our obedience.)

3. What can we give to others that money can't buy? (Friendship. Honesty. Patience. The good news about Jesus.)

School Uniforms

Look for ways to be kind to and care for others.

Teacher's Materials

Bible with bookmark at Matthew 5:7, uniform from a school or sports team.

Introduce the Object Talk

It is important to always look for opportunities in which we can be kind to and care for others. Let's find out some ways one woman found to be kind to and care for others.

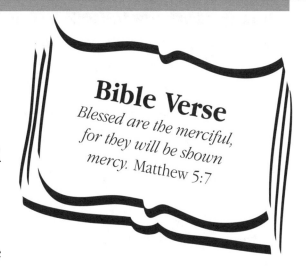

Bible Verse

Blessed are the merciful, for they will be shown mercy. Matthew 5:7

Present the Object Talk

1. Show uniform. (Optional: Volunteer wears uniform.) **When do kids your age wear uniforms?** Children tell. **In the early 1900s, school children in China wore uniforms. Schools even had contests to see which school had the best uniform.**

The children in one school, however, were embarrassed because they did not have uniforms like other children. This school was so poor the teachers could hardly buy school supplies. And because the children in the school were orphans (their parents were no longer alive), they couldn't afford to buy uniforms.

2. Grace Chang was a missionary teacher at this school. She cared for the children at the school so much that she decided to help them get uniforms. Grace planned to use her sewing machine to make the uniforms, but she didn't have any cloth! Grace prayed and asked God to help her.

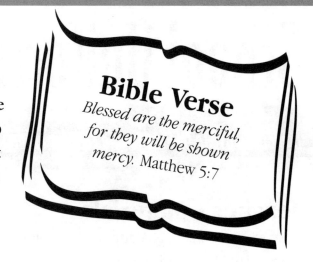

Bible Verse

Blessed are the merciful, for they will be shown mercy. Matthew 5:7

God answered Grace's prayer. Soon another missionary gave her some cloth, and Grace started sewing uniforms for the children. Then Grace got women in a nearby village to help make cloth shoes for all the children. (At that time, Chinese children typically wore cloth shoes.) Soon the jackets, skirts and shoes were ready. The children excitedly wore their uniforms to school. And when they won the contest for the best uniform, the children were even more pleased!

Conclude

Read Matthew 5:7 aloud. **When we show mercy to others, it means we are kind to them—even when they don't deserve it. How did Grace Chang show mercy and kindness to others?** Children tell ideas. **Let's ask God to help us find ways to be kind and care for others this week.** Close in prayer.

Discussion Questions

1. Grace Chang used her sewing machine to be kind to others. What could you use to be kind to someone?

2. When has someone been kind to you? Why do you think that person chose to be kind? How did you feel as a result of that kindness?

3. Who are some people you could be kind to and care for this week?

Additional Information for Older Children

Grace Chang trusted that God would help her show kindness to others. Once, another missionary became ill and needed someone to take her home to the United States. Grace was asked to help her, but neither woman had any money for the boat ride! Grace prayed and prayed and then felt sure God wanted her to borrow money from a bank. Even though Grace had nothing to give the bank in return, the bank manager loaned her the money!

Service with a Smile

Be ready to serve others with a gentle attitude.

Teacher's Materials

Bible with bookmark at Galatians 5:13, scrub brush, bucket.

Introduce the Object Talk

Being ready to serve others with a gentle attitude helps us show God's love. Let's find out how someone showed God's love with a scrub brush.

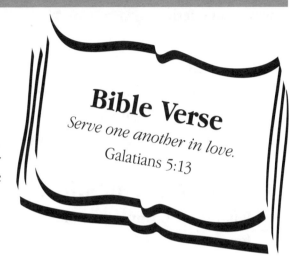

Bible Verse

Serve one another in love.

Galatians 5:13

Present the Object Talk

1. Show scrub brush and bucket. **When have you used a scrub brush or bucket?** Volunteers tell. **Some people don't like to wash floors or cars, because they think it's not very important work. In 1895 a woman named Amy Carmichael had to scrub something dirty to show what it meant to serve others.**

2. Amy had gone to India as a missionary. She noticed that many children needed a safe place to live. Some of these children came to live with Amy. Soon Amy was taking care of 17 children! Sometimes Amy wondered if she had been right in giving up important work in other places to take care of the children. But Amy remembered that Jesus showed God's love by serving His disciples and washing their feet. Taking care of the children was valuable, because it was a way she could serve others and show God's love!

3. One day a new woman came to help care for the children. Amy asked the woman to serve by washing the nursery floor. The woman refused, because she wanted an easier, better job. So Amy took the bucket of soapy water and

got down on her hands and knees and scrubbed the dirty floor. Because Amy was willing to do this hard work, she gently helped the woman learn how important it is to show God's love by serving others in whatever way is needed.

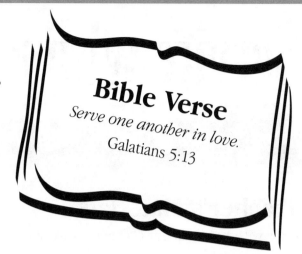

Bible Verse
Serve one another in love.
Galatians 5:13

Conclude

Read Galatians 5:13 aloud. **What are some ways Amy Carmichael served others with love?** Children respond. **Let's ask God to help us serve others with gentle attitudes.** Lead children in prayer.

Discussion Questions

1. **What do you think the verse means when it says to "serve" someone with love?** (Be kind and gentle when we help. Don't have a bossy or proud attitude. Pay attention to the needs of others.)

2. **What are some ways to serve others?** (Get a glass of water for someone who is sitting down resting. Set the table without being asked. Help your mom by taking care of younger brothers or sisters while she cooks dinner. Make a card for someone who is sick.)

3. **What can you do this week to serve others at school? At home? On the playground?**

Additional Information for Older Children

Amy Carmichael broke her leg when she was older. Her leg didn't heal correctly, so she couldn't walk for the rest of her life. Instead of being angry that she couldn't do the things she had done before, Amy still served others by writing many books that helped people learn more about missionaries and about God's love for people all over the world.

Talented People

Use the talents God gave you to serve others.

Teacher Materials

Bible with bookmarks at Psalm 145:10 and 1 Peter 4:10, large sheet of paper, marker, masking tape; optional—paper, markers.

Prepare the Activity

In the middle of large sheet of paper, vertically print the word "talents," leaving space between each letter. Tape to wall.

Bible Verse

Each one should use whatever gift he has received to serve others. 1 Peter 4:10

Introduce the Object Talk

Each of us can use the talents God gave us to do good things for others. Let's talk about different talents and how we can use them in ways that please God.

Present the Object Talk

1. Show children paper you prepared. **Let's make a kind of acrostic to see how many talents we can think of that begin with or use each letter of the word "talents." What are some things that kids your age like to do or are good at?** Print ideas on large sheet of paper next to the appropriate letters. (Optional: Give paper and markers to children and ask them to make individual acrostics using their names and talents.)

2. Some psalms are written like acrostics also. Psalm 145 is called an alphabet acrostic because in the Hebrew language the verses of the psalm begin with the letters of the Hebrew alphabet in order. King David wrote this

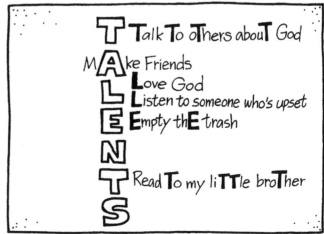

Talk To oThers abouT God
MAke Friends
Love God
Listen to someone who's upset
Empty thE trash

Read To my liTTle broTher

psalm a long time ago. In this psalm we can read a reason we have all been given special talents. Read, or ask a child to read, Psalm 145:10. When we use our talents to help others, it's a way of serving and praising God.

Conclude

Read 1 Peter 4:10 aloud. **What does it mean to serve others?** (To help them. To give them what they need.) **What are some ways kids your age can serve others?** Pray, thanking God for the talents He's given us and asking for His help in finding ways to use our talents to help others.

> **Bible Verse**
> Each one should use whatever gift he has received to serve others. 1 Peter 4:10

Discussion Questions

1. **How has someone used a talent to help you?** (Helped me learn to read. Helped me make friends.)

2. **What kinds of things do you enjoy doing? What are you good at doing?** (Being friendly. Playing soccer. Reading. Singing.)

3. **When have you used a talent to serve others?**

Additional Information for Older Children

Read, or ask an older child to read, Romans 12:6-8 aloud. **What are some of the talents, or gifts, this verse describes?** Volunteers respond. **In this verse, the word "gift" comes from the Greek word *charismata* (kah-rees-MAH-tah). This word tells us these gifts are special, freely given by God to meet the needs of His family.**

The Lady with the Lamp

Generous and kind attitudes help us build friendships.

Teacher's Materials

Bible with bookmark at 1 Timothy 6:18, kerosene lantern or a flashlight.

Introduce the Object Talk

We can build friendships by being generous and kind in our attitudes and actions. Let's find out what one lady did because she was so kind.

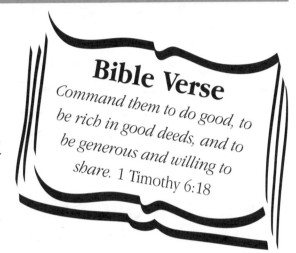

Bible Verse

Command them to do good, to be rich in good deeds, and to be generous and willing to share. 1 Timothy 6:18

Present the Object Talk

1. Show lantern or flashlight. **When do people use lights like these? How might a light like this help when you are afraid in the dark?** Children respond. **In England during the 1800s, a woman named Florence Nightingale became known as "the Lady with the Lamp."**

2. When Florence Nightingale lived, hospitals were nothing like they are now. There were very few doctors and nurses, and people didn't understand that germs make people sick. Hospitals weren't kept very clean. Many people who went to hospitals became sicker instead of getting better.

When Florence became a nurse, she believed God wanted her to change things! She used her own money to buy clean clothes for patients. She hired people to wash sheets and blankets. Florence often worked until late at night, carrying a lamp through the hospital as she checked on her patients. She was never too tired to help someone.

As Florence worked, she also talked to people about Jesus. Florence—"the Lady with the Lamp"—helped people learn about Jesus' love and saved the lives of many sick or injured people because of her kindness and generosity.

Conclude

Read 1 Timothy 6:18 aloud. **How was Florence Nightingale kind and willing to share? What does it mean to have a generous attitude?** Children tell ideas. **Let's ask God to help us build friendships by being generous and kind this week.** Lead children in prayer.

Bible Verse

Command them to do good, to be rich in good deeds, and to be generous and willing to share. 1 Timothy 6:18

Discussion Questions

1. **What are some generous or kind actions kids your age can do? How might these actions help to build friendships?**

2. **Read 1 Timothy 6:18. How can we "be rich in good deeds"?** (Do good things often.)

3. **How would obeying 1 Timothy 6:18 help the kids in your school?**

Additional Information for Older Children

Because of the help Florence Nightingale gave soldiers during the war, she became a national hero in England. The Nightingale School of Nursing in London was started to honor her kind actions. In addition to the many honors and awards Florence received, she was the first woman to receive the British Order of Merit, a very important award.

Traveling School

Goodness includes using what God gives you to help others.

Teacher's Materials

Bible with bookmark at 1 Peter 4:10, peanuts.

Introduce the Object Talk

Using what God gives us to help others is a big part of showing goodness. Let's find out how one man used what God had given him to help others.

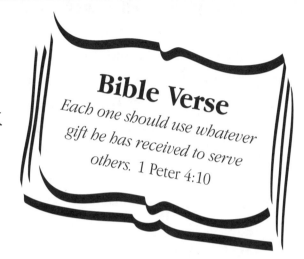

Bible Verse

Each one should use whatever gift he has received to serve others. 1 Peter 4:10

Present the Object Talk

1. Show peanuts. **What are some things that people use peanuts for?** (To eat. To make peanut butter.) **Before the early 1900s, few people grew peanuts because they didn't know how to use the peanuts. But a man named George Washington Carver believed that God had given him a brain to help him discover how the peanut could be used. Dr. Carver discovered over 300 things that could be made from peanuts, including printer's ink, a milk substitute, face powder, soap and candy.** (Note: If child indicates he or she is allergic to peanuts, comment, **While some people are allergic to peanuts, there are other good uses for them besides eating them.**)

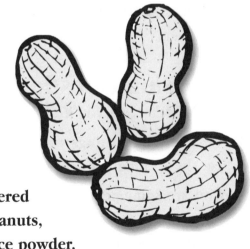

2. Dr. Carver also discovered many things about the best ways to grow plants. And he didn't keep what he learned to himself! Dr. Carver used what he had learned about plants to help others.

Dr. Carver and a friend got a horse and wagon and set up a portable school. They traveled to poor farms all over their county to teach African-American farmers better ways to grow plants. He also taught them new ways to use the things they grew so that they could make money selling new products. Some people complained that Dr. Carver should make people pay to learn the things he was teaching. But Dr. Carver insisted that money was not important. Dr. Carver told people that it didn't matter how much money they had or how fancy their clothes were. He said that serving others was more important than money or clothes. In fact, in one of his jobs, Dr. Carver didn't accept a pay raise for 40 years! All that mattered to him was helping people.

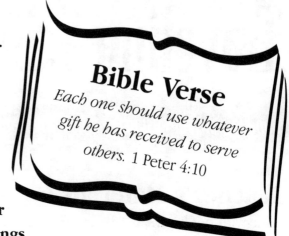

Bible Verse
Each one should use whatever gift he has received to serve others. 1 Peter 4:10

Conclude

Read 1 Peter 4:10 aloud. **How did George Washington Carver show goodness and obey 1 Peter 4:10?** Lead children in prayer, asking God to help them find good ways to help others.

Discussion Questions

1. Who is someone you know that shows goodness? What does he or she do?

2. What are some things you enjoy doing or are good at doing? How can you use these things to help others?

3. Who are some people you can help or serve this week?

Additional Information for Older Children

When Dr. Carver first began teaching people how to grow better crops, some of the farmers didn't believe what he said. So as part of his teaching, Dr. Carver would show them sample plants and patiently explain how to grow the plants. Sometimes Dr. Carver would even cook a good-tasting meal to show people how they could make food from their crops. (Optional: Volunteers taste chickpeas (garbanzo beans), one of the foods Dr. Carver taught others to eat.)

Will Work for Free

Humble and gentle attitudes help us not to look down on others.

Teacher's Materials

Bible with bookmark at Philippians 2:3, money (coins and/or bills).

Introduce the Object Talk

When we have humble and gentle attitudes, we won't look down on others. Let's find out how one man showed a humble and gentle attitude.

Bible Verse

Do nothing out of selfish ambition or vain conceit, but in humility consider others better than yourselves. Philippians 2:3

Present the Object Talk

1. Show money. **What are some ways people get money? Why do you think some people want to have lots of money?** Children tell ideas. **When do you think someone might NOT want to have lots of money? In the country of Japan, a man by the name of Kagawa** (kah-GAH-wah) **chose not to be paid a lot of money for his hard work.**

2. Kagawa lived in a shack in a poor part of his town. He lived there so that he could help the people who lived there learn about Jesus. While Kagawa was living in this part of town, a terrible earthquake destroyed most of the city. An important city leader told Kagawa that the city needed him to help people rebuild their homes, to make sure people had food to eat and water to drink and to help the poor people find good jobs. The official said, "The job pays a good salary and you will be given a car."

Kagawa surprised the official when he said that he would be glad to do the job, but he would not take money or a car. Instead, Kagawa asked that his salary be used to help poor people. Kagawa's actions showed that he was

humble. He believed that the needs of poor people were just as important as his own needs.

Conclude

Read Philippians 2:3 aloud. **How did Kagawa show that he was humble?** (He lived in a small house. He asked that poor people be helped with the money he worked for.) Lead children in prayer, asking God to help children have humble and gentle attitudes.

Bible Verse

Do nothing out of selfish ambition or vain conceit, but in humility consider others better than yourselves. Philippians 2:3

Discussion Questions

1. **What are some ways to describe a person who is humble?** (Cares about others. Remembers that other people are important. Wants to do what is best for other people.)

2. **How do you feel when someone acts like he or she is better than you are? How would you want to be treated instead?**

3. **What are some things you could do to show a humble and gentle attitude?** (Let others go first. Don't act better than everyone else. Listen carefully when others speak.)

4. **When we have humble attitudes, we don't spend our time comparing ourselves to others. What should we think about instead?** (Ways to love God and others. How we can help others.)

Additional Information for Older Children

A teacher, poet and scientist, Kagawa wrote 150 books. Kagawa was known to repeat three prayers: "Father, forgive"; "God, let me live to serve"; "O God, make me like Christ." These prayers showed how much Kagawa loved God and how much he wanted to obey God by helping others.

An Itchy Situation

God's gift of joy can help us be thankful in any situation.

Teacher's Materials

Bible with bookmark at Ephesians 5:19-20, anti-itch cream or lotion; optional—cotton swabs.

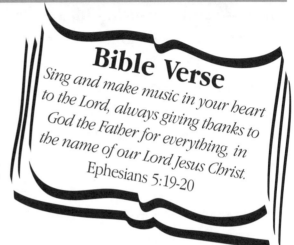

Bible Verse

Sing and make music in your heart to the Lord, always giving thanks to God the Father for everything, in the name of our Lord Jesus Christ.
Ephesians 5:19-20

Introduce the Object Talk

We can be thankful in any situation, because of the joy God gives to us. Let's find out about an unusual situation in which two women found that they could be thankful.

Present the Object Talk

1. Show anti-itch cream or lotion. (Optional: Use cotton swabs to dab a small amount of cream or lotion on hands of volunteers.) **When might someone need an anti-itch (lotion)?** Children respond. **Many years ago, during World War II, a woman named Corrie ten Boom and her sister, Betsy, could have used a (lotion) like this.**

2. Corrie and Betsy were living in a prison camp because they had helped Jewish people hide from the Nazis. The two sisters worked hard all day and slept in a crowded, smelly room at night. Corrie often felt like complaining— especially because the room in which they slept was full of fleas. Fleas hopped everywhere. They even lived in the straw that the women had to sleep on. The itching was awful. Things seemed terrible!

   Betsy reminded Corrie that God could do good things in any situation. They thanked Him for the fleas. But they must have wondered how God could

make something good happen in their terrible situation.

Each night Corrie and Betsy read the Bible aloud to the other women in the room. At first, they posted lookouts to keep watch for the guards because anyone caught with a Bible would certainly be killed! But one day they found out that no guards ever came to their room—because of all the fleas! Corrie and Betsy thanked God because the fleas made it easier to read the Bible and teach others about God's love.

Bible Verse

Sing and make music in your heart to the Lord, always giving thanks to God the Father for everything, in the name of our Lord Jesus Christ. Ephesians 5:19-20

Conclude

Read Ephesians 5:19-20 aloud. **What do these verses say about thanking God? Why do you think Corrie and Betsy ten Boom were able to thank God, even in a very bad situation?** (Because they knew God would always be with them and help them.) **God gives us good things and loves us, even when we are having hard times.** Invite children to pray, telling God things they are thankful for.

Discussion Questions

1. **When are some times that it is hard to thank God? Why?**

2. **What could you give thanks for when you have a bad day at school?** (You can read. You have a school to attend.) **When you are sick?** (You have a bed to rest in.)

3. **What are some ways to show God's gift of joy?** (Singing or playing an instrument in a song of praise. Telling others about God.)

Additional Information for Older Children

Corrie, Betsy and the other members of their family were arrested by the Nazis for hiding Jewish people in their home. On the top floor of their house, a small secret room was built behind Corrie's bedroom. In that tiny room, they hid Jewish people. Even though all of Corrie and Betsy's family were arrested, none of the Jewish people they hid were ever found. After World War II ended, Corrie wrote many books. One book, *The Hiding Place*, is about her family's adventures hiding Jewish people from the Nazis.

Cornucopia of Thanks

Give thanks to God for His care for us.

Teacher Materials

Bible with bookmark at Exodus 15:2, cornucopia or large basket, magazine pictures of good things God has given us (food, family, friends, church, parks, school, nature items—one picture for each child, including several examples from each category).

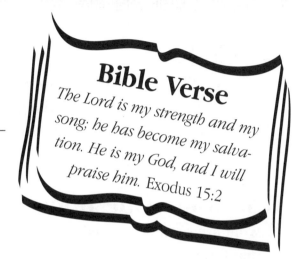

Bible Verse

The Lord is my strength and my song; he has become my salvation. He is my God, and I will praise him. Exodus 15:2

Prepare the Activity

Place pictures in cornucopia or large basket.

Introduce the Object Talk

As we learn about God, we discover the many wonderful ways He cares for us. God's care for us is something we can celebrate and thank Him for! Let's find out some of the gifts He gives us.

Present the Object Talk

1. Ask a volunteer to take a picture from the cornucopia or basket, identifying the picture for the entire group. **What is one thing about this picture that makes you want to thank God?** Repeat, using a different volunteer for each picture in the cornucopia or basket.

2. At your signal, children group themselves into categories according to their pictures. Repeat as time allows, having children select new pictures.

3. What are some of the things people do to show their thankfulness?

(Say "thank-you." Write thank-you notes.)

In several countries around the world, such as the United States, Canada, Brazil and Argentina, Thanksgiving Day is celebrated to thank God for the good things He gives. (Optional: If your children celebrate Thanksgiving, invite volunteers to tell about their family celebrations.)

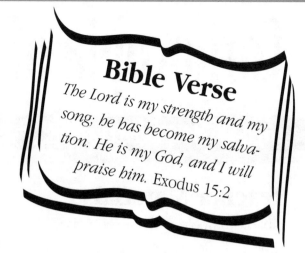

Bible Verse

The Lord is my strength and my song; he has become my salvation. He is my God, and I will praise him. Exodus 15:2

Conclude

Read Exodus 15:2 aloud. **What are some of the ways we can praise God for the good things He gives us?** (Sing songs that thank God. Read God's Word. Pray to God.) Pray, thanking God for His loving care and the good things He has given us.

Discussion Questions

1. **What are some ways God cares for your family? For what would you like to thank God?**

2. **How can you show God that you are thankful for His love and care?** (Name the things you are thankful for when you pray. Write God a thank-you prayer. Sing praise songs to Him.)

3. **What are some ways to give thanks to God?** (Sing Him a song of thanks. Tell Him what you are thankful for when you pray.) **What is your favorite way to thank God?**

Additional Information for Older Children

The United States and Canada celebrate Thanksgiving Day in similar ways but on different days. In Canada, Thanksgiving Day is celebrated on the second Monday in October. Canada's Parliament, in 1957, decreed it should be "a day of general thanksgiving to almighty God for the bountiful harvest with which Canada has been blessed." In the United States, Thanksgiving Day is celebrated on the last Thursday in November. President Abraham Lincoln issued a proclamation in 1863 to set this day aside "as a day of Thanksgiving and Praise to our beneficent Father."

Making Music

We can thank God for all things and in all circumstances because we know He is always with us.

Teacher Materials

Bible with bookmark at Ephesians 5:19-20, six identical clear water glasses, pitcher of water, spoon.

Prepare the Object Talk

Fill the glasses with water as shown in sketch.

Bible Verse

Sing and make music in your heart to the Lord, always giving thanks to God the Father for everything, in the name of our Lord Jesus Christ.
Ephesians 5:19-20

Introduce the Object Talk

We all have times or situations that make us feel sad or happy. Because we know God is good and always with us, we can thank God for all things. Let's try a fun way to give thanks to God.

Present the Object Talk

1. Demonstrate how to play musical notes by gently tapping the glasses with the spoon. Point out to the children that different amounts of water in glasses cause different notes. (Optional: Invite volunteers to experiment with tapping the glasses.)

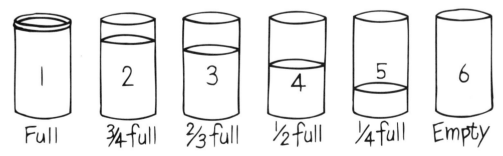

2. It's fun to make up our own music with these glasses. Listen to Ephesians 5:19-20 to see what it says about music. Read verses aloud. **Making music in our heart means we're so glad and thankful that our prayers to God are like**

songs. Many of the songs we sing in church are prayers of thankfulness and praise to God.

3. Choose a phrase from the verses such as "giving thanks to God the Father" or "Sing and make music in your heart" and tap the glasses as you say or sing the words. Invite children to say or sing the words with you. (Option-al: Invite several children to tap the glasses for these or other phrases from the verses.)

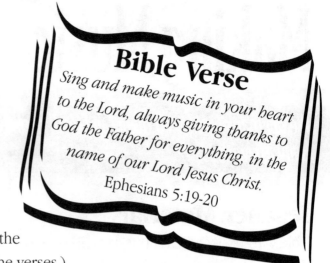

Bible Verse

Sing and make music in your heart to the Lord, always giving thanks to God the Father for everything, in the name of our Lord Jesus Christ. Ephesians 5:19-20

Conclude

Lead children in a prayer of thanks to God.

Discussion Questions

1. **What are some ways of giving thanks to God?** (Saying prayers. Writing prayers.)

2. **What are some things you are thankful for?**

3. **When might you and your family give thanks to God at home?**

Offering It All

Our offerings of love, time, abilities and money are ways we show our thankfulness to God.

Teacher Materials

Bible with bookmark at 1 Chronicles 16:29, objects used by your church to collect offerings (boxes, bags, plates, tithe envelopes, banks, etc.), large bag, blindfold.

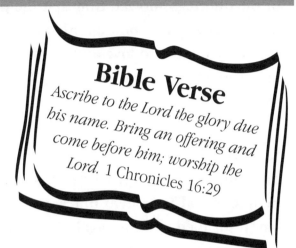

Bible Verse

Ascribe to the Lord the glory due his name. Bring an offering and come before him; worship the Lord. 1 Chronicles 16:29

Prepare the Activity

Place in bag objects used to collect offerings.

Introduce the Object Talk

An offering is anything we give to show love for God. We can give offerings of love, time, abilities and money to show our thankfulness to God. In the Old Testament, people gave many different types of offerings to God, too. Let's look at different ways to give to God.

Present the Object Talk

1. Invite a volunteer to wear a blindfold. Then take one object from the bag, hand it to blindfolded volunteer and ask him or her to identify the object. **What is this object used for?** Volunteer responds. Repeat, using a different volunteer for each object.

2. We use all these objects in our church to collect offerings. Explain use of objects to children as needed. **What are some other ways people give to show their love and thankfulness to God?** (Bring canned foods. Give used clothes. Volunteer time to help or teach others at church. Sing in the choir.)

3. In Old Testament times, people gave different kinds of offerings, too. They gave animals, grains, oil, fruit and vegetables. God's people brought their

offerings to the Tabernacle and later to the Temple—the places where the people gathered to worship God. The offerings were burned at a special place called an altar. These offerings were called sacrifices. (Optional: Read, or ask an older child to read, Leviticus 1:1-2; 2:1-2; 3:1 aloud.) **Some of the offerings showed God that the people were sorry for sinning; others showed that they wanted to love and obey God and were thankful for His good gifts to them.**

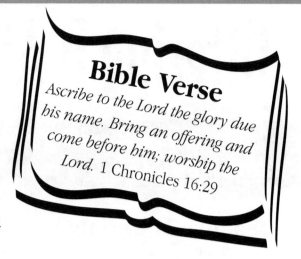

Bible Verse

Ascribe to the Lord the glory due his name. Bring an offering and come before him; worship the Lord. 1 Chronicles 16:29

Conclude

The Bible tells us to give offerings to God. Read 1 Chronicles 16:29 aloud. **Unlike people in Old Testament times, we don't have to make offerings because of sin. Jesus died and rose again for ALL our sins. His sacrifice was the most important offering ever. Now we bring offerings to show our praise to God.** Pray, thanking God for the good things He gives us.

Discussion Questions

1. **What kinds of offerings can you give to God?** (Money. Time helping others. Love for God and others. Singing songs of praise.)

2. **What attitude should we have when we give offerings to God?** (An attitude of thankfulness. A happy and willing attitude that shows we are glad to give to God because we love Him and want to help the people He loves.)

3. **When have you or your family given money or other things you own to show thankfulness to God?** (Given books to a missionary family. Given money to church to help other people learn about God.)

4. **Why is it important to give offerings to God?** (Helps us remember God's gifts to us.)

Additional Information for Older Children

Provide several children's Bible dictionaries or encyclopedias. Invite children to read information about the different types of offerings described in the Old Testament: burnt offerings, grain offerings, fellowship offerings, sin offerings and guilt offerings.

Songs of Joy

God's gifts to us bring joy and cause our thankfulness to overflow.

Teacher's Materials

Bible with bookmark at Psalm 28:7, hymnal.

Bible Verse
The Lord is my strength and my shield; my heart trusts in him, and I am helped. My heart leaps for joy and I will give thanks to him in song. Psalm 28:7

Introduce the Object Talk

Remembering God's gifts to us helps us be joyful and want to thank God. Let's look at a book written by people whose thankfulness to God couldn't help but show.

Present the Object Talk

1. Open hymnal and show it to children. **What is in this book? How are books like this used?** Volunteers respond. **Hymnals are books of songs about God. These songs were written by many different people who loved God and wanted others to love Him, too. One hymn writer's name was Francis Crosby. (She is often called by the nickname "Fanny.")**

2. Francis Crosby was born in New York in 1820. When Francis was only six weeks old, she became sick and eventually became blind. Then shortly after Francis became blind, her father died and her family became very poor.**

In spite of the bad things that happened to her, Francis Crosby didn't feel sorry for herself. When she grew up, Francis became a teacher at a school for the blind. She also was a concert singer and played the piano and the harp. And Francis wrote songs, thousands of them! During her lifetime, Francis Crosby wrote over 8,000 songs and poems—and many of them were written to show her love and thankfulness to God.**

Conclude

Read Psalm 28:7 aloud. **Among the good gifts God gave Francis Crosby were some special talents. What were some of her talents?** (Francis could play the piano and harp. She could sing well and write songs. She was a teacher.) **How did Francis use her gifts to show her thanks to God?** (She wrote and sang songs about God. She taught others about God.) Lead children in prayer, thanking God for His gifts to them.

Bible Verse

The Lord is my strength and my shield; my heart trusts in him, and I am helped. My heart leaps for joy and I will give thanks to him in song. Psalm 28:7

Discussion Questions

1. **What are some of the good gifts God gives us?** (People who love us. Food. Clothing. Forgiveness of sins. Talents.)

2. **What can you do to thank God for these gifts?** (Tell Him words of praise and thanks. Tell other people how great He is. Sing songs of thankfulness to Him. Use the gifts to praise Him.)

3. **The best gift God ever gave us was His Son, Jesus. Jesus makes it possible for us to become members of God's family. What are some ways to show we are thankful for Jesus?** (Say prayers of thanks to God. Sing songs about Jesus.) Talk with interested children about becoming members of God's family (refer to "Leading a Child to Christ" article on p. 8).

Additional Information for Older Children

In a church hymnal, use bookmarks or Post-it Notes to mark several hymns written by Francis Crosby. Her hymns include "To God Be the Glory," "Blessed Assurance," "I Am Thine, O Lord," "Praise Him! Praise Him!" and "Redeemed." Volunteers find and read or sing hymns written by Francis Crosby. **What do these hymns talk about? What did Francis Crosby want to thank God for? What words or phrases remind you of being happy or joyful?**

Index

Bible Verse

Biography

Holidays

How to Use the CD-ROM

Getting Started:

• Insert the CD-ROM into the CD-ROM drive.

• Double-click on The Really Big Book of Kid Sermons and Object Talks pdf icon located on the CD-ROM.

• Once the file is opened you can manually scroll through the pages (using the scroll bar on the right of the Acrobat window), or you can access any chapter by clicking on the chapter title in the table of contents. At the bottom of each page the Return to Main Menu link will take you back to the chapter index.

• You can print single of multiple pages. In the Adobe Acrobat Reader print Dialogue box select the appropriate button in the print range field. (Before printing please read "How to Make Clean Copies from This Book" on page 2.)

Problems?

If you have any problems that you can't solve by reading the manuals that came with your software, please call the number for the technical support department printed in your software manual. (Sorry, but Gospel Light cannot provide software support.)

Big Bible Learning Fun!

The Big Book of Bible Games #2

150 active games that combine physical activity with Bible learning. For Grades 1-6. Reproducible Manual 176p
ISBN 08307.30532

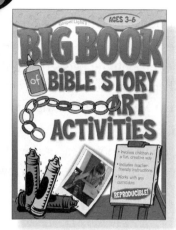

The Big Book of Bible Story Art Activities for Ages 3 to 6

Instructions for puppets, collages, chalkart, and more! Bible stories included. Reproducible Manual 213p
ISBN 08307.33086

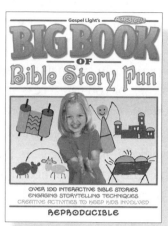

The Big Book of Bible Story Fun

Over 100 interactive Bible stories for kids ages 6 to 12. Creative activities to help get kids involved in the Bible stories. Reproducible Manual 228p
ISBN 08307.30591

The Big Book of Christian Growth

Engaging ways to lead preteens in discussing and applying Bible truth to life. Reproducible Manual 176p
ISBN 08307.25865

The Big Book of Games and Activities for Young Children

Learning activities for preschoolers at church and at home Reproducible Manual 276p
ISBN 08307.28821

The Big Book of Kindergarten Puzzles, Vol. 1

104 fun Bible puzzles—mazes, dot-to-dots, matching, counting, letters and shapes! Reinforces Bible learning. Reproducible Manual 216p
ISBN 08307.27574

The Big Book of Kindergarten Puzzles, Vol. 2

104 fun Bible puzzles—mazes, dot-to-dots, matching, counting, letters and shapes! Reinforces Bible learning. Reproducible Manual 216p
ISBN 08307.28848

The Big Book of Service Projects

Gives students practical opportunities to show God' love to others and encourages students to begin a lif time of Christian service. Reproducible Manual 176p
ISBN 08307.26330

Gospel Light
God's Word for a Kid's Wor

Available from your Gospel Light supplier.

www.gospellight.com

How to Teach Children to Think and Act Like Jesus

"If people do not embrace Jesus Christ as their Savior before they reach their teenage years, the chance of their doing so at all is slim."

George Barna
Transforming Children into Spiritual Champions

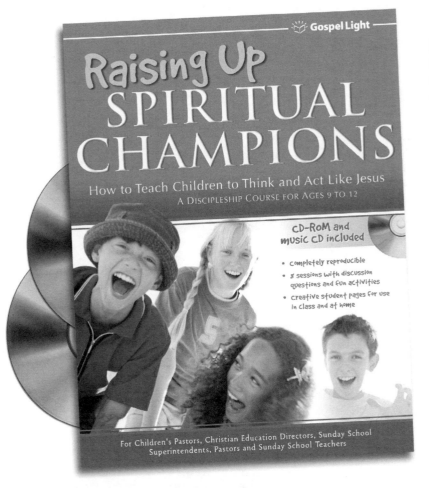

Raising Up Spiritual Champions
How to Teach Children to Think and Act Like Jesus
A Discipleship Course for Ages 9 to 12

Help kids answer the big questions about what it means to think and act like Jesus every day of their lives! This eight-session discipleship program provides the tools teachers need—from meaningful discussion questions to creative activities, from student pages to parent pages—to nurture lifelong spiritual growth in their students. Because most children's spiritual beliefs are in place by age 13, it's crucial that they acquire a biblical foundation for how they view themselves and the world. This program will help leaders teach God's truth during these all-important preteen years!

ISBN 08307.36638
Reproducible Manual
with CD-ROM and Music CD

Available at your
Gospel Light supplier.

Raising Up Spiritual Champions Includes

- CD-ROM containing everything in this book, including awards, **Student** and **Parent Pages**, publicity flyers, customizable forms, clip art and more!
- 8 reproducible sessions with discussion questions and fun activities
- Reproducible music CD with 12 praise and session-related songs
- How-tos for setting up the program
- 12 teacher-training articles
- **Student Pages** for use in class and at home to build discipleship habits
- **Parent Pages** that support parents in their role of spiritual teachers
- Teaching resources, including skits, discussion cards, games and more!

Gospel Light
God's Word for a Kid's World!™
www.gospellight.com

THE ALL-PURPOSE CHILDREN'S MINISTRY SOLUTION!

For Grades 1 to 6

KidsTime is perfect for those times of the week when teachers need a **flexible, easy-to-use program**, or when there aren't enough teachers and children of different ages need to be combined into one group. These "year in a box" programs are an unbeatable value!

Use **KidsTime** for: Any number of kids • Any number of teachers • Limited budgets • Second hour on Sunday • Children's church • Midweek programs • Evening programs • Whenever you have a group of kids!

52-Lesson Kit
Grades 1 to 6
Reproducible
ISBN 08307.23455

Now teachers can make sure their kids get **God's Big Picture**—not just bits and pieces. With **KidsTime: God's Big Picture**, teachers can show them how the whole Bible fits together, the way God meant it. This course is packed with fun activities for kids and brings Scripture into focus as a beautiful portrait of God's love for His people and His interaction with them.

52-Lesson Kit
Grades 1 to 6
Reproducible
ISBN 08307.25415

KidsTime: God's People Celebrate gives kids the big picture of worship as they celebrate His gifts to us. Each lesson includes Bible stories, worship, music, games, art, puzzles and object talks. Includes Old Testament holiday celebrations, church calendar and seasonal holidays.

52-Lesson Kit
Grades 1 to 6
Reproducible
ISBN 08307.25792

KidsTime: God's Kids Grow Kit gives teachers a whole year's worth of fun-filled lessons that help kids explore the **fruit of the Spirit** through art, songs, games, Bible stories, service projects and more! Plus, kids can discover real-life stories of how Christians have shown the fruit of the Spirit. It's a great way to help kids grow the fruit of the Spirit in their own lives.

Gospel Light
God's Word for a Kid's World!™
www.gospellight.com

Available at your Gospel Light supplier.